D0056847

NORTH

of

CRAZY

NORTH
of
CRAZY

A MEMOIR

NELTJE

ST. MARTIN'S PRESS • NEW YORK

NORTH OF CRAZY. Copyright © 2016 by Neltje. All rights reserved. Printed in the United States of America. For information, address St. Martin's Press, 175 Fifth Avenue, New York, N.Y. 10010.

www.stmartins.com

Library of Congress Cataloging-in-Publication Data

Names: Neltje, 1934– author.
Title: North of Crazy : a memoir / Neltje.
Description: First Edition. | New York : St. Martin's Press, 2016.
Identifiers: LCCN 2016010632 | ISBN 9781250088147 (hardback) |
    ISBN 9781250088161 (e-book)
Subjects: LCSH: Neltje, 1934– | Painters—United States—Biography. | Women
    painters—United States—Biography. | Ranchers—United States—Biography. |
    Women ranchers—United States—Biography. | Doubleday, Nelson—Family. |
    BISAC: BIOGRAPHY & AUTOBIOGRAPHY / Personal Memoirs.
Classification: LCC ND237 .N443 A2 2016 | DDC 759.13—dc23
LC record available at http://lccn.loc.gov/2016010632

Our books may be purchased in bulk for promotional, educational, or business use. Please contact your local bookseller or the Macmillan Corporate and Premium Sales Department at 1-800-221-7945, extension 5442, or by e-mail at MacmillanSpecial-Markets@macmillan.com.

First Edition: October 2016

10 9 8 7 6 5 4 3 2 1

— CONTENTS —

For all serious daring starts from within.
—Eudora Welty

Prologue

My cabin here at the base of the Bighorn Mountains in Wyoming fronts on the rising sun yet allows me to watch light fail behind the granite peaks each evening from my living room chair. What an apt metaphor for my life, as I was born in New York City and when I die, my ashes will be spread on this ground. I sit on the cabin's deck as I have weekend mornings for the past twenty-two years, drink coffee from the same mug and let my mind roam free as the herds of buffalo used to do and the elk still do. I shade my eyes and look east to Pumpkin Buttes, eighty-five miles away. The breadth of this land stuns me still, after forty-eight years in Wyoming, and the ever-changing subtle to brilliant light soothes and provokes my mind. How lucky I am to be where I am, to be who I am.

The Little North Fork of Crazy Woman Creek, aptly named for my life, tumbles out of the mountain passes through this land of mine, meanders across the plains, marries into the Powder River, the Yellowstone, the Missouri, and finally the Mississippi. I think on the pioneers, the guts it took to travel this tough country in the 1800s. And I remember the courage it took me to leave the East, the comfort of the familiar, to make a life out of the scraps of myself.

I set out for the waterfalls with my dogs, my constant companions: Gypsy, a basset hound, and Tara, an almost blind Australian shepherd mix. This afternoon is perfect for a walk. On one side of the Little North

Fork of Crazy Woman Creek, huge granite teeth pierce the sky. They are the uplift of Sisters Hill. On the other side of the creek lie the forested flatirons of Red Dog. I think of these foothills as guardians of the wilderness beyond: cliffs, pools, boulders, rocks, trees, pinecones, and singing cascades. Dry grasses crackle beneath my feet. It is late August 2013. We have had a drought for ten years. The dogs lead me down a cow path to the creek where water burbles, glazing the rocks. I bend and crouch to avoid the clawing limbs of dead trees and poking shrubs that nip at my legs.

Down through a young aspen grove, up over huge ragged rocks, along the narrowest path, where I must put one foot right in front of the other or fall into the creek far below. The dogs turn to make sure I follow, continue on when I say "Go." I stop to sit by a pool, watch the dogs snuffle tree trunks and grasses. They swim like toddlers in the mountain stream and then shake their bodies, spraying me with water.

Farther on, I gaze up the vast canyon walls, a creamy rose in the softened light. They are well over a hundred feet high and many hundreds of feet in width. I must throw my head back as far as it will go to take in the plummeting drop of these cliffs.

I cross the creek on a rickety wood bridge, hike straight up the hill with the help of a blue nylon rope attached to a ponderosa pine above. I come to an area of ill-sorted rock of different shapes and thicknesses, some at odd tilts. The perfect spot to twist, sprain, or break an ankle; no one would find me for days. No one knows where my weekend wanderings take me. It is a terrain I fear. After scrabbling up on hands and knees over more rocks and boulders, I find a faint path in a pine-needle forest. Two years ago I saw a mountain lion at the mouth of the cave on the other side of the creek. He appeared to be napping in the sunshine. I walked over. It was very early spring and the creek still had a thin coat of ice. Each footstep was a challenge. No flies buzzed about the lion, but he was absolutely still. I hugged him, stroked his curled body, scratched his ear. He was dead. I wondered why.

I hear the roar of falling waters reverberate in this tight valley, and a short distance away, half hidden by cottonwood and ponderosa pine trees, I see the waterfall. Hollowed-out cups of granite give me footholds on the final boulder. I reach the pool's edge, stand tall before the pounding water, the spray, and watch droplets dancing in the sunlight. I take off my boots and socks, shirt, jeans, and underclothes. The stone is rough to my bare feet. I take a step down to a granite ledge just beneath the water. In one motion I turn, face the falls, and dive flat into the water. Oh my god, it is cold. I swim a few strokes toward the falls, think of the power and cold, turn back and swim seven strokes to the granite ledge. I have to kneel before I can stand. I let out a howl. I am damned glad to be alive. I am seventy-eight years old and not proud of every moment.

ONE

Plantation Living

Today we are going fishing. I am excited because I like being in the flat-bottomed boat with Jimmy paddling, gliding along beside the tall rice grasses. They line each side of the narrow canals, wave and rustle, making a comforting sound in the still air. Jimmy is my friend. He says he takes me fishing as a treat for both of us. I trail my fingers in the soft warm water as I wonder how Jimmy knows where to find the best fishing spots. One canal looks just like another to me. I am six years old. It is Christmas vacation, 1940, and I am so happy to be at Bonny Hall, our plantation in Yemassee, South Carolina.

I wear my deep blue corduroy jacket and pants. This is my favorite set of clothes and will keep me warm on the water. Mademoiselle Van Toch, my new French governess, will be coming, too. This past summer Nana, the Scottish nurse I have had since I was born, left us to work for the Roosevelts. My brother, Nelson, and I cried. I am too old for a baby nurse, according to my mother, and besides, she says, I need to learn to speak French.

This is Mademoiselle's first year at Bonny Hall. I feel superior because I have been fishing with Jimmy and Nana many times. Nelson, who is a little more than a year older than I, almost never comes fishing; he prefers to play with his go-cart and trains. And he never rides horseback, either. Sometimes I miss his being near me, but I like having Jimmy all to myself. We meet down at the landing beyond the three pecan trees.

I like the sound of the pecan shells cracking against each other in my hands. Each shell holds two nuts, like two people in a pod. I talk to them when no one is around.

We climb into the flat-bottomed boat, which is painted a deep green. Jimmy sits down on the back bench, takes up a paddle, and strokes evenly through the water, maybe letting a drip fall into the boat as he switches the paddle from one side to the other. This "each side paddling" keeps the boat steady and straight in the canal, Jimmy tells me. He will choose the lure. The lures are made of two brightly painted pieces of wood hinged in the middle, so that each part wriggles like a fish or some kind of bug. Four hooks dangle off the metal rods in each section of the lure. All the lures have names: Scrubber, Pirate, and She-Devil. Jimmy says it matters which one he chooses. It all depends on the time of day, where we are and the sun is. I am glad Jimmy knows so much about fishing and hunting and about the alligators and snakes—which are poisonous, which harmless. I feel safe being with him.

I am part of this rice field now. I inhale its musty damp smells, sometimes sour and at other times pure, almost sweet. I like peeking between the grasses. Occasionally we round a bend to find a flurry and flap of ducks squawking as they lift off, annoyed at having their peace disturbed. Jimmy paddles. We glide almost noiselessly. For the moment I bask in the world of water, sharp-edged rice stalks, slime, and dreams. No "You have to" or "You are wrong" or "When will you ever look where you are going? Have you scraped your knee again?"

Jimmy and I let our line out, not too far, to keep the hooks from getting snagged. You have to wiggle or jerk the fishing pole softly to make the lure at the end of the line seem alive to the fish. I want to catch one at least, so Nelson won't be able to tease me. Mademoiselle swats at flies, asks, "When will we go back?"

"Not for a long time. We only just got here," I reply. At that instant the line zings as it slices through the water. Jimmy stands and cries out, "We gots one on da line." The boat rocks. He reels in the line steadily, not too fast. The fish darts from one side of the canal to the other, to the front of the boat and back, making the line sing out. Sometimes the fish breaks through the water to get away, twirling its body in a spiral that shines bright in the green-blue-brown water as Jimmy reels the fish alongside. When he lifts the tip of his rod, the fish flies, wriggles, squirms, flips, lands with a *slap* in the bottom of the boat. One eye stares up at the sky. The painted orange-and-green lure with one hook lost in the fish's mouth rests like a broken toy on the boat's bottom. Jimmy whacks the fish on the head with a stone. I catch two bass and Jimmy gets two more. What a good day.

Jimmy and I walk up the hill, cross the wide lawn, climb the back stairs to the kitchen, and hand over our catch to Betsey, the kitchen maid. Mademoiselle goes to the front of the house to get to her room. I watch Betsey run cold water over the bass, then slide them whole into ice trays and put them in the icebox. I listen to Betsey and Jimmy talk about fishing when they were kids as he and I stand on the small porch outside the kitchen door. Jimmy is in charge of the gun room. He takes care of all the hunting clothes and equipment, polishes the riding boots and everyone's shoes. Betsey helps Anna, the Swedish cook, prepare staff meals as well as our children's meals and all the meals served in the main dining room. Jimmy and Betsey are cousins.

Christmas is such a busy time—a houseful of guests and family, small tissue paper–wrapped presents in stockings opened in my parents' bedroom. My mother is still in bed, having breakfast. My father sits in his chair by the fire, which spits and crackles like the tissue paper in my hands. In my father's office, I play the slot machine over and over while my parents dress. I open my big presents with Nelson here. Sometimes I feel I belong as I stand alongside the Christmas tree, covered with shiny ornaments and colored lights, behind the sofa. I like this red-painted room lined with books and a fireplace. I don't believe in Santa Claus anymore. The night before Christmas, I used to try to stay awake, cozy in my flannel pajamas, dreaming I would hear the clatter of reindeer and a sleigh on the roof. Now that dreamy time as I fall off to sleep doesn't happen.

Most of the year, I live in our house, called Barberries, in Oyster Bay. I don't like that place as much as I do being here, where there are wide-open spaces, a canal and swamp to explore, and live oak trees laden with Spanish moss to climb. At Bonny Hall, the furniture is not formal like it is at Barberries, but comfortable, with pillowed sofas and large, cozy overstuffed chairs. Only the dining room is formal. I ride my pony, Tuffy, and feel the whole world belongs just to me. My two half sisters, Madeleine and Pucky Violett, are here. They are twelve and ten years older than I am and have a father named Atwood Violett. My mother was married to him before she married my father. My mother and her first husband, Atwood, and my father, Nelson Doubleday, and his first wife, Patty, met in Nassau in 1923 or 1924. They became friends and traveled together often, even to Paris. My brother, Nelson Doubleday Jr., is my best friend. He, too, is here. Everyone adores Nelson because, well, he's a boy. He will inherit my father's business. I will do something else.

My father is Nelson Doubleday, head of the book-publishing business with that name. He lives and works down here from November until May, along with my mother, Ellen. They entertain a lot of business guests. Here I don't have to wear dresses. I can wear overalls, climb fences, make cave houses with tree limbs and, best of all, ride horseback and feed the farm animals. I go fishing with Jimmy when he can get away. I have a friend, eight years older than I am, named Haskell. He has been my playmate since I was two. When I was in the sandbox, he was there up a tree, he was there and in the pony cart as well, he was there. Haskell is a Negro.

Every morning at exactly seven o'clock, Mr. Jaycock, the plantation farm manager, walks from his house to the cow barn with a long-legged, easy stride. Haskell and I cannot keep up with him. I feel the cool air against my face and the warmth of Haskell's hand in mine. Eight cows patiently stand in their headstalls, munching hay while they are milked by Little John. "Mawnin, Miss Neltje. Can ya name all da cows dis mawnin, Miss Neltje?" Little John asks as he rubs the hindquarters of a pale brown cow. He has to speak loudly because the Victrola, a large wooden box that stands on four legs in the corner, plays classical music very loud. Mr. Jaycock believes if he plays symphonies for the cows they will relax and give more milk. This morning they are listening to Beethoven.

"Let's see. This one is Betsey, then Bell, then Clarissa, then Annie. On the other side is Beulah in the rear, then Flora, Maybelle, and Magnolia. I did it. Good for me," I say with a little jump for the pure pleasure of feeling proud.

I like the sweet sweat smell of the cows, the milk, the feel of the humid air on my face, the crunching sound of cows eating hay, and the *ssssssssssttttttt* of the milk hitting the pail. Little John is a Negro, too, like Jimmy and Haskell. He is short and stocky. Now he leans the side of his face against the cow's side belly and hums his own tune to her as his brown fingers pull on her teats. Her bag is full. The third cow, Clarissa, drops a huge plop of poop. That smell I don't like.

After all the cows are milked and the milk has been put in tall metal milk cans, the cows are let out into the west pasture. They follow Little John through a gate one by one, in a slow, lazy walk. Haskell and I bring up the rear with willow switches to keep them moving, mosey them out to mid-field. After we see the cows settled, eating grass or lying down, brown splotches on a lush bed of green, we return to clean up the cow barn. I push the leftover hay down to the end of the trough while Little John, with Haskell's help, washes down the concrete floor and shovels up the manure to use in the garden.

Mr. Jaycock turns off the music and carefully puts the records in their box on top of the Victrola. He is a quiet man who seems lonely, even though he has a wife and grown children. A leather cap covers his silver hair. Every morning when Haskell and I meet him, he brings up his right hand to the peak of his cap when he says "Morning" to me, yet he doesn't tip his hat for Haskell because "Haskell is a Negro," my mother says. The way she says "Negro" tells me she feels he is different. Something she does not really like. I am supposed to feel that way, too, but I don't. My mother doesn't like me being at the farm in the early morning— "unladylike," she says—but she is never awake until nine or ten, and milking starts early.

We feed the pigs after the milking is done. Five huge hogs grunt and snort. Three of them are sows with litters of squealing, skittering piglets. The boars are kept in one pen and the sows and piglets in another. Each pen has a wallow, a wet muddy space for the boars and sows to lie in. "Mud is cool," says Mr. Jaycock, "and they need to cool down from being in the hot sun. Being so fat makes them hot also."

Their bristly hair is rough to touch.

"Don't rub it the wrong way or you'll hurt yourself," says Haskell.

Haskell at fourteen is taller than Little John. Each now puts one foot on the bottom rail, hoists himself up, and throws pails of smelly kitchen garbage into the pens—not cans or paper, but practically everything else: fish bones, vegetable trimmings, potato peelings, corncobs, eggshells. I sit on the top rail, my toes tucked behind the rail below, listen to the snuffling, watch the hogs. They can run surprisingly fast. Piglets nurse; they are too young to eat garbage. Sometimes a sow will lie down on her piglets, crushing them to death. I felt scared when I heard this from Haskell, but I didn't let him know that he had frightened me. If a mother pig can kill her piglets, could a human mother kill her children? I wonder about this. We go on to feed the chickens and collect the eggs.

We pick up the heavy sacks of chicken feed in the back shed. I drag mine along. We toss the feed, making half-moons, wide arcs of seeds in the air. Chicks, hens, and roosters cluck and scurry, pecking hungrily as the seeds touch the ground. They squabble, pushing one another out of the way, pecking to get at the food. Their feet make imprints in the dusty road. I feel sorry for the little ones, who get beaten out each time.

Little John, Haskell, and I walk down the slope behind the five houses for the Negro household help, down to the chicken nests made of wood and wire at the edge of the woods. Each of us probes into the nests with careful searching fingers. We place the eggs we find, some still warm, in a bowl. This ritual gathering we do together feels good. Little John will put fresh straw in the chicken nests that need it and then go to paint the corral fences white. Eddy, the new horse hand, will hay the horses, and I will go to the schoolroom. Haskell walks with me to the kitchen, carrying the bowl of eggs. He hands the bowl to Betsey at the kitchen door. Negroes who work outdoors do not set foot in the house. That is the rule. The household help feel superior to the outdoor help. They let me know that.

Sunshine fills the schoolroom this morning; I am alone here. I sit in the straight ladder-back chair and feel the empty space around me. I let in all the morning's pleasures, a continuous stream of pictures, like a movie. The scent of bacon floats up the stairwell from the kitchen below. I hear my brother, Nelson, coming up the stairs. "Why didn't you come to breakfast?" he asks.

"Just because," I reply.

Mademoiselle bustles into the schoolroom with an armful of books. She had to send for them, and she mutters about how hard it is to get the school supplies that she needs here. We go to Yemassee only once a week for supplies. The phone is the kind you have to crank up, and it only works from time to time. I don't mind being cut off from the rest of the world, but it annoys my mother because of the difficulty involved in getting food and other necessities for entertaining.

This morning my brother is in a foul mood. He lost at cards yesterday and behaved badly, so he is not allowed to play today. I doubt my mother will stick to her rule. She usually caves where Nelson is concerned. I pore over a book about bugs. Their hairy legs fascinate and repel me. I would like a book on butterflies, because I love their bright-colored patterns and their freedom dancing in the air. They suck sugar from flower blossoms. I watch them on the camellia and azalea bushes in the gardens below my window sometimes when I am meant to be taking a nap. I am thin and everyone fusses at me to eat more and rest more. Eating is the only thing I can control about my life. Adults have the say about everything else. They fuss over me less when I am outdoors and out of the way.

When returning to Bonny Hall, I look forward to so many pleasures, like watching Mattie, one of the maids, light the fire in the fireplace to warm up my room in the morning. We have no other heat system, and sometimes we get snow. I ring the bell to let her know I am awake. She and the other maids wait in the pantry, where there is a black box on the wall with numbers for all the rooms; a light flashes when a bell is rung. My bedroom is right over my mother and father's bedroom and looks over the gardens my father had Umberto Innocenti, a well-known landscape architect and friend, designed for him. Nelson's bedroom, next to mine, is directly over my mother's office, where she spends hours and hours "balancing the books" of the farm. We live in a wing of the house separate from the center square section, which houses all the living spaces: my father's office, the gun room, the living and dining rooms. The hall downstairs from our rooms joins up with the center of the house at my father's office, which is awkward. If he is in his office and the door is closed, we have to go around outside. Not fun when it rains or snows.

The pantry, where Ephrom, the butler, is in charge over his younger cousin Frankie, opens into the dining room on one side and the kitchen on the other. Ephrom comes to work at six in the morning and walks a mile home between the canal and swamp each night, after the dining room table has been cleared and all the dishes are done. Once, he was bitten by a rattler on his way home. We teased him and said the rattler died instantly. But Ephrom was hurt. He was away from work three days and limped rather badly when he came back. His helper Frankie loves to tell jokes and tease. I like him best. The two-story kitchen house has three storerooms, a staff dining room, and a kitchen. Anna, the cook, has a bedroom upstairs, because she is white. Our schoolroom is upstairs, too. The rest of the household help, all Negroes, sleep in what used to be the "slave quarters." Ephrom is the only one I don't feel close to. He thinks I am in the way and hates when I ask questions. I like to ask "Why?"

My father's office, as well as the front hall, gun room, and the guest rooms above, face out over the lawn to the rice field and, in the far distance, the Combahee River. When my father goes to his office in the morning and closes both doors, no one dares enter. But I have seen Ephrom many mornings with a tumbler of whiskey on a silver platter, making his way to my father's office. My father calls that drink a "phlegm cutter." At lunch, "builder-uppers" are served from a silver-rimmed crystal bucket. My family and guests drink two or three buckets of builder-uppers before lunch every day. Their glasses are small, but they drink several. I don't think grapefruit juice and whiskey tastes good, but the grown-ups do.

My bedspread is pale blue like the flowered curtains on the windows overlooking the gardens. The room is large, with a cozy stuffed chair next to the fireplace. When I was little I sat on Mattie's lap in this chair, listened to stories about when she was a little girl, stories about her and her mom and her brothers and sisters. I lay against her breast, listening to her heartbeat, her voice; felt the soft warmth of her flesh beneath her uniform. And her laugh made her whole body jiggle. A toy box sits in the corner of the bedroom. It has a few toys and dolls from years past in it. I don't remember them, but I know that everyone gives me a doll at Christmas because little girls are meant to like dolls. I don't play with dolls and haven't since I was three years old.

Each November when my mother and father leave Barberries, our place on Long Island, to spend the winter at Bonny Hall, the house goes dark and feels hollow. I feel unwanted. Until I was four and began school, I would spend winters with them on the plantation. Now Christmas and Easter vacations are the only times I get to ride horseback, explore the swamp, and fish the canals with Jimmy. I feel happy and free at Bonny Hall, an open sense of the world around me—from books to builder-upper drinks, horseback rides to cracking pecans, the swamp, the animals, the vast sky, all feed me. I never have this sense of total belonging to everything around me when I am up north unless I am prowling the woods, but even then it is different. Nelson and I come down by train to Yemassee, either on the Silver Meteor or the Havana Special, with who-ever is taking care of us. When I turn seven or eight, we might get lucky and travel with one or both of our half sisters, Pucky or Madeleine. They play cards or I Spy or I Pack My Grandmother's Trunk with us. With them, we are real people, instead of charges. I hate always being taken care of by someone hired for the job. Why doesn't my mother want to take care of me or Nelson? We are like toys to her, to be seen as attrac-tive playthings, then put back in the chest, well out of sight.

The Sunday before Christmas in 1942, when I am eight, my mother and I take the baskets she has made up for the children at the Church Street School. We did the same thing the previous year, and the year be-fore, too. We take them to the church at the end of Church Street, where all the Negro field hands and some house Negroes live. The baskets full of toys and candy are for boys and girls of all ages. Each is exactly the same, which seems odd to me. But the same is true of Christmas here at the house. Last year I watched my mother wrap six belts that were just alike, four for the business wives and one each for Pucky and Made-leine. It made me sad. It meant my mother didn't care about anybody enough to get something just for them. When I told her my feelings, she said there were just too many people to have special presents for. The sharpness in her voice made me flinch. There was a cruelty in the timbre of her voice that alarmed me, made me feel I had to watch what I said or that sharpness would pierce me. Dare I question anything my mother says or does? Sometimes I think she wants me to have no voice at all.

Haskell opens the trunk of the gray Buick to dozens of brightly colored baskets. My mother climbs the worn wooden steps of the church just as the steeple clock rings noon. I follow, and Haskell and Ephrom mount the steps behind me, arms loaded down with baskets. The teacher, Miss Wright, bespectacled and wearing a light blue dress, meets us at the church door with a kind welcome. She always tells me how much I have grown. Why do adults say such dumb things? Of course I have grown. I am a year older.

My mother and I walk down the wooden aisle, children crowded into the pews on each side. One by one, my mother passes a basket down the pew to a girl or a boy, and always the soft "Thank you, ma'am" echoes back. Ephrom and Haskell keep us supplied with baskets; suddenly at the end, there are not enough. Three girls in the front pew have no basket. They look down at their shoes as my mother stammers and promises to bring three baskets down the next day. She is flustered. One of the three girls, all teenagers, says, "That's all right, ma'am. Don't worry yo' self." We turn, walk back down the aisle, say Merry Christmas to the teacher, and walk down the steps. "No lingering," my mother had said to me earlier in the morning when she was dressing.

My mother sits behind the wheel. I sit next to her on the front seat, at her insistence. Haskell and Ephrom get in the back. My mother puts her finger to her lips to communicate to me to say nothing. Is she afraid I might criticize her or make some comment about the three missing baskets? That would be like me. She takes out a Benson & Hedges cigarette from a gold case and lights it with a small gold lighter. She takes a puff and slowly lets the smoke slide out before starting the car.

My father's guests at Bonny Hall are his friends, brothers or sisters of my mother's, along with their spouses, some authors, but most are men who work at Doubleday and their wives. The women do not bother me; few of them go out with the guns in the morning, although my mother gets all dressed up in hunting gear every couple of weeks to go quail shooting. Some of the men do bother me. I watch them put on their new hunting jackets slightly self-consciously, wondering if it is as good as the next guy's. Jimmy is steeped in platitudes. "Yes, suh, you sure to get a bunch o' quail t'day. I knows yo'se gwoin to git a big deer this mawnin. Shua goin' to happin." The hunters go out the gun room door in their brand-new hats, vests, jackets, and the best boots from Abercrombie & Fitch—rubber boots when they go hunting in the bogs, but canvas and leather boots for quail shooting. They will hunt in the big field south of the main road. That field stretches all the way past the "darkies' graveyard," almost to Church Street. One of the hunters might get a deer in that field, because it lies next to the forest where the deer bed down.

The four Negro beaters left an hour earlier, before dawn. They will line up at the wooded edge of the cornfield, and when the hunters are ready, a whistle will signal; they will slowly start walking forward toward the hunters, flushing the quail from the rows of corn. They have a very responsible job, my father says—to flush out the birds at just the

right time, so the guests get a good shot at them. It seems a bit unfair to
the birds, I think, but do not say so.

I tell my mother later that morning, "I don't like anyone killing animals or birds. I think it is an unfair and mean sport. Besides, it scares
me. They could shoot me if they got mad." My father could shoot me, I
think, but I don't dare say this last sentence.

"Hunting is one of the main reasons for Bonny Hall. Your father loves
to hunt," my mother replies.

He and his business associates, family, or just friends go hunting early
mornings maybe three or four times a week. Not all of them have that
slimy, self-satisfied look, but the ones who do really scare me.

The ruddy-faced men beam with satisfaction when they come in from
the day's hunt. They take off their outdoor clothes, boots, canvas pants,
and new hunting jackets, which separate the "real men" from those who
hunt in old clothes. They leave their outerwear, from boots to hats, for
Jimmy to clean and polish, as well as their guns. Milo Sutliff, who
works for Doubleday, as do all the other men—Barney Brownell, Cedric Crowell, and Charlie Marshall—says, "Oil this coat, Jimmy; I got
some bird blood on it." He pulls off his leather jacket and lays it over the
back of a bench.

Cedric Crowell, already in the dining room with my father, stands at
the buffet table and removes the cover from a large silver dish. He says
over his shoulder, "Nelson, you made a splendid shot by that dead tree.
You hit the quail perfectly, blew his head right off." He mounds scrambled eggs, biscuits, and bacon onto his plate. When he sits down, Ephrom
serves him a bowl of oatmeal with cream from our cows, then pours him
a cup of coffee. Barney Brownell joins in: "Yes, Nelson, great shot." My
father sits at the head of the table after all the guests are seated. "Enough,
fellas," says my father. "I felt good about the shot; now let's eat." The china
looks too fragile for the men and their piles of food.

I sit by myself in the corner at a card table. Mademoiselle Van Toch
and Nelson are nowhere around. They must have had breakfast while I
was out in the stables. I nibble on toast and jam, listen to the men talk.
In my mind I see the quail fall from its flight, headless. I hate my father
for killing birds. They have a right to live. And I am afraid of him, but I
love him and want him to love me. He is fearsome. My opposite emotions

upset me. When they are all busy eating and talking, I ease myself up, silently open the door to the back hall behind me, and run out the front door, straight back to the stables.

As I stroke my horse's flank, I mull over the satisfaction I saw on some of the men's faces, a smug and cruel look. I don't like those men, those few, no matter how much they sweet-talk me. If they can kill an animal, I am afraid they could kill me—the same way they killed the deer I saw hanging upside down from the big old live oak tree two years ago. Those lifeless eyes stared right into mine. There was no difference between us then, nor in my memory now. My stomach turns with fear. I have no one to talk to about this. My father would either laugh at me or get mad. My mother had waved her hand and laughed, saying, "Oh you foolish child," when I told her my worries while she had her breakfast in bed that morning, after the men went hunting. Puck and Madeleine are back in New York at school, and Nelson thinks I am crazy to be afraid. He always tells me not to say anything because it will just make our parents angry.

I love Nelson and depend on him, but we are so different. He hides everything, so you never really know what he is thinking. At times I think he doesn't like me at all, especially if I win at gin rummy. Cards are his department; animals are mine. We get quarters to play the slot machine. I lose a lot and he wins a lot. Once, I stole his winnings and told him and Puck that a big black witch came in and took his quarters. Nobody believed me, but I didn't give up the quarters. He and I play other card games like Go Fish, Old Maid, or hearts with my mother. My mother says he "has good card sense." I have no patience waiting for others to make up their minds on what card to play, and when I can't decide what to play, I just throw down anything. But Nelson truly is better at every card game, which makes me jealous and angry. I am best at horseback riding and fishing, anything to do with the outdoors or animals. There I shine. Nelson just doesn't like animals, so he never goes to the farm part of the plantation. We do love each other—like most siblings, sometimes lots, sometimes not at all. I think of us as one against the grown-up world most of the time. We live a strange life, isolated from parents, being with them only briefly, always with a caretaker, then alone again until another caretaker is hired. We have to be dependent on each other for comfort at least. There are no others. We often talk about feeling lonely and left out, usually in a whisper, afraid someone will hear and report us to my mother or the caretaker.

Nelson plays cards with the adults on occasional afternoons, gin rummy with my mother and Mr. Maugham, a well-known author who lives down the road. But I don't because I can't concentrate. My mother gets exasperated with me because I would rather play outside than sit at the bridge table. Sometimes I want to ask her why she bothered to have us, as we are always sent off to live with a caretaker, but I would be called impertinent and sent to my room. When I asked why we don't live like other children do, at home with their parents instead of being alone with a governess up north, her answer came back like the crack of a whip: "You make so much noise, you annoy your father."

TWO

Barberries at Oyster Bay

The Long Island house, Barberries, is the main home for the rest of the family, but not for me. I like the more comfortable furniture and surrounds of Bonny Hall. At Barberries, the upstairs hall stretches from bedroom to bedroom, connected by a red-carpeted hallway lined in places with bookshelves and my mother's closets. I am supposed to be very quiet when near my parents' bedroom. That area is out-of-bounds until well after they have rung their bell for breakfast.

My earliest memories are of the nursery, where I live with Nelson and Nana. We have our meals here, brought to us by Hilda, the upstairs maid and housekeeper, or Tillie, the new maid from Ireland. Nana bathes us and feeds us; she dresses us, plays with us, takes us for walks, and watches over us in the sandbox and pool. At night after our supper, when we are in our pajamas, she reads us a story or sometimes two. From my bed I can watch Nana undo her long silver hair, brush it with her head tilted to the side, so it looks even longer. She makes a braid and flips the braid to the back of her neck outside her nightie. She is constant. She does the same thing every night. I like that.

Occasionally in the morning, after my mother and father wake up, Nelson and I are taken into their bedroom, where we can stay for a few minutes. We are not allowed up on the bed to hug and play with our mother. She has her breakfast on a tray in her bed. My father eats his breakfast sitting in his blue chair by the fireplace, his tray on a suitcase stool in front of him. I want to climb up on his lap and be hugged, but he says he is busy with the newspaper. He has to learn something important in the newspaper.

My mother is unreachable, so far away in the big bed, dressed in a pink bed jacket, her glasses down almost at the tip of her nose, *The New York Times* tucked in the left tray cubby. Her boiled egg sits up in a blue china eggcup. I watch her thin, blue-veined hand slice the top of the egg off with a knife. She dips a very small spoon into the egg, then raises the spoon to her pursed lips, opening her mouth only slightly to take it in. She wipes her lips with a white linen napkin, then catches the bit of yolk on her lower lip with the index fingernail of her right hand and presses the slippery bit of yolk into the napkin. I study her every move, waiting and hoping she will pay attention to me. She puts butter and marmalade on her toast, lifts the toast to her mouth. She bites cleanly into it, leaving teeth marks in the toast. I tell her I think it is pretty enough to draw.

She laughs, then puts down the toast and says, "Let's have the Clark-sons to dinner tonight, Nelson. You will be working at your Garden City office, so traffic won't make you late."

"If you want," he answers while still reading the paper.

I don't exist to her. I feel the air around me cool and heavy. I reach for Nelson's hand behind me, but he is not there, he is way over by the sofa. The curtains on the windows are drawn back. Sun floats across the blue carpet. Tears rise up. As I run down the hall to the nursery, I hear my mother say, "What is the matter with her now?"

In the evenings, after our supper and before my parents have dinner, we might get to have a visit with them. Nana gets us all dressed up. I wear a dress; Nelson wears short pants, a shirt, and sometimes a tie. Today I have on a flowered dress with a white background; Nelson wears blue short pants and a white shirt. Nana walks downstairs with us to the landing, where the cannonball sits by the grandfather clock.

"The cannonball is special," my father told us last year. "General Abner Doubleday, your great-great-uncle, shot the first cannonball from Fort Sumter. That was the beginning of the Civil War in America, between the North and the South. This is the cannonball," my father said, holding it up in his hand. Nelson and I both touched the cannonball, but I could not read the inscription on the brass plate. I was four then.

Now Nana takes our hands. As she bends over to whisper to us, the big clock right next to us strikes six. Nana says in her Scottish brogue, "Yer mother and father are sitting on the patio outside the library. Go now and be good. Remember to behave, no fighting, or ye won't get time visiting another day. Yer parents won't tolerate any noisy chatter. Off you go now." She kisses Nelson on the cheek. "Be a good boy, now. You are Nana's boy, remember."

I want to say, "What about me? Whose pet girl am I?" But I know better. I keep still; I am afraid of the answer. Nelson is the most loved, by everyone. Nana has told me so many times when I have seen her hugging him and not me. I ask why he gets all the attention from my mother and father and even the businessmen from the company. "Why not me?" I ask.

"It is because he is a boy and ye are just a girl. Girls don't matter, lassie. Ye'll learn that as ye grow older. All they ever want is fer ye to earn yer own keep and have boy babies to help work with the dad. Never ye mind. As long as ye do what the men say, ye'll learn ways to make yer'self happy."

Nelson and I walk past the front door on the right, down the wide carpeted hall, and into the paneled library. Through the glass door, we can see our parents sitting on the terrace, a glass-topped table between them. They sit in the shade of the dogwood tree, now covered with pink blossoms. My mother has a glass in her right hand, and as she tilts it to her mouth, a sprig of mint seems to stick up her nose. I start to giggle as Nelson opens the glass door. I look down at my patent-leather shoes and white socks, so my parents can't see me giggling. My feet are not happy in these shoes. What will my mother find wrong with me today? I wonder. And will I cry? Both my knees are covered with ragged scabs, from falling off my bicycle on the gravel driveway.

"Here come the 'babes,'" says my mother. "Don't they look sweet!"

"Hi, you two hooligans," says my father as he gets up. "I'm going to get a drink. Do you want another, Y'Ellen?" he asks. "Y'Ellen" is his pet name for my mother, what he calls out every afternoon when he gets in the front door. His call can be heard almost anywhere in the house.

"Please, Nelson," she answers, while stretching out her arm and hand with an almost empty glass. "Well, what have you two been doing all day? Did you have a swim with Nana in the pool?"

She is hugging Nelson, runs her hand down his shirtfront. "My, you look handsome tonight."

Nelson throws his arms around her neck. "We swam lots today. I stayed in the water forever. I can swim the width of the pool many times, and even the length. Nana says I am the best swimmer she has ever seen. Neltje got cold. She is a sissy. Her lips get blue. Nana wrapped her in a towel, then made her lie out in the sun. Nana says she gets cold so fast because she is skinny and she won't eat." The words spill out from his mouth, one on top of the other.

I hear all he says, every word. I want to defend myself in some way to gain my mother's approval, but instead I watch her put her arm around Nelson, pulling him close to her in her chair.

"Come sit on my lap," she tells him.

I stand in awkward silence by an empty chair across from her. I rub the top of my left shoe against the back of my right leg and press the fabric of my flowered dress between my forefinger and the thumb of my right hand. The cloth slides easily back and forth in a rhythm like a soft drumbeat. Moving my fingers back and forth calms me. I don't know what to say. I can't chatter like Nelson. I feel all knotted up, and my chest and belly hurt.

My father comes out the library door, leaving the door open because he has a drink in each hand. "Here is your Tom Collins," he says, handing the drink to my mother. "I rang for Tony to get more Collins mix and limes. He will bring them in a minute, along with some hors d'oeuvres to nibble on before we dress for dinner." He finishes his sentence as he sits down with a glass of bourbon and water in his left hand, then places the glass on the table between their chairs.

"Close the door for me, daughter," he says while running the ice cubes around in his glass.

Later they will have old-fashioneds for the real cocktail hour. This drink time now is called a "prelude." When they have old-fashioneds, my father occasionally gives me the maraschino cherry as a treat. Sugar and bitters and an orange slice are mashed down in the bottom of the old-fashioned glass by our butler, Tony, the ice next, then the bourbon. The cherry comes last, just decoration. If my father gives me the cherry from his cocktail, does that mean he loves me a bit? I wonder. He talks to Nelson much more than to me. And he takes Nelson on many more drives in the car.

Back on the terrace, my father turns his body to face me. "Well, daughter, what have you done today?" he asks in a businesslike way. He terrifies me. He is six-five-and-a-half, so tall, and his deep voice rumbles like trucks on a railroad track. At times he has been sweet with me, talking to me in my room when Dr. Schloss, my baby doctor, said I needed to be quiet and not use up energy because I was too thin. I was put to bed at five in the afternoon. My father would pour 4711 aftershave on his huge handkerchief and trail it across my brow and the back of my neck on summer evenings. He told me stories about Mike and Ike and Hemoglobin, characters he made up, who ventured all around the world. But then, too, he can be so cruelly mean. I do not know how to tell him of my day's activities, so I stumble over the words *swimming* and *racing*. I did both with Nelson today. I am not allowed to hit him back or beat him at a game or a race. My mother says boys are fragile and we have to treat them gently, never threaten their superiority.

"I swim, swimmed, swam in the p-p-pool with Nelson and we r-r-r-r-raced each other across the pool and the long way, too," I stammer, feeling foolish and ashamed.

"So, little lady, you went swimming with your brother. Did he beat you in the race? Yes? Well, good. He should, you know. He is a boy and older and stronger than you."

"Oh, but this morning before it was warm enough to swim, I climbed way high in the cherry tree over the sandbox. Nana got very cross with me because she couldn't reach me and couldn't climb the tree. But I felt happy and safe up there," I say, excited, hoping my father will tell me that I, too, am strong and brave.

"You are going to break that neck of yours climbing trees one of these days. Let's have Mr. Kenny give you a tennis lesson, as well as Nelson. Let's use up your energies there. What do you say to that, missy?" he asks as his gray eyes shift to Nelson.

"Fine," I reply, thinking I will get really good at the game by practicing every moment I can and then I will be strong enough and good enough to beat Nelson. My mother says I am always jealous of Nelson and have to get over it. But he gets everything his way, so why wouldn't

I want what he has? My mother does not understand. She turns her head away from me and tells my father about Nelson's swimming accomplishments.

"He can make it to the end of the pool and back without a pause," she says, her voice warm with admiration. My father holds out his arms to Nelson, who immediately slips off my mother's lap and runs over to my father.

"Well, son, tell me about your swimming. It sounds like you are a champ."

I move to the right. I need to get away. I take a small step down from the patio onto the flagstone path, then slowly move on past the path to the driveway. I like how the yew trees are trained to make a covered archway, and the color of the mottled redbrick house, old bricks, not new. There are flagstone steps to the left that lead down a wide alley lined with tall, evenly trimmed hemlocks. All of a sudden, the air smells lusciously sweet. Wisteria blossoms pungent with perfume grow everywhere on the brick library walls. Yellow and white tulips stand tall in the eight rectangle beds, each rimmed with boxwood. Dogwood trees, two white, two pink, hold down the garden at the four corners. I walk along the path, careful not to trip. On the right lies an uneven rock wall four feet high, with nooks and small spaces that allow for a variety of tiny flowers and green-leaved plants to grow, mosses, too. The wall stretches to the corner of the garden, beyond where the white dogwood tree grows. I step over the low boxwood border into a flower bed, careful to avoid stepping on young plants. I find a single rock that sticks out farther than the others, giving me a ledge to lean on but not big enough to sit on. I look around the garden, then up at the wisteria, all shades of purple now in the warm evening sunlight. I look at the boxed-in rectangles of tulips and, in the distance, the woods, my favorite place to play. I touch tiny forget-me-not blossoms and the velvet moss that grows between the stones. I make up stories about a little girl in a world of animals and birds who lives and plays in this garden land of sunshine and soft smells, where squirrels and chipmunks, bunny rabbits and I play cards and drink old-fashioneds.

Just in front of my right knee lies a small, thin snake on a rock barely big enough for his body. He is basking in the sun, unaware of me at his side, or else unconcerned. I stay quiet, not wanting to scare him. A breeze moves the dogwood leaves behind me. I know their rhythm: a slow back-and-forth movement. I know because I have watched them many times before.

I put my forefinger down only an inch away from the snake's head, then slide it slowly toward him till my fingernail is a paper-thin slice from his head. He does not move at first, but continues soaking up the sun, seemingly unaware of my finger. I tilt my hand a bit to the left, not even half an inch. My finger presses gently on the snake. "I will call you Sam," I say in a whisper. Sam lifts his head, his tongue darts in and out, and then he lies back down over my finger and moves his body into the palm of my hand. I look at the silvery-gray scales of his skin and the dark line down his back. I admire his sleek beauty. His skin does not feel slimy, only cool.

I would like to take him over to show him to my father, but I know my mother, and Nelson, too, would shriek just looking at Sam. I stay where I am—safe, apart.

Nana appears on the patio, her white uniform a signal that tells me I have to go back in. I tilt my hands. Sam slithers back to his spot on the rock and I walk slowly in answer to Nana's call. I say my formal good nights, receive the ritual kisses. Just for once I long to feel the kisses as real. I follow Nana up the stairs.

Over the summer, I learn to swim better and better by going to swimming class at Piping Rock Beach Club. To this day, I can smell the salt seawater, see Nana bent over me in her white uniform, her head of silver hair tied back in a neat bun. I lift my foot and press it against her leg. My nose is running and she hands me a Kleenex. "Blow out all that salt water," she says in a disapproving voice. I adore Nana, for she is my day-to-day mother. She wipes out the sand from between my toes with great care, so not a grain of sand is left to irritate. Once Nelson and I are dressed and the wet suits and towels have been put in the beach bag, Nana slides back the half-rusted lock of the white wooden door, and the three of us walk out along the corridor with dressing rooms on both sides. The smell of seawater is strong. In this narrow space I feel the humid, damp, salty air, hear the playful cries of other children still on the beach. Maybe they are lucky, have ice-cream cones, don't have to be bundled off home so the car and Sweeny, the chauffeur, can be at the ready in case Madame, my mother, should need him. We know she is at the bridge table playing cards with her friends, and she will stay there until ten minutes before my father is due home. The time now is only four o'clock. I am cross. "Why should we have to give up swimming with our friends just in case our mother might possibly want to use the car?" I say, knowing it will do no good. I continue even so: "You know she doesn't go anywhere when she has friends over to play bridge."

Nelson now chimes in: "I want to watch the bridge game. Maybe I will get to play a hand or at least kibitz." I have lost my ally.

"Don't ye be smart-talking like that about yer mother," Nana says as she shushes me with her hand. I wish Nana would love me like she loves Nelson. I love her. She is all I have.

My anger does not go away, but seeps through me, becomes a sense of helplessness. The chain of my mood is familiar. I become silent, look out the window at the passing trees, then at the other cars on the road. I notice the back of Sweeny's neck, how thick it is. We pass Locust Valley High School. It is midsummer, so no teenagers stroll about. I feel lonely. I am sent to my room for being "cheeky" and "selfish and willful." I am always being called selfish and willful.

This is Nana's last summer. Next week she will move away to a Roosevelt family to take care of their newborn baby. She tells Nelson and me that is what she is trained to do. Nelson is seven and I will be six in October. The fear of being alone and uncared for swallows me up. I am silent. On the appointed day I watch as she leaves the nursery. The good-byes and clinging kisses I give her, the lingering tears and pleadings, none of it helps. Beside me, Nelson sobs. Earlier, he tried to steal and hide her glasses so that she would not leave, but she found them. As Nana goes down the stairs with her small brown suitcase, the butler, Tony, ahead with her large case, we two stand at the top railing, waiting for her to turn around and say "I love you" or wave a last good-bye. She doesn't. She just goes away.

Mademoiselle Van Toch is our new French governess. We have French lessons every day. She is tougher and meaner than Nana and her voice is sharp. But at least she doesn't think Nelson is such a prince, doesn't tell him how wonderful he is, as Nana did daily. One morning, I felt sick. I said I didn't want to go to school feeling sick. I threw up on the carpet in the nursery, Mademoiselle's room. She made me eat my vomit off the carpet and sent me to school. That afternoon when I came home she locked me in her closet as punishment. She said I was pretending to be sick to get out of school. I wished there were scissors in her closet. I would have cut her clothes in half. Maybe I did. I don't remember.

Years later, in 1942, toward the end of summer, seven English children with parents and nannies arrive to live in Oyster Bay. They come from London, which is being bombed by the Germans. The mothers and fathers are book-publishing friends of my father's, and my father wants these children to be safe during the war. The house he has rented for them sits at the end of a gravel road on the far side of Oyster Bay, right on the water. It is called Ramsbroke, has three stories, and is painted gray, with white trim. Sea grasses grow on the sand and gravel dunes just beyond the white wooden fence surrounding the house. They all live there, Simon, Annabelle, and Susan Bott, Timothy and Jeremy Wagg, and the Frère children, all with their nannies. Their parents have to return to London, even though they will be in danger. They have businesses to run.

Nicholas Paravacini, who is the writer Somerset Maugham's grandson, is being taken care of by his mother, Liza Paravacini—Liza to all of us, because who can pronounce Paravacini? Nicholas is the envy of all us children because his mother takes care of him. He has no nanny. He is four years old, younger than all of us except Jeremy Wagg, who is the same age. Nicholas has a crown of bouncy golden curls and the sweetest smile. We call him "Nicky." Everyone says we girls should be jealous of Nicholas because of his soft skin and good looks, but Annabelle and I are tomboys and care more about doing stuff than about what we look like.

Annabelle is the eldest. She is eleven. Simon is almost ten and Susan is six. The Frère kids are young—five and six—and round-faced; Timothy Wagg is seven; Jeremy, his younger brother, is four. For a while, I cannot get their names straight. I stumble and fumble and blush, but they don't seem to mind at all. They just giggle at my confusion and make a hash of my name in return. Many times I have wished I had a more normal name. I am named after my father's mother, a naturalist who wrote books about birds and wildflowers. It is said she wrote those books to keep the presses rolling in the early days, when my grandfather started the book-publishing business called Doubleday & McClure.

I bicycle the five or six miles down to Ramsbroke as often as I'm allowed, to play and swim with leggy, dark-haired Simon and tall Annabelle, sweet Timothy and soft-eyed Jeremy, who is my favorite. Nelson doesn't enjoy our new friends very much. He rarely bikes down. I think it is because he is no longer the oldest or the big cheese, but maybe he just likes playing with Peter Stehli, his best buddy, more. They have been friends for years, in school and out.

On the beach we build sand castles, whole towns of them, then watch the tide sweep them away. And the swing and jungle gym are much bigger there than the little set at home, which has been around since I was small. The only tree to climb is a good-size, gnarly copper beech. Climbing it is fun. Its thick leaves hide Annabelle and me, allowing us to watch and listen to the nannies and neighbors. The neighbors have kids who come play with us. One family has a tree house with a deck, where you can look all the way across the bay to Centre Island. I have to be home by five-thirty for supper. I hate to leave. We have such fun.

In late August, before school starts, all the children have to get inoculations against various diseases. My mother tells me at breakfast on Tuesday morning that I have to go first. "Because you are not afraid of having shots and you don't cry. Set a good example for all the children and they will try to be as brave as you."

I am so thrilled at being called brave, I say, "Yes, I will do it," without really thinking the idea through, not that I could do anything to change the plan. I am always accused of not thinking, just bulldozing ahead and doing, and here I am, doing it again.

That afternoon, Sweeny drives the three of us, Mademoiselle, Nelson, and me, down to the office of our pediatrician, Dr. Wickers, where we meet all the neatly dressed English children huddled together on the wide gray-painted porch. We file into the waiting room without talking, but only the nannies and governesses sit down on the dark-patterned chairs and sofa. We children stand by the big window, chattering and giggling, our voices pitched higher than normal. The talk keeps our fears outside the window. The room is quite drab. Nelson stands off to the side. I feel bad for him, since he's not part of the Ramsbroke gang. Nicholas, the lucky one, will come with his mother on another day. The nannies and Mademoiselle Van Toch talk among themselves. Mademoiselle will tell me later that she thinks she is better, more educated, than the Scottish and English nannies. I think she is just being "uppity."

I am called first, as planned. I walk down the long hall into the dispensary room, my shoulders back and my head held high. Dr. Wickers sits writing notes at her little desk. Her nurse says, "Neltje is here for her shots, Doctor." Dr. Wickers stands up very tall; she stretches up like my father. She is a gentle white-haired lady with softly wrinkled skin. Her thin-lipped smile broadens into a wide welcome. She glides across the room, her hands outstretched. She holds my face close to hers and says, "I am so glad to see you, Neltje." And I believe her; I can feel she is glad to see me. The shot hurts, but I won't ever say so.

Mademoiselle is let go at the end of that summer of 1942. Tillie, the upstairs maid, will take care of Nelson and me now. We go to Green Vale School, a private school, over on Route 25A, about fifteen miles away. In October I turn eight years old. We go by school bus, which picks us up at the end of the driveway. Greenhouse, the chauffeur who replaced Sweeny, used to drive us to and from school, but with gas rationing due to the war, it is no longer possible. When the bus drops us off at the end of the day, we walk up the curving drive, now bare-limbed and dreary except for the droopy-leaved rhododendron bushes. The front door of our house can be hard to open. It is made of heavy glass with a carved bronze screen overlay of mythical and real animals. It is far heavier than even my tomboy arms can manage.

This afternoon at four-thirty, darkness enfolds the large house surrounded by tall shrubs and trees. Day ends in a frosty gloom. We wipe our feet on the bristle mat before opening the inside glass door. Silence greets us. We climb the three red-carpeted stairs, walk past the grandfather clock and the precious cannonball. It sits on a square block of wood. The red carpet continues in a sweep up the curved staircase to the second floor and leads to the pantry on the first floor as well. The grandfather clock chimes once for the half hour. Lights are on, but I hear no voices.

Tony, the butler, all four feet eight of him, stands on the top step of a ladder in the pantry. He is lifting down heavy silver platters from the pantry cupboards one by one. He hands them down to Tillie and her sister Ethel, who stand below with outstretched arms. He already has much of the silver—the knives, forks, spoons, the serving spoons, some bowls, water pitchers, and platters—lined up on the mahogany table in the dining room. I can see them all laid out in neat rows through the open dining room door. Tillie and Ethel carry the platters to the table—round tray platters, oval platters, rectangular platters, small, medium, and large platters, plain silver platters, ornate sculpted platters, simple silver trays—along with sauceboats, salt dishes, and pepper shakers, dozens of relish dishes.

"What is going on?" I ask.

"Your mother telephoned. She wants all the silver packed and shipped to Bonny Hall."

"Why? I don't understand. We have silver there," I say.

"She said she read in the papers that there are going to be air raids in New York City, which means we don't know what. We are just doing what she told us," says Tony.

Some of the silver pieces, like the wine coolers, are badly tarnished. They haven't been used since the last big party in the summer. Ethel has the silver polish and cloth in her hand. Tony stops her from picking up a large platter. "No point polishing any of this silver before it is shipped. It will only tarnish before the next use. I doubt Mrs. D. will use this silver down south; I think she just wants it safe," Tony says.

Nelson says nothing. He often just goes silent and stares, says, "No, nothing is wrong," but I know he is angry or upset in some way. He usually tells me later—sometimes the next day—what was bothering him. We sit quietly at the oval table by the window, eat our cookies, drink our milk, and go to our rooms to do homework. The house even smells empty when my parents go south. Life goes out of *home.* Tillie, Tony, and Maggie Burns, the cook, are fun to be with—more fun than Mademoiselle or even Nana—but the space around me seems more hollow. They play cards with us, tell stories, and we get to eat with them in the help's dining room, instead of alone in the main dining room. We giggle and tease each other. But we can't let our parents know we eat with the help.

Two weeks later, my mother phones on a Sunday night. She talks to Tillie for a long time. "Yes, ma'am. I will, ma'am. When will this be, Mrs. Doubleday? . . . She will not be coming out from the city? . . . We are to meet her at the train? . . . Yes, ma'am. I will get all their things packed. . . . The children are right here. Will you speak with them?"

Nelson gets the phone first. He doesn't say much more than "Hello . . . How come? . . . What is her name?" After a long pause he goes on: "I will miss all my friends, particularly Peter Stehli. Could he come down for Christmas? . . . Ya, well, okay. Thanks, Mom."

He hands me the phone. My mother explains to me that Nelson and I will spend the winter at Bonny Hall because of the war. She doesn't want us to be living near New York City, but she doesn't say why, nor does she say she misses us.

"I miss you and Daddy," I say.

She tells me my father is busy with his business, and with the house full of guests, she, too, is very busy. She has to plan all the meals, difficult with ration books now, and keep the business wives amused, which she says is a chore. Miss Luckin has been hired to care for us, and to be our teacher. We have to continue with school. At the end of our school week, she will meet us at the train gate in Pennsylvania Station. "You will have a drawing room, difficult to get now, you know, because of all the army and navy troops moving about the country. You will be taking the Havana Special. You are to get off at Yemassee, not Green Pond. Be sure to remember. Do not get off the train at Washington. They shunt the train around a good deal now, guests tell me, splitting off sections. Do stay in the drawing room, or who knows where you might end up." She laughs. "Tillie will take you to the station."

We are huddled in the upstairs phone room. Nelson and I look at each other, but nobody speaks until Tillie looks at her watch. "Bed," she says.

Perhaps sensing I am upset to be going on a long train ride to Bonny Hall with someone I don't know, Tillie comes into my bedroom to say good night, but she stays. She sits near me on my bed, says, "Well now, what do you think of going to Bonny Hall for the winter?" Tillie is Irish. Her voice feels soft, with a bit of a lilt, as she talks in the darkness.

"I am scared. I have never even seen Miss Luckin, and to have to travel with someone I don't know on the train frightens me. What if she is mean? We will have no one to defend us."

Tillie tries to reassure me by saying, "Your mother would not hire a 'not nice' woman," and we giggle at the phrase. She gets up, gives me a kiss on the forehead, says good night, but leaves the light on by the door in her room and my door open a crack. I don't ask her how she knows Miss Luckin will be nice. I understand that she is just trying to reassure me. Strange things are happening to me without my knowing why, like the hormones I started taking so I will get my "period" and then stop growing. My father does not want me to be six feet tall. I am five-nine now, and I have just turned nine. But why does he care how tall I am?

— THREE —

Winter at Bonny Hall

At Bonny Hall I am given a new horse, a grown-up horse, named Little Dan, son of my father's horse. I can't believe he is mine. He is so beautiful, and I can ride twice a day sometimes, like on weekends. Oh! What a difference in the way he handles, like quicksilver, immediate and smooth. He is a rich deep brown with a long black mane and the gentlest brown eyes. He nickers when I first get near him and his velvet nose nuzzles my neck. Almost every day, I bring him carrots from the kitchen and apples from the tree by the three greenhouses where my father grows his special camellias. I am not meant to pick them, but I don't care. After feeding him two ripe apples, a little of his spittle lies in the palm of my hand. I wipe it off on the seat of my jodhpurs and tell him not to be "so sloppy." I brush and curry him, comb out the burrs and odd bits of grass and hay from his mane, then halter him and take him out of his stall. I tie him up to the corral post, pull some green grass by the fence, and give him a treat until I can return. Whenever I can, I ride. Eddy, the stable boy, saddles him up for me because I can't yet lift the weight of the saddle high enough to get it up on Little Dan's back, but I can bridle him.

Haskell is no longer here. He just joined the army. I miss him, my hand in his, the easy way we had with each other, the adventures we shared since I was a baby. I worry about him in the war and wonder what to do with myself alone in the empty hours now.

Mr. Jaycock is gone, too, because there is no dairy farm, no cows. My mother said the government shut the farm down, particularly the dairy, because Little John had syphilis. A joke was made of this at the dinner table by my father, in front of all the guests. Frankie, the butler's helper, told me after lunch one day. That was mean of my father to make fun of Little John. He also teased my mother about the failure of her farm, for the farm was her baby; she "kept the books" but did not like the animals. I know what the disease comes from and that it should be kept private. But I am often told I am a killjoy, with "sanctimonious attitudes."

Bill Magill runs the plantation now. His daughter Angie is close to my age. We jump rope and play board games together, climb where we shouldn't climb: attics and creepy places under the houses. I am glad to have a girl to play with. Until now, I have been playing with Nelson and his friends—baseball and car racing, stuff like that. I get beat up from time to time by Nelson if I am winning. I don't understand why boys have to win all the time, like my mother says they need to do. Why are they so fragile that they can't cope with a loss or two? As a girl, I am meant to lose all the time? No, that's not right.

When the navy pilots now living in Mr. Jaycock's house or the guests at Bonny Hall want to ride, I accompany them and get to be the guide. My parents won't let me ride alone, which irks me, because my elder half sister, Pucky, is allowed to ride anywhere by herself. She is ten years older, but I am a better rider, I think. There are others who do not agree, like my mother. But she has never watched me ride, so how would she know? It is all an age thing, something I can do nothing about. I hate being the youngest.

My father is very proud of his purchase of the adjoining plantation. His neighbor didn't really want to sell. It took three years to get the deal done. My father is an impatient man. Before he bought the other plantation, none of us, including my mother, could mention it without being subjected to a tirade. There is no house; no buildings or fences other than a sketchy exterior fence; nothing but scrubby land with a few blades of grass, not enough for cattle or horses. The sparse wooded areas and grasslands have never been cultivated, so very different from the rice, corn, and rye fields of Bonny Hall. Tree branches and vines make riding treacherous. Once, while riding, I saw three turkey buzzards, proud as can be, on the belly of a lone bloated cow, her four legs rigid and up in the air at the edge of the big field. The insides of her belly could be seen. I was disgusted. When baked by the sun and with no rain, the one-track clay lane through the land becomes rock-hard, particularly when you fall off your horse. I think my father just likes owning land. I wouldn't dare say so.

I am nine. When I was very little, I sat in front of my father on his horse, Big Dan. For me to be allowed to ride with my father on his horse was a treat. He wore tan jodhpurs and tall black riding boots, which Jimmy polished. I had new brown boots on and I was three years old. I liked being so high up on Big Dan with my father's left arm around my waist, holding me close against him. I held on to the front of the saddle. Big Dan just walked slowly around the front driveway in a circle. My father told Nelson he could have a ride next. But Nelson said no and ran into the house. He really didn't like horses.

I liked looking far into the distance, over rice fields, enjoying the rocking motion and smell of the horse. Someone had to hand me up to my father. When I was four, I climbed up the four steps of the painted wooden platform that sat in the driveway in front of the house. The platform was to help guests, ladies and children, to mount their horses easily. Eventually I could swing myself up on Little Dan with a jump, like cowboys do in the movies.

On special occasions, my father asks the darkies to sing for us after dinner. It is a treat to be able to stay up so late. Before an evening of "Sing" when I was seven, I asked my father, "Why do you call the Negroes 'darkies' when you want them to come sing for you?"

"Why do you always ask 'why'?" he retorted, and moved away.

It is tricky asking questions, particularly after lunch or dinner. The adults, especially my father, act differently then, and what they say at night is often not even remembered in the morning. It's hard to know what is real. I am often confused.

Even though I am nine and Nelson ten, we still eat at the card table in the dining room with Miss Luckin at six o'clock, well before the grown-ups. After supper I go up to my sisters' room, which is above the boot room in the main house. Pucky and Madeleine are both trying on clothes, attempting to decide what they will wear tonight for the Sing. Four Marines are coming from Parris Island for dinner and the Sing, so there is much excitement. They try on dresses, skirts, and different blouse combinations. The two beds are a jumble of clothes.

"Which skirt? My blue one with the red tailored blouse, or the black with the gold blouse? Which?" Puck asks.

"You can wear my black dress with the white piqué collar, Puck. It will look so good with your tan," says Madeleine, who is twenty-one.

"I can't fit into that dress. You know damn well I can't." Puck grabs her robe off the bed, sticks her arms in the sleeves, and wraps the belt around her waist.

"First dibs on the bathroom. I am going to fix my face," she says. She walks out of the bedroom into the hall, and then into the bathroom. I follow her, barely squeaking in as she closes the door. The bathroom is not big, so I sit on the toilet. I love to watch her ceremoniously "putting on her face."

First, Puck uses a washcloth with soap and water to remove the iodine and baby oil mixture that she has used as a tanning lotion, then pats her face and neck dry. She tips the bottle of face foundation into her left hand, rubs both her hands together, and carefully smears the foundation goop evenly over her face and down her neck. She tells me it is important that her neck and face be all smooth and one color, otherwise she would look silly. Puck finds her powder compact on the bottom shelf in the medicine cabinet, which is jammed full of cosmetic stuff. She powders her face carefully, around her eyes and plucked eyebrows, across her forehead, down around her cheeks, chin, nose, and mouth. I say, "Pucky, this takes a lot of time, and you are pretty without all this stuff. Why do you gunk up your face so?" She powders her neck and all the chest that would be seen and says, "Darling Nelch, I want to look the best I can, so everyone will think I'm gorgeous." She laughs a little and smiles down at me on the toilet. She then puts on something called blush. She has several different shades of blush, different for day and night and depending on how much of a suntan she has. Her eyes will be next. When she begins her eyes I lose patience and go to check in on Madeleine, who sits on the bed, putting nail polish on her toes.

"Have you decided what you are going to wear for dinner and the Sing tonight?" I ask.

"Yes," she replies. "That pretty skirt over there on the chair with my white eyelet peasant blouse. The two together will show off my tan."

"How come you and Pucky are getting so fussy about what you wear, just because a couple of Marines are coming over from Parris Island for dinner? I mean, why the fuss? There is no place to dance, and you won't see them ever again," I say.

"Oh, honey, you'll know when you are older. I promise you will."

I hate when people say "You will know when you are older." It makes me feel small and stupid. I wander off downstairs and go into the living room. No one is there. I don't want to run into Nelson, so I head toward the pantry just as Ephrom comes out the swinging pantry door to ring the gong for cocktails before dinner. It is seven o'clock. Dinner will be at seven-thirty, but they never go in to dinner until quarter to eight or even later, which makes Anna, the cook, very cross. I wonder if Madeleine and Puck will make it down in time, decide not to wait around to see, because tempers will flare, my father's in particular, if they are late.

I stop by the kitchen, where all the help are busy chopping vegetables, stirring pots, or filling the muffin pan with cornmeal. We will be having turkey Southern style, Betsey tells me before saying, "No time to talk now, Miss Neltje. Sorry, hon." She refocuses on the mush in front of her and I leave for my room. I want to dress up, too, so I'll look older. I meet my father coming down the hall from his room. He is dressed in my favorite jacket, white linen, the design showing Chinese junks with aqua sails.

"Where are you going, Josephine?"

My father calls me "Josephine" when he is in a sweet mood. He calls me that because he often calls Nelson "Joe."

"Up to change into a dress. Pucky and Madeleine are getting all dressed up because the Marines are coming for dinner. So I think I'll put on a dress, too," I reply.

I hear the dinner gong sound just as I put on my party shoes. Miss Luckin says, "Come, let me brush your hair and put on the pretty red velvet ribbon."

My hair is short, just so the tip of my ear shows. I always have to have it cut this way, my mother says, and always at the barber's in Best & Co. by the office in Garden City. When I grow up, I am going to have long hair and wear pigtails. I have on my red velvet dress with a white lace collar. As I start down the stairs, Nelson comes out from his room. He is dressed up, too. We, all of us, are dressed up for these dumb Marines, I think, but I feel good that I look pretty.

"Do you want to play rummy while they eat dinner?" he asks as we walk through the office.

"Of course," I answer.

When the dining room doors open after dinner, my mother rises from the table, as do all the guests and my father. She leads everyone to the terrace, where it is still warm. She is wearing a long blue-and-magenta lounge dress from Hattie Carnegie. She is very proud of this dress. My father, in a rage because she was away visiting her mother and father, gave the dress to Ephrom for his wife. My mother made my father get it back, but she never again felt delight in wearing it. She sits down now next to the Crowells, whom she really likes, and the Brownells, who are nearly neighbors up north. The Marshalls are talking with Madeleine and the four Marines in dress uniform. I can watch them without seeming to. Puck runs upstairs to get a sweater, and my father calls for Jimmy to bring out the blankets and a few hunting jackets in case the women, in particular, get chilly. Nelson, Miss Luckin, and I sit off to the right in the front row of chairs. We have a perfect close view of the square metal box on the four-sided wooden post. A fire crackles in the box, sending sparks in wild disarray. A grouping of men stand around the fire in jackets, some with caps or hats, making them hard to identify in the darkness. I don't recognize any of them. I think most are field hands, except far off to the left I see Betsey. I have heard her sing a solo spiritual before. She has a deep, rolling voice that makes your spine tingle.

Once the guests are seated and have after-dinner drinks, my father calls out, "Let's get started. Ephrom, wet their whistles before they begin." Ephrom and Frankie appear from the bushes to the right, carrying trays full of drinks.

Below us, the Bonny Hall Negro Choir stands in a half circle before the fire. With a great deal of shuffling of feet, coughs, and humming sounds, they begin with the spiritual "Down by the Riverside." Their voices are mellow and full of emotion. I want to cry. They sing with such sadness but also with a joyful energy that seems to encompass us all, the whole world. I feel I belong somehow but don't know how I really fit. Their voices, rolling out like waves lapping on the beach, soothe and envelop us. We clap, and all the guests, including the four Marines, are smiling and nodding. They also have felt a connection.

The choir sings three more spirituals before they sing "How Dry I Am, How Dry I Am, Mr. Doubleday, He Know How Dry I Am": a signal for Ephrom and Frankie to come out again from the bushes with the tray of martini glasses full of clear liquid. Martinis? After dinner? Or Everclear, more likely. The singers stand around the fire, drinking and smoking, murmuring to one another. Nelson and I get a ginger ale and the guests replenish their drinks. "Joshua Fought the Battle of Jericho" is the next spiritual, and in that one I can hear Betsey's voice above all the others. Voices in the darkness meld into a chorus that could be twice as large, their words so clear. The throb of music in their voices speaks of a belonging I have never known.

The next day, four guests, a navy pilot named Dirk Winters, and I ride horses down to Parker's Ferry, where Mr. Maugham lives. We rarely stop to visit unless my father is along, which is almost never. Mr. Maugham hates to be disturbed when writing in the morning or when he naps in the afternoon. He has written a novel entitled *The Razor's Edge* and is now going over the galley proofs. Occasionally, when he hears the horses, he will come out of the small white clapboard house where he writes. Today he stands in the doorway, says hello in a distracted, halting manner. He holds his right hand above his eyes to shade them from the sun. Mr. Maugham stutters badly at times, strains to get the simplest words out. I feel embarrassed watching him struggle. When he plays bridge or gin rummy with my mother after teatime most afternoons, he is more relaxed than when first meeting someone. He stutters far less then. He likes to play cards with my mother, who is also a good cardplayer. I pay attention to his nicotine-stained fingers and wrinkled hands when he picks up the cards. These are the same fingers that hold the pen he uses to write books. Special hands. He can be very snappish and mean. Although he scares me, I have a secret liking for him because when I was very little, he gave me a teddy bear bigger than I was. That was my best present ever. Last Christmas, Mr. Maugham gave me five dollars. I had never had money of my own before that.

I am hot from the ride in the full sun. The guests and the navy pilot chat with Mr. Maugham. There is a cool breeze here by the Combahee

River. I gently kick Little Dan's side with my left heel and head him up front to Mr. Maugham. I lean down from my horse, hand Mr. Maugham an envelope, and say, "This is from my father. He said you needed it right away." He takes the envelope and says, "Th-th-thank you, N-N-N-N-Neltje." We say good-bye, turn our horses, and head back down the road.

At the fork, Dirk stops and says, "Everyone, let's go to the picnic ground. It is not far, just a short ride through the woods."

The guests, two business couples who have not ridden a horse since the year before, say they are tired and will just head home. Dirk says, "Neltje, come along. You and I will go."

Dirk often takes me riding on his day off. His wife is pregnant, and his kids are too young to ride. He gives me Hershey bars from the commissary at the naval Air Force base where he works, and gives them to Nelson as well. I wish he would give them just to me. They are a big treat in wartime. He gives me a small locket with his picture in it, a present I treasure. I think he loves me. He is tall and strong. He hugs me.

In mid-December 1943, Dirk and I go off for a ride alone. I am nine years old. I think I am grown up. I tell Miss Luckin I will be gone more than two hours, riding over to the other plantation with Dirk. Our horseback rides have been getting longer. I'm on Little Dan, as always. We often ride over there, make the loop back past Church Street, Maugham's drive, Harper Landing, and the Negro graveyard. In the woods, Dirk stops suddenly, gets off his horse, and tells me to get off mine. He tethers the horses, takes my hand, and leads me over to a big boulder, where he tells me the story of how the Earth came to be. While he talks to me, he pulls me close, runs his hand over my hair, touches my cheek, and kisses me on the lips. I don't know what to do. I can't run away; he could catch me in a second. I like the feel of his hand on me, on my hair, my face. He is being very gentle, different from the way he is at Bonny Hall with my father. He talks to me about what I am reading, tells me about his flying, about how much he likes being with me.

He unbuttons my jodhpurs, says, "Well, what do you think of that?"

"I don't know," I reply, but don't ask why he does this.

He feels me between my legs, says, "You feel so soft and good. Do you like me touching you?" I nod my head. He stands right behind me, holds me against him, with his left arm across my chest. Many years later, I remember that embrace and recognize with shock that it was exactly the same embrace as my father's when I was a small girl, riding with him on his horse. I am tall and rangy now and have not stopped growing despite the hormones I have been given to halt my growth.

On New Year's Eve, Dirk comes over from his place across the lawn to have dinner at our house. His wife isn't feeling well and stays home with their children. Champagne flows. The house is bursting, with every bed taken. Puck and Madeleine are home, and two business couples and Don Elder, a bachelor editor at Doubleday, all are visiting over the Christmas holidays. I am trying to stay awake long enough to "bring in the New Year" but am having difficulty because everyone is talking and laughing at the same time. The noise is overwhelming. No one is listening. I, too, sip champagne but don't like the way it fizzes up my nose. I watch the living room fire, feel bored with the chatter around me. But I often feel that way. I'd rather be alone with my thoughts.

Dirk sees I am falling asleep. He says, "I'll put Neltje to bed." I try to hide in the bathroom to get undressed, but Dirk comes in, watches me take off my undershirt and underpants, get into my pajamas. I need to pee. I want him to go away but don't know how to say so. It is past ten o'clock and I am very sleepy. When I climb into bed, Dirk kneels on the floor next to my head. My eyes close. I drift in half sleep. "Here, suck this," Dirk says softly. His hand caresses my back. Soft flesh presses against my lips. "Open your mouth, like that, yes. Yes, that is it. Suck it like a lollipop."

— FOUR —

Sealed Door

My mother calls up the stairs wanting to know what is taking Dirk so long. "I am telling Neltje stories. I'll be right down." He pulls away quickly, zips up his fly, kisses me on the forehead. "Don't tell anyone. It is just our secret," he whispers. I try to spit out the sweet smell of him but fall asleep.

The riding, the touching, and sometimes the demand to suck Dirk's penis continue for the rest of the winter. I say nothing to anyone. Before I leave to go back north to school, Dirk threatens me. "If you tell anyone, I will come kill you. Do you understand that?" He never waits for an answer.

Once, he asks me to come into his house with him and takes me to the summer porch off the main living room. I am nervous to be there. He comes back into the room, tells me to lie down on the daybed against the wall. I do as he says. His wife and children are there at home. They might walk in, any one of them; it is midafternoon. Dirk undoes my pants, rubs me, caresses me between my legs. His caresses arouse me, make me ache down there. He pushes his finger barely inside me. I tremble. He wants me to suck his penis. I would have, but we both hear footsteps. He zips up and says harshly, "Fix your clothes," as his wife, Jenny, comes around the arched opening into the room. He tells her, "Neltje was tired after a ride, so I let her nap there on the daybed." Lies stream out of him with such ease; I am frightened.

My father puts Dirk in charge of the plantation when my parents go north in May. Dirk phones my father every Sunday evening with a report on the workings at Bonny Hall. He always asks to speak to me, and my parents think, How nice.

"Have you told anyone our secret?" he asks.

"No," I reply.

"I will come kill you if you tell." And the phone goes dead.

Dirk doesn't talk to me anymore when he calls. He just threatens. I keep thinking he loves me. He is scared because he has a wife and children. I can be strong, pretend it is not happening. I avoid being around on Sunday evenings.

In August, I visit Puck in her room after dinner. She is propped up in bed, reading a book. It is late. We talk about last winter at Bonny Hall. As she questions me about my riding with Dirk so often, I open up, tell her about what he did with me. Part of me so wants to believe he is making love to me, that he loves me. But I know what we did together is wrong. I feel guilty because he has a wife. I beg Puck not to tell anyone, especially my mother. I am scared of what her reaction might be.

The next day, Puck says we need to tell my story to Dr. Wickers. She tells me that what Dirk did with me was not right at all. At Dr. Wickers's office, Puck sits over on the right on a straight-back chair between the windows. Dr. Wickers sits in front of me, maybe a long arm's length away. I sit on a wooden chair facing her. We sit in silence. Dr. Wickers begins in her soft voice by asking me if I enjoyed riding with the navy pilot. I burst out crying and never stop. She asks intimate questions about what happened, especially about when Dirk made me suck his penis. I feel such shame and disgust.

Puck is crying, too. She looks appalled. Is it because I have to answer these questions or because she is disgusted with me? I can't bear to lose her love.

When we leave Dr. Wickers's office, Puck takes my hand, says, "Sorry, darling. That was rough."

My mother greets me at the door, does not send me to my room as punishment for sassing her the night before, so I know she knows.

From then on, I have little memory of being at Bonny Hall. It is as if I don't exist when I am there, and I will be there two more winters. Snippets of a scene or a conversation float in my mind, but certainly the joy of being in the moment in the wild has left me. I feel disoriented from time to time, ragged, with gnawing anxieties unrelated to any current circumstance. I say nothing. My emotions freeze, and I see myself from the outside, as though I am watching a movie—as if it is not about me.

My mother takes me to a psychiatrist in New York City that summer. As we drive to the city in silence with Greenhouse, the chauffeur, at the wheel, I fantasize I have an invisible sword that goes through the glass window and fells all the telephone poles along the parkway. The police cannot find me. I say nothing to Dr. McGraw, the psychiatrist, during our excruciating times together. In silence I stare at the Rorschach tests put in front of me. All I see are penises, but I am not going to tell him that. My mother would think I am disgusting, and he would surely tell her when she goes into his office after I finish. I don't trust him. He is a man.

Dr. McGraw offers to have me live with him and his family on Block Island for the rest of the month of August so that I can learn to trust men again. But my mother refuses his offer, saying the family will take care of its own. My mother never mentions Dirk or what happened, other than to tell me never to mention Dirk to my father. It would make him angry. She also says on the way home, "Dirk has been moved from his base in South Carolina and from the plantation. Admiral de Florez, your father's great friend, made that happen." My being molested, my fears and guilt about all that went on in the fields and woods, the threatening phone calls—nothing of what had gone on is ever mentioned again. I feel I am an animal in a cage of glass. I can see out, but nobody wants to be in here with me. I don't exist for them. The air around me keeps me apart. I feel this way a lot of the time but say nothing.

When I am fifty-four years old, with many therapies behind me, I walk into a coffee shop in Washington, D.C., on the way to see a Joan Mitchell exhibition at the Phillips Gallery. Three construction workers sit at the counter. They turn to look at me, as guys do when a woman enters what they consider their domain. For the very first time since the Dirk business, panic does not grip my belly, nor cause saliva to juice my mouth. I stop just inside the door, smile, approach the stainless-steel counter, and in a clear voice ask the guy behind the counter for a cup of coffee and a bagel with butter and jam. I sit at a table and wait. The men look at me, case me up and down. They don't bother me. I have no anxiety.

This is new. Before this time, I would have panicked. For instance, in a cab coming from Kennedy Airport the previous year, the cabdriver took a different route, one I did not know. I was terrified. In my mind, he was kidnapping me. How and where could I get help? He could take me to an isolated area, sexually abuse me, and kill me. The voice saying "I will come kill you" remains. In my seventies, I still hear it.

Later in August, my mother and I sit on the terrace in Oyster Bay. "The apartment I found for you and Puck is a good address, Thirty East Seventy-first Street, close to Central Park. The apartment has four bedrooms, all with baths, except for yours, Nana's, and Nelson's; you three have to share a bath. Nelson will be away at Eaglebrook boarding school."

This is all new to me, my going to live in New York City. Why can't we still go to Green Vale and have Tillie care for us? I never ask that question, but I do ask, "Why is Nelson going away to school? Has he misbehaved? Is that why?"

"Of course not. Anyway, you will be living with Puck, who will be going to college at Barnard."

My mother seems anxious to get us children out of the way, giving her time to be with my father. It is an anxiety I have sensed before, but this time the pressure has increased. Because of what? Dirk's molesting me? Puck's need for a place to live while going to Barnard College in the city?

"I have rehired Nana to take care of you and any guests, and there will be a cook and maid, probably Tillie, as well. Madeleine is still hell-bent on joining the navy; she wants to be where the boys are. Won't that be nice to have Nana back? You didn't like Miss Luckin much," she says in a half-questioning tone.

I say, "She was a liar. Remember, she told you I pushed her down the stairs from the schoolroom. I wasn't even in the house. I was out riding with Dirk. She was standing there by the front door when I walked in the house, crying and sniffling into her hankie. She said she had told you what a nasty child I am, that you must punish me. Remember?"

I remember so clearly seeing Miss Luckin at the front door in her blue jumper and gray sweater. She was indeed crying into her handkerchief when I returned from riding that afternoon with Dirk. "You pushed me down the stairs. I know you did. Nelson was there. He saw you do it," she said, sniffling into her hankie. "I have told your mother what a nasty child you are. She will punish you. I told her she really must. You are out of control, willful, disobedient, and horrid."

"But Miss Luckin, I haven't been in the house for hours. I just got off my horse. I have been out riding with Dirk all the way over at the other plantation. What is going on?"

"You are such a little liar."

I ran down the hall, heading for my room. My mother, who was in her office, saw me start up the stairs and called out, "You come in here right this minute."

I stopped on the third step, turned back, and walked down the three steps slowly.

"Miss Luckin told me that you pushed her down the stairs by the schoolroom. What were you thinking? What you did is mean and horrible. She could have really hurt herself. How could you? I am ashamed of you. She is a nice older woman who has tried hard to be a good teacher and companion to you. There will be no riding for a week. That is the end of it. Your father will be very disappointed in your behavior."

"But that is not true, what she says. I was—"

"Don't make it worse. Don't make it worse with more lies. Enough. Go to your room."

Later my mother came into my room and found me sitting astride the windowsill. She told me that Dirk had come over for a drink and confirmed that I was with him. I was glad she found me, because I had been trying to figure how to land in the camellia bed and not on the iron railing of the stairs leading down to the camellia garden. I didn't want to hurt before I died. I told her that I didn't want to live anymore because she never listened to me or believed what I said. She said that she was tired of my crying wolf, of my being such a drama queen. I wanted to tell her that I made scenes to get her attention, so she would listen.

Now, discussing my new living arrangements, I want to say, You believed Miss Luckin without listening to me, and that hurts. But I can't. Instead, I say, "Yes, I am glad she is gone. Where did you find her? I mean, where did she work before she came to us?"

"She worked in a prison," my mother replies.

When I give her an astonished look, she says, "Well, darling, you need to remember I was in South Carolina, and you know what the phone is like down there. Your father wouldn't let me come north, and I probably couldn't have gotten a berth on the train because of all the troops moving about the country." My mother draws on her cigarette and waves her right hand in the air in explanation. Her fingers are delicate. The two nails on her right hand are stained by cigarette smoke. She does not use nail polish but does spend time at her dressing table in the morning, creaming her nails and pushing back the cuticles.

The summer of 1944, the weather is beautiful. I ride my bicycle as far as allowed and farther. Miss Rand is the new governess-companion for the summer. I begged my mother to hire someone young, but it didn't happen. I spend a good part of every morning watching the new French chauffeur wash and polish the cars. He is handsome and has green eyes. Greenhouse also helps, but he doesn't interest me. I miss Sweeny, our old chauffeur. He has cancer, the disease everyone talks about now. But André, the new chauffeur with green eyes, makes my body tingle.

In the afternoon, I go to the pool. My mother sits under the green canvas canopy by the swimming pool in her white sharkskin bathing suit. The pack of Benson & Hedges cigarettes lies on the arm of the Adirondack chair. A sweating highball packed with ice and a sprig of mint sits on the table to her left. My father is playing tennis on the clay court behind us with Mr. Kenny, the pro; Malcolm Johnson, who works at Doubleday; and John Martin, a man with one arm. The other he lost in the Great War. Despite that injury, he is merry, always telling funny stories. He won my heart by secretly showing me how to light a match in a book of matches with one hand.

I look across the pool to the wide view of Oyster Bay and Centre Island. Our butler, Tony, stops by to see if my mother needs anything.

"Do not take the drink cart back to the house, Tony. The tennis game is not finished," my mother says over her shoulder.

"No, madam. I brought out more ice and the beer for Mr. Kenny," he says, and then turns away toward the house. Tony is shorter than the canopied drink cart, which is about five feet high and two and a half feet wide. The two shelves are of thick glass to bear the weight of glasses, liquor, an ice bucket full of ice, a large pitcher of iced tea, plus bottles of quinine and soda water. I know he struggles to push it out here from the pantry, but he never lets my mother or father see how he grimaces when he has to push it up the hill or through the thick grass.

I climb on the frame of the canopy. I like to hang upside down. My behavior scares my mother. She is not athletic at all. Occasionally, she does the breaststroke across the pool, but she does not really swim. It is strange, because my father is athletic, plays tennis and baseball at Doubleday Company's field days, held on our croquet field, and Mr. Kenny comes every evening at four in the summer. I have a half-hour tennis lesson now, Nelson has an hour, and then the men play doubles when my father gets home from the office.

Nelson paddles the length of the pool and back on a reversible red-and-blue air mattress. He looks funny from my upside-down position. We have been growing apart since he went away to school. I no longer have someone to talk to, to tell about my loneliness.

FIVE

Living Apart

In the fall of 1945, Nana, Puck, and I move from the very dreary Seventy-first Street apartment to a swank two-story apartment in the Carlyle Hotel. It has fewer bedrooms, just three. There is no pretense that my mother and father will spend time in the city, as had been suggested last year. The largest bedroom goes to Puck. As usual, Nana and I share a room, which is right next door. The third bedroom has only a single bed, a bureau, and a small comfortable chair by the window. After a couple of months, Nana moves into the single room because she snores so loudly, I can't sleep. I got up the nerve to tell Puck about Nana's snoring, but felt guilty that I was being disloyal to Nana, telling on her. Puck called our mother, and this time she listened.

The apartment is on the twentieth floor. That winter I often run up the twenty flights of stairs after school and sometimes continue to the very top floor of the building, the thirty-fifth floor. Shoes are put out to be shined before many of the hotel rooms and apartments. They are too alluring to a ten-year-old girl. I swipe a shoe from one door, take it two flights down and to the far corner, then mismatch it with another shoe and take that three floors down. The game goes on until I become bored or find some other deviltry.

One day that spring, I make an ink bomb. I made water bombs before, but an ink bomb will make a most terrific splash. From the window at the back of the large living room, I look down on the patios behind the brownstone houses twenty floors below. On the first patio, a woman dressed in old clothes is painting a table white, reviving it. I say to myself, That table would make a perfect target. I make a water bomb, folding each section with great care. I blow air into it, put it in a thin paper box, and pour in the ink. It leaks a little, so I have to work fast. I open the big window as wide as I can. The woman below steps back to admire the work she has done. I drop the bomb, close the window quickly, and race up to peek down from one floor above. The bomb hit right on target. That is all I see. Ten minutes later, the doorbell rings. A manager comes to the door of my bedroom with Nana. I sit at my desk, doing my homework. He asks me very politely if I threw an ink bomb below. I lie, of course: "I've been here in my room doing homework. You can come in and see if you want."

During the summer months, Nelson and I are sent to live with my mother's brother, Thomas N. McCarter Jr., and his wife and children in Marion, Massachusetts, Buzzards Bay. My parents stay at Barberries in Oyster Bay and clearly do not want us around. My father has rented this large house on the water for all of us: my three cousins, Tommy, Sue, and Patrick, who is just a baby; Clare, Patrick's nurse; and Aunt Sukie and Uncle Tom. We live in a wonderful disarray of gin and whiskey, sailing, swimming, and playing tennis at a small club. Sue, Nelson, and I go by cab to the movies many nights in the surrounding villages, as far away as Wareham. We know we are spoiled. I love the sense of belonging, the delight of having friends who live across the street or a bicycle ride away, something I have never known on Long Island, where friends live miles away. I bike downtown every day and to the nearby tennis club, where many of us kids gather just to be together.

Sue and I crew for Uncle Tom in his Herreshoff Twelve sailboat in the Saturday races on Buzzards Bay. He drinks far too much whiskey before lunch every Saturday and is usually quite plastered when he gets into the sailboat at the yacht club at about two in the afternoon. It is always a bit dicey crewing for Uncle Tom. He has a brazen attitude and a loud voice when drunk. That he makes up his own rules about crossing the starting line should not be a surprise to any of us, but it leads to some terrifying moments when twenty-two sailboats just like ours come bearing down on us as we cross the starting line. And twenty-two sailboats are left in our wake with flapping sails. "GODDAMN SON OF A BITCH. What do they think they are doing? I have the right-of-way," bellows Uncle Tom. Sue and I just keep our heads down and bail water.

In midsummer, my mother phones to tell me that in the fall I will be living with Aunt Virginia and Uncle Uzal, my mother's youngest brother and his wife. I do not know them really. I have met them at McCarter funerals and birthdays, and at my grandparents' house and farm in Rumson, New Jersey. There is no explanation of why them or why I am not continuing to live with Nana. Puck, I know, will graduate from Barnard this summer. "They said they would take a chance on you. They have no children." This is all my mother says. I am used to being shoved around like a pawn on a game board with no explanation, but each time it hurts. I take in the news this time as if I have been told I will have chicken soup for supper. I don't know where Puck will be. Nana has been let go.

Before I move in with them, Aunt Virginia and Uncle Uzal give a party for me, an early birthday party, they call it. The party is held at their house in Rumson. They have wound string all over their yard, creating web upon web for a treasure hunt. No one has ever taken this much trouble over a party for me before: clowns and puppeteers, magicians and movies, yes, but not an intricate game that took preparation, thought, time, and caring to create. I am thrilled that they care enough to do that for me. I don't know how to express my delight. I feel loved for the first time.

At the end of September, I move back into my old room in the same apartment as last winter in the Carlyle Hotel. Aunt Virginia and Uncle Uzal move in the same day with Bessie, the cook, friend, and dog walker, and their dog, Fuzzy, a medium-size poodle. I have a home.

In late October of that year, 1946, my father is taken to the hospital in Glen Cove because he has had trouble breathing. They find his left lung has collapsed. After more than a week's stay and endless tests, he is sent home with an order to stay in bed until Christmas, maybe longer, depending on future tests and X-rays. The doctors have no idea why his lung collapsed.

My mother asks me to come to Barberries every weekend. She wants time for herself apart from my father, to talk on the phone with her friends, take a walk, or read a book. My father, like most men, Tillie says, is a lousy patient. My job these weekends is to keep my father company for an hour or two. I enjoy having time alone with him, because he is always curious. He has an early-model TV, thanks to his good friend Admiral de Florez. The images are very snowy and there are only a few shows to watch. But my father loves watching baseball, though the entire game is gray and fuzzy, and wrestling, with all the fake moans and groans. He thinks it is hilarious fun. I don't think it is so hilarious; I am taken in by their performances of torture.

He is fascinated by what is advertised on these sport shows, for he has never heard of many of the items. He orders everything advertised: boxes of Brillo and Pepsodent toothpaste, Ajax and Clorox, literature on John Deere tractors and other farm equipment, folders of information on Ford trucks and cars, and Chevrolet ones as well. Boxes and boxes arrive in the bedroom, are opened, examined briefly, then put away somewhere. What interests him is how the products are merchandized. My father is not a reader of books, not a book publisher in that sense. He is a marketing man; his interest is in selling lots more books to lots more people. That was how his career began. He bought month-old magazines for almost nothing and sold them for a profit the following month. In his own way, he is a snake charmer. He then got Emily Post's book on etiquette, including the right to sell it by mail, which was the beginning of the Doubleday book clubs. His endeavor became such a success that his father took him into his firm, Doubleday & McClure, rather than face the competition, or so the story goes.

We have a large new Scott phonograph, along with yards of 78 rpm records of show tunes, musicals, ballads, and love songs. My father wants me to put on *Annie Get Your Gun*, with Ethel Merman. He wants the whole musical played over and over again. He laughs till he chokes every time she sings "Anything You Can Do" or "You Can't Get a Man with a Gun." I love hearing his laughter.

My father, larger than life in size, stride, gesture, a man with a wild imagination, is now felled and scared, although he never has admitted it. I just think so by the way he acts, always asking when the doctor is coming and "Why the hell do I have to stay quiet in bed? Why can't I be quiet at the office?" He is bored and cranky, unused to being told what to do. I tell him how much I like the flowers he sends me every school day. I feel respected and very grown-up. He sends me *Cymbidium* orchids, those small velvety flowers in a wide range of colors, so delicate. I feel his love, new for me to know. And I love him and tell him so. Aunt

Virginia thinks his present strange but lovely. I have been careful not to let my mother know, as I have a feeling she would not approve. I am right. When she finds out in mid-December, she has the flowers stopped. She tells me it was silly and inappropriate of my father to give me or-chids—in fact, any flower. I feel my mother is jealous of my relationship with my father, his love for me, mine for him. She doesn't like that my father is loving with me.

My time caring for him, making him as physically comfortable as being bedridden can be, jousting words and ideas with him, forms a storehouse of good memories for me. It is a new sensation—our conversa-tions, our shared laughter. I dare just be, without defenses at the ready.

Aunt Virginia, whom I adore, serious Uncle Uzal, an intense man, particularly about golf, Bessie from Scotland, and Fuzzy are my new family. Aunt Virginia takes me to the bus stop on Park Avenue with Fuzzy each morning, and is there to meet me with Fuzzy when I get off the bus in the afternoon. During cocktail hour, Aunt Virginia and Uncle Uzal drink black coffee or tomato juice, like me, while they talk endlessly about putts and wood shots, traps and hopeful birdies. Bessie calls us to dinner at six-thirty on the button. The three of us eat in the dining room at the end of the big mahogany table, with Fuzzy under the sideboard. After dinner, if I have finished my homework, we play cards. They have taught me a rummylike game called Oklahoma. At dinner after a week or so, I say, "I know what is wrong with you two."

They both look startled, but cheerfully reply, "So, tell us."

"You are not drunk. I don't know how to behave around you."

They laugh and tell me they met each other in a "drying-out" sanitar-ium and that they no longer drink. I am so relieved. My evenings will not be spent trying to judge what I can or cannot say that might incur rage or derision from my father, or sniping from my mother. I am home free.

The following spring, before my mother and father return from the South, where they had been able to spend some time after my father's recovery to full lung power, my mother tells me on the phone from Bonny Hall, "Aunt Virginia and Uncle Uzal don't want to live with you anymore. They are getting to love you and have decided they just don't want to be with you anymore. We have to find a place for you to go to school in the fall." The pain of those words and the meanness in the way she addresses me deadens my joy in life. Nothing matters. I refuse to feel the hurt; the rejection is more than I can handle. I go into "do it" mode, frozen inside. I say nothing to Aunt Virginia and Uncle Uzal, and they never mention the subject to me. Many, many years later, when I was well into my fifties, I realized why Aunt Virginia and Uncle Uzal, who could not have children, understandably did not want to become too attached to me. They did not approve of the way my family treated me. They knew I felt abandoned. Over the year we were together, they made every effort to be real parents, to know me, to enjoy me, to want to please me and watch me flourish. They knew my mother would remain in control, make all decisions about my life. They would have no say over my future, or their place in it. Did they stop loving me? I have to believe they did not.

I find a coed school in Montana advertised in a magazine. The ad reminds me of Western movies I had seen with Ethel Crow years before, the wide-open space, the sunshine, leather, and laughter, the cattle and no cowards. I beg my mother to look into it. She replies, "Your father would never agree to a coed school, so put it out of your head right now."

In the end, my mother decides on an all-girls school in Switzerland, where I will at last learn French. All classes are in French. My cousin Mimi Kelly will be going there as well. She will travel by ship with other girls and a chaperone, but I will go with my mother on the *Queen Mary* ten days later. We will go to London first. I don't know whether to be pleased that I will have time alone with my mother—does she really want to be with me?—or feel sad that I will not be going with the other girls, which might be more fun. I ask if I can go see Mimi off on the ship in New York, and to my surprise, my father agrees. His permissions are peppered with puzzling riddles, totally dependent on his mood of the moment and guided by criteria no one really knows, not even he.

Rankin, the new chauffeur who replaced Greenhouse and André, drives me to the dock in the city at five in the afternoon. It is the first time I have been alone with a man I do not know in a closed-in space since Dirk. I am anxious and edgy.

The ship is huge. In the stateroom, I laugh and talk with Mimi's mother and father, her brother Carlie, and her friends from Rumson. The other girls who share the cabin with Mimi also have family, so the cabin is a crush of people. When it's time to go, the ship's horn blasts and a British voice comes over the intercom, requesting visitors to leave. I realize an elderly couple, Mimi's relatives, have to catch a train to go home to Queens. They are worried about getting to Penn Station in time for the last train of the night. It is late. We will drive right through Queens on the way home, so I offer them a lift. When I am late getting home, my father yells at me in a fit of rage and says, "No flying up to Marion to see your summer friends tomorrow."

I am crushed. "All I did was give a ride to two old people who didn't have money for a cab. Why was that so bad?"

My father never answers. He gets up from behind his desk and unsteadily moves through the living room to the front stairs.

"Please let me go. I want to see the friends I played tennis with this summer. I won't see them again until next summer. I will be in Switzerland at school. Please."

"No, and that's final. No more, or you'll get a hide tanning," my father growls.

I see him from behind, his right foot on the bottom step, his red-white-and-blue jacket creased from sitting in a chair, his left hand reaching out for the banister rail. I howl inside with the injustice of his response. The joyous excitement of being on a big ship and of trying to be kind to two elderly people is sucked out of me. He is a drunk, I know. But that just infuriates me more.

"He is a drunk. A lousy drunk," I scream at my mother, who stands in her Florentine taffeta long gown by the library door. "No," she says with vehemence. "He is not a drunk. He has alcohol poisoning." In my book, that is not an excuse. He is a drunk and I hate him for it. I have no idea how my mother feels about my father's drinking. She will only say, "He will crawl into bed with me during the night and make it all better."

In mid-September 1947, my mother and I depart on the *Queen Mary* for England, where we spend two days before going on to Lausanne, Switzerland. I am to spend the school year there at Château Brillantmont. The long blasts of the ship's horn and the vibration of its engines as they reverse this enormous grand vessel out from the dock and into the open waters of the Hudson River make my heart race with excitement. From the deck, I watch a fiesta of colored balloons, many with ribboned tails, float high above. Cheers of good-bye ring through the air from dock to shipboard and back again, and faces that once were clear quickly become a blur. I lose sight of the tall but stooped frame of my father. He vanishes into a kaleidoscope of colored scraps. Nelson, his round face frozen in sadness, refuses to look up at me. He fastens his eyes on the churning waters below. He will be alone now to deal with our parents. I have felt separated from him after the events with Dirk. I think he knows about what happened, but it has never been mentioned between us. Pucky screams a happy "Bye-bye, Mummy. Bye, baby." She blows a bundle of kisses with her right hand and waves a long bright red scarf in arcs above her head.

I see that dot of red for the longest time. The ship's bow turns to face the Atlantic Ocean. Bodies that were pressing me against the wooden rail cap move away now, and my merriment is gone. Like a movie jazzed to great speed, glimpses of the past summer—games of tennis, days at the stony beach in Marion with my cousin Sue, ice cream at Peterson's, even sailing on Buzzards Bay with drunk Uncle Tom—all are tangled together, and I cry inside because I miss the fun of being with friends. I turn to smile at my mother. She stands beside me, her face unreadable.

England is still on rations for meat, butter, sugar, and eggs, but on shipboard every luxury is available in abundance. We are fed breakfast in bed in our cabin; beef or chicken bouillon on the promenade deck at ten with crackers and cheese; tea with a feast of cakes, cookies, and tea sandwiches neatly displayed on silver trays with lace doilies at four in the main salon. An orchestra of ten plays dreamy songs by Cole Porter and Jerome Kern, show tunes, and waltzes by Johann Strauss while we nibble. Cocktails are at seven, with elaborate hors d'oeuvres, even caviar. Dinner follows in the main dining room with a four- or five-course meal beautifully prepared and elegantly served. The whole gustatory performance is capable of occupying every hour of the day if you let it. After dinner, coffee and liqueurs are served by tailored stewards up in the main salon. The green felt racetrack is laid out on the carpeted floor; tall painted wooden horses for running the course stand in wait.

Bets are called, written up, the dice rolled, and the race is on. As the races continue, bets get higher. The drinks change to highballs, and the air thickens with the smoke of cigars and cigarettes. Very few children are on board, so I sit with my mother and her bridge pals or with congenial people she has met. Everyone changes for dinner, which means long gowns, jewels, and possibly long white gloves are in order, the finer the better, and for the men, tuxedoes are required, heaven help the tweed jacket. Sumptuous satins and silks with matching evening slippers and striking jewels, including diamond tiaras, sparkle against aging skin and powdered faces. The dress code is "de rigueur," my mother says, which means everyone knew beforehand what is acceptable and expected. This dress code was "a must" in all "good houses" in England and America in Victorian and Edwardian days, my mother tells me before we dock. Most nights, I flee to bed after dinner, jumping in with my book, *Green Grass of Wyoming*, where I fall into a world of mountains, rolling green hills, horses, and wide skies. The simple, uncomplicated way of life feels good to me.

Following bingo in the grand salon one night, my happy and gay mother gathers up the folds of her gray gown as she rises from her chair and, with a regal air, glides across the patterned carpet to the area where the serious betting takes place. "Come along if you want to watch. We bet on how many miles the ship will travel from midnight tonight till midnight tomorrow night," she says.

A portion of the grand salon has been cordoned off for the serious gambling, and the bets begin. "One hundred, two hundred. Do I hear three hundred in the rear left?" The numbers ring out. "Four, five, six hundred." The numbers climb. I stop listening. I am frightened that we will not have enough money to eat if my mother keeps betting. They are talking about English pounds, not dollars. There are almost three dollars to the pound. My mother's first husband was a gambler who lost a good deal of money, as my mother has told me. She said she often did not have money for food. I go to our cabin, get into bed, and worry. What will happen to us if we have no money? I don't dare say anything to my mother the next day, or be vulnerable before her, for fear of being ridiculed, particularly in front of others. She never tells me whether she wins or loses. I have no idea how to talk to her.

In London, we stay at the Savoy. My mother has accepted a luncheon invitation from a well-known author of the time, Clemence Dane, so off we go the first day to the Ivy. It is a renowned meeting place for book publishers and writers especially. We get there first and are seated at a banquette, the prime place, my mother says. Again she reminds me not to order meat because it is "fearfully expensive" and not very good, according to Miss Nerney, the head of the London offices of Doubleday.

Clemence Dane sails into the Ivy in a cloud of rich blue patterned Chinese silk with billowing flowers and small sailboats. She is a very large woman with twinkling blue-gray eyes, white hair, and a hat at half cock. Her fingers, when she pulls the bread apart, are quite pudgy but not unattractive. Her rings certainly could never come off. She whoops and chatters with my mother, each trying to outdo the other in a friendly story competition. They are old friends. As I have been made conscious of continued meat-rationing in England, I order a pig's ear from the very large menu. A fuss is made at my odd request, but I want to order an unknown kind of meat, something strange. I wonder what it will look and taste like. I know I am just being a bit naughty, but I do not want the adults to have all the fun.

The restaurant is decorated with wood paneling, probably mahogany. Large gold-framed still lifes or landscape oil paintings, darkened over decades from cigar and cigarette smoke, hang from the walls. The ambience is of cozy elegance, but I think everything in the restaurant needs a good cleaning. The literati of England find the restaurant a gourmet haven, with suitable atmosphere.

The pig's ear arrives, served wordlessly by the waiter. There is a hush at our table and at the next table. I see before me a blanched ear covered with hairs still attached. It sits alone in the middle of a large gold-rimmed white plate, with no parsley or other decoration. I have no idea of how to go about eating this. "Oh dear," says Miss Dane. "That is indeed a pig's ear." Then she breaks into a rollicking laugh that sets off everyone close by. I get frowns from my mother. I look at my plate and, with all the courage I can muster, take my fork and knife and cut the ear in half. It is not as difficult as I thought it would be. The skin is soft, easy to cut and peel back. The meat, on the other hand, tastes of greasy nothing.

In Lausanne, Switzerland, the night before I go to school, my mother and I have dinner at the hotel Beau-Rivage, where we are staying. We eat a pleasant meal, avoiding all possible points of tension, such as my anger at being sent away to be cared for by others, or my father's drinking. I hated even the idea of school in Switzerland, and it was never my idea, like you always say it was. It was always yours, dear mother. No, I don't say those things. I talk about who might be going to Brillantmont, where would they come from.

We spent the day going to a back doctor for me. I have scoliosis. My spine wriggles like a snake, and I have had to do back exercises to avoid serious pain ever since I was four. In bed after dinner, my mother starts talking about how difficult it has been to find the help—governesses and companions for me. I lose my temper and retort, "Why did you bother to have children? You never spend time with us, or even have us live with you. How do you think that makes me feel? UNWANTED!" I switch off the light on the nightstand between us and roll away from her in my bed. Hot anger sweeps through me, unleashed and in the open now. I don't sleep for a long time. I hear my mother crying but feel no compassion. I have finally said what I've felt for so long, rather than continue the dance of pretend. I have no power, but have said my piece.

The following morning, after unloading my suitcases at school, I kiss my mother on the cheek and say good-bye. She tries to hug me but I stand back. I do not believe her show of affection. My last view of her in the car is of her brown eyes, red and pleading, with tears rolling down her cheeks. I steel myself to be unmoved.

A princess from Portugal comes to school almost a month after the school year began. We are the same, many of us, unwanted or inconvenient children of selfish parents with no loving skills. I meet girls from England, Greece, Italy, Spain, and South Africa. I settle quickly into the routine. My main pleasure is mail from home or ice cream from the cart man down at the corner. During this year, I have a hug-and-kiss affair with a Greek girl, one of three roommates. Two lonely girls feeling lost.

On a trip to Paris for spring vacation I get caught stealing a towel from the hotel, but I do not get caught hiding in a sarcophagus at the Louvre. I don't want to spend time looking at Greek and Egyptian carvings. I want time to look at the paintings, the *Mona Lisa* most of all. The painting seems dark and formal, her smile not as mysterious as books say. The many paintings in that gallery are all portraits of royalty, dark and formal, with little to no sense of life.

At school our classes are in French except for arithmetic, which is first taught by an inept Scottish minister. It becomes evident quickly that he doesn't know how to do a square root. He is dismissed and we, all five of us, get a free period for almost two weeks. One morning after breakfast, Mademoiselle Poullin, niece of the headmistress, tells us our new math teacher will be Miss Pratt, who will teach "off campus."

We have to walk down four very steep blocks to Miss Pratt's apartment. She greets the five of us at her door, an elderly and fragile-looking woman with long white hair that she ties in a knot on top of her head. One very long white hair, quite coarse and scraggly, hangs down from under her chin and wiggles when she talks. Her dress is dark green velvet with a white Peter Pan crocheted collar. She appears to have stepped out of a book by Dickens. The entire apartment has that same feel, with a vague rose-smelling mustiness throughout the living-dining room area, where we are to work. The smell reminds me a bit of my grandmother, my mother's mother, who uses rose-smelling soap and perfume. She has always been sweet to me, so I feel comfortable here.

The round table where we are to work is by a window that lets in a little natural light now at ten in the morning. A large Tiffany-style chandelier hangs above where we sit on dining room chairs with seats that have been embroidered in needlepoint. In this apartment time seems to have ceased in the far past. I don't much like math, but I sink with comfort into Miss Pratt's world, which is much warmer than the bare classroom at school.

I enjoy the chatter of my three roommates. Greek Vanda barely understands or speaks English. Like me, she is one of the youngest in school. The others are Barbara Tierney, half sister of the movie actress Gene Tierney, and a blond American girl. (She was so sweet, but I can't remember her name.) At meals we are supposed to speak French, but there is always a twitter of Greek or Italian, Spanish or German going on. My ears become attuned to the various languages over the year. Many of us speak English when not in class, and most girls on my floor are American.

The views outside the schoolrooms and my bedroom take in the full length of Lake Geneva and the Italian Alps. The mountains in all their varying lights are a prison as well as a comfort in their steadfastness. Days, weeks, and months pass slowly.

Mail is so important. Each of us attends mail call in hopes of letters from family or friends, news of home. We, the youngest at school, are perhaps the most in need of letters from home base. My father writes me weekly from his office, dictating to his secretary, Mrs. Robbins (whom my mother hates), about business things that are happening in the office and about the new plant in Virginia and the machines Luis de Florez has invented for book printing and packaging. The letters are not long, and are usually about business, but I can count on them. I write my parents and Nelson daily. I am so hungry for connection, so hopeful of return mail.

Nelson writes me almost daily, and I love hearing even what annoys him about school. My father has given Nelson's school, Eaglebrook, Ben Franklin's printing press and the building to house it. Nelson is dying of embarrassment. He is teased and verbally bullied about being the "rich kid." I can understand the embarrassment over my father's grandiose gesture with such a big gift. It shows my father's insecurity, I know, and that makes me sad. Nelson, too, is insecure. Poor guy. He hates the non-school emphases: winter sports, ski jumping, and downhill skiing. Nelson is heavyset and loathes exercise. He tells me news of his buddies, the trouble they get into, and about classes, teachers, and his dorm masters, who sound "pilly" and mean.

Puck and Madeleine write, and so does Aunt Virginia a time or two. But my mother writes me only three times the whole year.

I felt my childhood coming to an end and my adult life beginning. Just before the official end of school, my cousin Mimi and I left to spend a week in London before returning home. We had a room to ourselves in the Athenaeum Hotel, facing onto Hyde Park. I was thirteen, and Mimi had just turned fourteen. We dressed up with lipstick and eyeliner, foundation cream and powder, testing for the best and most sophisticated image. Mimi was more interested in fashion and appearance than I was. She knew about many different cosmetics. I liked to have time to write in my spotty journal or read a trashy novel. Before going out we stuffed our bras with Kleenex, but when we had to make fresh padding, we happily used toilet paper.

Most of the time we traipsed around London, sightseeing with gentle Miss Nerney, the head of the London Doubleday office. We were taken to the theater and to the Tower of London, where Anne Boleyn lost her head, as well as to Shakespeare country and to Oxford and Cambridge universities, where we made quick stops. No museums and no cathedrals were on the schedule, at our request; Mimi and I had decided no more after our Parisian trip, which had included visits to cathedrals, statues of the famous, and museums, to the point of exhaustion. Our trip to Windsor Castle was to be different, a personal event.

My father was friends with the well-known English author Daphne du Maurier; Doubleday published her thrillingly gothic novels *Rebecca* and *Frenchman's Creek,* among other of her books. She was married to Sir Frederick Browning, who was the chancellor of the exchequer in the household of Princess Elizabeth, newly married to Prince Philip. Daphne and Tommy, as he was called, enveloped us two American girls with so many kindnesses, dinners, theater, and rare sights of the royal family. One Saturday at the end of June 1947, we were taken to Windsor Castle by Miss Nerney to watch a cricket tournament of Princess Elizabeth's household against the king and queen's household. Prince Philip and Tommy would be playing in the game. Tommy, a handsome man with a clipped mustache and a comfortable manner, insisted we call him by his first name. We stood in the sunshine, looked up at the imposing castle on the knoll, and tried to imagine life at court over the past centuries. I wished I knew more English history for those few moments: who lived there, when, whether they'd had children. I said nothing because I didn't want to appear dumb.

I wore a dress bought from a girl at school, because none of my clothes fit anymore. Always skinny, I had blossomed by thirty pounds on the school food, which relied heavily on pasta and country bread with butter. Very occasionally, bread and butter was all we were given to eat. I had bought, with Mimi's encouragement, a pair of high-heeled blue spectator pumps to go with the dress I was wearing. My bra was stuffed to a full roundness, and I wore deep red lipstick. My eyes were done up by Mimi. I was thirteen and in my view a grown-up.

Guests of the royal households moved about a manicured wide lawn with an easy grace; their voices could barely be heard, so softly were they speaking. An electric tension passed through me. The king and queen of England came walking slowly down the knoll to our left. They nodded to friends as they passed by. I had been told to curtsy as they walked by, so as they approached, I bowed deeply. The left heel of my new high-heeled shoes caught in the bottom bar of the canvas lounge chair behind me. In a split second, I went over backward, presenting my slip and underpants to the king and queen of England. Recalling it now, I laugh.

Prince Philip and Princess Elizabeth came next, and I curtsied without mishap. A bit later, Prince Philip and Tommy came up to us. The prince bowed to Mimi and to me. He shook our hands, welcomed us to England and specifically to Windsor Castle, and invited us to a cocktail party at his house after the match. "Of course we'd be delighted to come," Mimi said. I was too cotton-mouthed to speak. The team members arrived, dressed in their white uniforms. Their white pants were knickers that came below the knee, and they wore tall white socks. They trotted onto the field and I lost sight of who was who. Only a thin gold stripe on the knickers defined the king and queen's team. The balls cracked on the bats and the players ran between wickets. I had no idea what the game was about. The small but enthusiastic audience cheered politely. After an hour and a half, the final score was announced; Princess Elizabeth's household had won. Relief, the game was over.

Silk and chiffon floated softly as guests moved toward their cars and chauffeurs, who stood at rigid attention. A jubilant Tommy came trotting over to us. "Off we go," he said, signaling to his chauffeur.

Princess Elizabeth's house had a gray facade, with a featured staircase, elegant in its simplicity. Tommy took each of us by the arm, and we entered a room full of people talking and laughing. He guided us over to meet the princess, who was evidently pregnant—with Prince Charles, we later found out. We curtsied. I didn't know if it would be rude to ask when the baby was due, so I remained silent. We curtsied before the smiling king. Tommy went off to get us drinks, leaving Mimi and me in the middle of this new world, feeling awkward and shy. The queen came up to me. She was dressed in a soft gray-blue dress with a loose jacket of the same material. A beautiful spray of diamond leaves and flowers covered her left breast.

She said hello and extended her hand. "Tell me about school in Switzerland. What was it like?"

I curtsied and said, "How do you do, Your Highness. School in Switzerland was difficult, but I learned to speak French quite well and even dreamt in French." At that moment, a waiter in black tie offered us deviled eggs on a round silver tray.

The queen, who was not a tall woman, looked up and said, "Thank you, William," as she took an egg from the tray. I took an egg and promptly popped it in my mouth, finishing it in two bites.

The queen brought her egg up to her opening mouth, but something distracted her off to her left. The egg slipped from her fingers and fell to the floor. We looked at each other. I, much taller than the queen, quickly bent down to pick up the egg, but partway down, I bumped heads with the queen, who was also trying to rescue her egg. We stood up and smiled at each other over the silly situation but said nothing. I again tried to get the queen's egg, only to bump heads with her once again, this time quite hard. I was embarrassed and did not know what to do. We stood facing each other in silence. Simultaneously, we turned the palms of our hands up and laughed. I noticed the queen's hat of twisted silk, which matched her dress, was a bit askew. She righted it with both hands. I decided I would let the queen pick up her own egg.

At that moment, Prince Philip appeared at my left shoulder, and it was he who picked up the egg and placed it on a silver platter that just appeared. He wiped his hands with a napkin passed to him by a footman, then extended his hand to me. He did not seem like royalty at all, but more like a friend's older brother who had just won a tennis match. "How are you doing?" he asked. "I am glad you had a chance to see Tommy play. He is good."

He talked to me about the possible similarity between early English dances and American square dancing. I tried to sound knowledgeable and sophisticated, but I truly knew nothing to add to this historical comparison. Mimi was off talking gaily with a group of guards by the window. Tommy came by and said, "We must go." We said our farewells to all the royalty after scooping up Mimi, much to her displeasure. We were driven back to London with Tommy in an elegant black Rolls-Royce.

Daphne joined us for dinner. She said she just "would not do any of those stately things." She spent her time down at her house, Menabilly, in Cornwall. That was where she lived and wrote. She rarely came up to London. Tommy obviously enjoyed the royal social life. They had figured out how to keep a good connection between them even though they lived apart. The two of them were such fun with each other and with us, easy in a way my parents were not. Conversation flowed and their laughter was infectious. Mimi and I returned to the Athenaeum Hotel that night full of excitement.

SIX

Going Home

Two days later at Heathrow Airport, we embarked on an evening Pan American flight to LaGuardia Airport in New York, with Daphne and Tommy. Mimi and I were going home after almost a year away. I was filled with expectation and joy, yet anxious that I would be treated like extra baggage and shipped off again. Would my family be glad to see me? We were traveling first-class. I was impressed by the sumptuous feast created by the onboard chef for our dinner, served on white china plates with the Pan Am logo. I have never flown first-class again.

The plane landed in Iceland to refuel and once again for more refueling in Newfoundland. Mimi and I found the trip long and frustrating; sixteen hours of sitting made us antsy. We were eager to be home. I had missed the companionship with Nelson most of all. We had been best friends to each other all of our lives.

My father had spent the spring in the Hartford Retreat, drying out and learning to live without alcohol. His consumption had apparently gotten way out of hand, to the point that my mother joined forces with Aunt Dorothy Babcock, my father's sister, and Mr. Black, president of Doubleday, to have the ability to block actions or decisions that my father might make within the business and even to limit his access to the business if necessary. The agreement among the three was called a voting trust, whereby any two could outvote the other, which put my mother in a most vulnerable position. She might have to vote against her husband and even further risk our family's control of the business and our financial future. The Hartford Retreat was one of the earliest institutions to take on the problem of alcoholism. While there, my father became fascinated with silk mills. His letters to me from there were full of descriptions of the mills themselves, the sad state they were in, and what a good buy they were. His runaway passion did not result in the purchase of one or three mills, as he had planned. But when I got home, two tall stacks of silk were presented to me; I could select patterns for four dresses I liked, and they would be made to my measurements.

We landed to great cheers from everyone, for this flight was one of the first transatlantic ones on Pan American Airways. It truly did take over sixteen hours but was considered a speed miracle, in comparison to the seven-day sea voyage.

Mimi fled to the ladies' room. The excitement of coming home, along with the bumpy flight, had finally gotten to her. She threw up all over herself. I went in to help and found her in tears, her dress sopping wet down the front, where she had washed off her vomit. I searched my purse for perfume, scented skin lotion, anything to take away that unmistakable smell. Mimi wept, terrified her mother would be angry with her for making a mess of her dress. I was horrified. Her mother would be so cruel? Daphne said brightly, "Come along. I will handle your mother," a no-nonsense approach to a severe case of the jitters. We left the ladies' room and walked and walked along yards of white hallway until I saw them. "There they are, ahead of us, the whole family!" I yelled.

I saw my father in the distance, taller than everyone, and on his face was a grin. I broke away, ran, purse and carry-on bag flapping in wild smacks against my hip, my arms stretched forward. I saw no one else as I ran. I slammed into his big body, laid my face against his chest, felt his arms enclose me, and heard him say, "Aw, daughter, I am so glad to have you home." I can still hear his voice resonate in my ears sixty-some years later. How I needed to know he missed me. The rest of the family, my mother, my sister Madeleine, my sister Pucky, all were there, but where was Nelson? Then I saw him against the far wall, looking at the floor.

"Hi," I said as I reached him, towering over him in my high heels.

He looked up at me. "You changed. You're different, grown up."

I looked down at my navy blue suit, my stockings and spectators. My hand went up to my long brown hair, which was curled into a soft pageboy. "Well, I guess I did a bit, and so did you. You look handsome in that seersucker suit." He was not appeased. He sulked, upset that I had left our childish world. I turned away and hugged Pucky, then Madeleine and my mother, looking each one in the eyes as I bounced from one to the next. My mother made no comment about my appearance, my high-heeled spectators or coiffed hair. Nobody did. Approval, disapproval, or shock? Who knew? Mimi went off home, her mother quiet and happy.

Steak, corn on the cob, asparagus, and blueberry pie with vanilla ice cream made up the menu for lunch, a request sent by me well over a month earlier. We ate on the terrace; sun shone through the trees, flickering bright light on the table and our faces. I couldn't believe I was home; I had been gone so long. I sensed I was in a movie. Words, no matter where they came from, seemed to float away. I felt happiness around me. I couldn't remember the word *fork,* so I said it in French. Madeleine, in a fit of pique, said, "N-N-N-Neltje [her stutter was always worse when she got excited], cut out showing off." She was right, of course, but I never would have admitted such a thing.

That afternoon when my father was resting, my mother took me aside. We sat together in the shade at the other end of the terrace, her favorite place to sit. She picked out a cigarette from the blue glass-topped cigarette box that sat on the table between us and lit it with the silver lighter.

"What is wrong?" I asked, for her face seemed fragile and thin, more deeply creased than before. Her small features were as perfectly formed and balanced as ever, giving her that air of stateliness. Her brown eyelashes, like mine, slanted straight down, but her eyes appeared more hooded than I remembered. Her skin was almost transparent, speckled with pale brown spots on the back of her hands, and the top side of her arms. I noticed this as she lifted the cigarette to her mouth. I remembered how a few years ago she, Nelson, and I had sat for hours while John Koch, a well-known portrait artist, painted our portrait; I perched on the arm of a white metal chair while my mother played cards with

Nelson. Her frontal gaze defined her as Madonna with Children, a scene out of what? A history of art volume from the library shelf? At the time, I resented the fakery of this portrait and was a sullen subject.

"Your father will be going into the hospital in New York in a few days. When he was up in Hartford, they found a tumor big as a baseball on his left lung. The doctors have told him he will die in three months if they don't operate. He has said he never wants to hear that phrase again." Her tone was matter-of-fact and distant, as though she were in another place altogether. And maybe she was. She was smoking a cigarette, looking out toward the bay, her facial features composed in a blank stare, disallowing conversation. I could not take in the fact that my father might die soon. They were words, not reality. I pressed her with questions. "What are his chances after the operation? How long before they can tell if it succeeded?" She would not speak. We sat in a dazed quiet. I felt a wash of pity for her, for all of us, but was afraid to let my feelings out, afraid the pain would never stop. I wouldn't think about it; that was best. I would freeze it out, like my mother was doing now, sitting as still as in her portrait.

Nelson and I were driven by Rankin to the Harkness Pavilion a week later, just after the Fourth of July. The process of getting to my father's room seemed an unconquerable hurdle. Nelson hung back in a mood of sullenness, a practice he had perfected in order to avoid coping. I entered the room first. My mother sat in an easy chair by the window, a book on her lap, eyeglasses askew. She had fallen asleep and her face, recently so tight with stress, appeared soft and childlike. My father lay in bed with a tube up his nose. Two needles bound side by side in his left arm allowed the liquid medicine in the two bags hanging off a metal medical stand to flow into his body. Two tubes drained liquids out of him, one dark yellow, the other bloody, into two containers, which sat on the floor under his bed. He had been operated on three days earlier. I touched my mother's arm to wake her. She shook her head, then looked at us and, easing herself up, said, "Oh, children. I am glad you are here. Did Rankin have trouble finding the hospital again?" She kissed us both on the cheeks and pulled me toward my father's bed. "He is doing well, and the doctors say the operation was a success. They got the lung out but do not know if the cancer has spread, and won't know until symptoms show up."

My mother put her right hand on my father's shoulder. "The children are here, Nelson; wake up, wake up," she said as she shook his shoulder gently. When he awoke, his talk was goofy. He saw a huge oil tanker in the room and gave us a list of instructions on how to steer the ship away from the dock and into the harbor, his voice tense. Quicker than he had come to, he vanished back into a drugged sleep. We met Bill Madden, a gray-haired male nurse, who was caring for my father during the day and would be going home with him, my mother told us. He was attentive, a quiet man who seemed to care. We kissed our mother on the cheek, said our good-byes twice. I don't think Nelson and I said anything to each other on the way home. My father's being so sick as to be next to death in three months if he hadn't had the operation staggered my mind into incomprehension and boiling anger. All possibilities were too frightening. Our world, gone.

The next day, Nelson and I boarded the *Scout*, a yacht my father had chartered for his recuperation. It could sleep six and had a crew of four. We took clothes and a few books that were on the reading list for school, tennis rackets, and sneakers. We were going to Marion, Massachusetts, again to live with Aunt Sukie and Uncle Tom. We stopped in the evening to refuel and spend the night at a town near New Haven, Connecticut. We were tied up at the dock. The air was warm, with a small breeze, just a breath from time to time. A guy, a bit older than me, who had been busy on the dock fueling boats, came over and started up a conversation. He was easy to talk to. We talked for a long time, watching the light change, the sun disappear. He said I was beautiful and that he wished he could see me again. His eyes were sincere. Nobody had ever said anything like that in that way to me before. I gave him my name and address. Years later, he phoned to invite me to Princeton for a weekend. I refused. I was getting married that Saturday.

The *Scout* pulled into Marion harbor about four-thirty on a Thursday afternoon during the second week of August. Our entire household, including Uncle Tom, who was on his vacation, waited at the harbor entrance, a grassy point only a block away from where we lived. My friend Kerry Luther and some of my tennis friends were with me. My father sat on the aft deck with my mother, looking like he used to before the drinking, the drying-out, and the operation. I felt he would live. Oh please, let him live.

The next day, a whole gang of us kids spent the afternoon jumping off the top deck of the *Scout,* screaming out the Woody Woodpecker call, *Ha ha ha ha ha.* It doesn't sound like anything in written words, but it was a happy, wacky call. No one said, "Hush. Don't disturb your father." My father laughed at our antics, joined in the fun with stories and jokes, laughed till he coughed. We had to be quiet then, but others, such as my father's nurse, Bill Madden, and friends, chimed in. My mother seemed a bit prim amid all the hoopla. I was proud of my father for taking part. Even Nelson loosened up, shouted out the Woody Woodpecker song like the rest of us.

And there were always gallons of ice cream to eat. I belonged to a family, and I blossomed. My father and I reminisced about when my mother had a croquet tournament in full swing and we sneaked in a goat. Attracted by the bright colors of the balls, the billy goat lowered his horns and raced to butt all the balls hard, well out of position. Ladies in their silk dresses or long flowing pants and large hats let out cries of disbelief; the men stood rigid and unamused. My father and I giggled. My mother was not amused at all. Another time, I flew with my father in the *Bonanza,* the small company plane, and he dive-bombed my mother's croquet tournament. The rush of air moved croquet balls yards and yards out of position, even from a wicket's edge. I loved flying with my father and his pilots. And my father adored flying; he had done lots of it in his youth, with his friend Luis de Florez. The combination of the speed earthward and the delight in being bad captured my heart.

Before school started, there was still no news about the cancer, but no sign of a return. In early September 1948, I was sent to Miss Porter's School in Farmington, Connecticut, where twelve female members of my family had gone before me, including my mother. My mother told me this with great pride. But the information was lost on me. I didn't care about the past and who had done what; my interest was in myself and my world and how and where I fit in. For years, I had been like driftwood, cast out to live with maids, nannies, governesses, sisters, aunts and uncles. They all told me what to do, how to think, how to be. I longed to belong, to be nurtured, to interest my parents in who I was. My parents thought it was their job to teach me who I should be as heiress to the Doubleday fortune, a gracious figure in New York society. Not so Uzal and Virginia, not so Pucky.

In the last quarter of November, I got a letter from Peter Stehli, Nelson's best friend, who was like a second brother to me. We three had fished in Beaver Dam, played pool, listened to music, and just been together all our lives. He started out by saying he had felt so sad when his parents told him the news that my father was dying of the cancer, which had come back. I was stunned. My heart hurt physically. I ground my teeth as I crossed the street, looked skyward from the half-read letter. I brushed at the tears that streamed down my face. I tasted their salt and felt bitterly bruised, as though I had been in a physical fight with someone bigger and tougher than I. As soon as I got to my room, I wrote my mother to ask what was going on with my father and why had I not been told that he was dying, when it was on the gossip trail? At Miss Porter's, we were not allowed to make or receive a phone call, ever. Three days later, I did get a call. I was allowed to take it, a home emergency.

My mother let fly in anger. "What were you thinking when you wrote that letter? I might have read it aloud to your father." She went on about the danger of his finding out that he was dying. There was not a space for me to speak. She was out-of-control angry. I listened, eventually said, "What did you want me to do? Nothing?" There was a pause. "No, of course not." Her voice softened. "I will arrange for you to come home for Thanksgiving this Thursday. Your cousin Sue and Nelson will meet you on the train Wednesday afternoon; that's just two days away, darling." This sentence came over the wires so gently, so different from the tone of fury that had begun the conversation.

What is really going on? I wondered. Why this silence? Nelson and I are not infants. We are talking about my father, yes, and your husband. Let us be part of what is going on.

Thanksgiving was held upstairs in the Pine Room, the room that had been my nursery. The table, festive with gourds and pumpkins and set for six, did nothing to obliterate the bad news. My father would die soon; the cancer had returned and there was nothing that could be done about it. Pucky came out from New York the night before Thanksgiving, after supper. She was tangled and fraught on arrival. We talked about my father's cancer until late that night. I wept. But in the morning, I was all smiles. I had been well trained to hide my feelings, and it served me well over the following days, though not without pain. Over lunch there was laughter and storytelling, teasing and prying goofiness.

My father came to the table with the help of Bill Madden and was returned to his room in his wheelchair. He had been told that scar tissue from the operation was impeding his speech, not that a cancer growth was the cause. This charade of keeping my father from knowing that he was dying, which my mother said was still necessary, seemed a pathetic gesture to me. My father was an intelligent man. Of course he knew he was dying. He could feel his body wasting away, his stamina collapsing, and his interest in the surrounding world diminishing. I was angry to be forced into playing this game of not telling, and even more angry that the summer's glimpse of my father would not continue. He was going to die very soon. The word *death*, end of being, nothingness, ran over and over through my mind. But I could not feel it, see it, or take it in. I only knew that brief moment on the *Scout*, that sense of belonging, would never be again. I couldn't concentrate on a book. I played rummy with Nelson and occasionally backgammon, but my mind was on my father. Could I will him to live?

In the back room or the playroom, which was our hangout, Bill Madden made us laugh with his stories. He was a spellbinding storyteller. He recounted his life of caring for wealthy people when a debilitating illness was at issue, the crazy things that happened—never with a name attached. He had a girlfriend, Sherry, whom he visited on his days off. They caroused in the jazz dives of New York City, danced wildly, and drank much more than enough. They sucked in as much life as their time allowed. His joy, frenzied at times, made an impression on me. Life could be open, not held down by mannered convention, and the love of life was a fine thing indeed.

We went back to our schools. A deadness, hard and heavy inside me, made classes difficult. I could not focus. I felt isolated, with no one to hear my sadness.

Most girls, including my roommate, Martha Walker, from Sheridan, Wyoming, were wildly excited about going to the dances in New York over Christmas vacation, but none of it interested me. I had a blue evening dress with a wide tulle skirt, low in front, in my closet. I was nervous about dancing with a boy anyway, even though I had been to dancing school and had danced with every boy there. Somehow, a real dance seemed a more intimate setting. It was still about Dirk, what he had done to me, the pain of his not really loving me, his threat, all jumbled in my mind. I still felt threatened and guilty, overcome at times with anxiety. The days passed. I wrote home and to Nelson at Deerfield Academy—the school he was now attending—every day, telling of the day's silliness, my homework, what I wanted for Christmas, anything to fill the page: short messages about the weather, the sun, or the clouds. I felt depressed and angry.

Christmas vacation came. My mother did not meet my train—the first sign of bad news. On the way home with Rankin, Tillie, our beloved Irish upstairs maid, who always sliced the air with an on-point zinger, gave me the lowdown on what home was like. "I just want to prepare you," she said as she rattled off how "Bill Madden thinks he runs the place. He is in charge of your dad and he lets me know that every day. He gives me a pain." My father was much worse, she said. "He sleeps a good bit, but he will get down the stairs, I will bet you, for Christmas presents and lunch." She was right.

I can see him now, these sixty-some years later, in his wheelchair in the living room. Sunlight washes over him. He is handing me a big box, wrapped in silver paper with a bow of silver ribbon. His hands are shaking. I look down at his pale skin, long fingers, and bony hands. I open the box slowly, all the while looking into my father's eyes. He is so excited. A half-smile flushes his face. I want to hold his head in my hands, bring him close to me, hug him while I stroke his head as I would that of a sick child. He sits in his wheelchair, his thin frame stooped, yet he holds up his head. My mother stands beside him, looks at me encouragingly. Out of the corner of my eye, I see Puck and Nelson waiting for me to open my present. I tear off the silver paper, the fancy ribbon. The crinkling sound of the tissue paper inside shatters the fragile silence. I see in the box a fur jacket in shades of light gray, sleek and silky to the touch. "A fur jacket! Oh! Daddy, how wonderful," I say, close to tears. I pull the jacket out of the box and put it on.

"It is goat," my father says, looking as pleased as a kid with tickets to the Rose Bowl.

Is this a goat joke between us? I wonder, but it doesn't matter. He has given me a fur coat, something special. That is what matters.

SEVEN

It's Over

The morning of January 11, 1949, I hear Pucky typing steadily. She is writing my father's obituary. My father is not hers. I love Pucky, and she is a writer, so of course she should write my father's obituary. But as he is my father, I want to write his obituary. Bill has told me my father won't last the day. What does that mean? I see an image of my father's body floating off the bed, disintegrating in the air and leaving not even dust. What is not being? Where does the soul go? The body is still there. What does it mean to be? Not be? Be? Not be? I sit on the sofa in my room. It is upholstered in a dulled-down blue fabric that blends into the pale blue walls. I am knitting argyle socks for my father, gray, with dark green and burgundy diamonds and white stripes, just a single stitch wide, that run crisscross through the sock.

My father will die today. Today is Tuesday, January 11, 1949. If I keep repeating it, will I know what dying means? I couldn't stay in bed with a tray and be alone this morning. I have not seen my mother or been allowed to see my father today. He has been in a coma since Saturday.

After an hour, Puck and Bill come down the hall. My mother has sent a message: We are to say good-bye. It is eleven o'clock. The three of us walk in a single file down the long blue-carpeted hallway to the telephone room, then round the corner past Nelson's bedroom. He is not here, but in the city getting a suit for the funeral. I am glad Aunt Al took me to Lord & Taylor on Saturday. She bought me a black wraparound wool skirt with three buttons that hold it together at my waist and a white silk blouse with a wide collar and cuffs. I will come to live in this outfit for the next five days. We walk, Puck, Bill, and I, on the red carpet in the front hall, past the curved staircase lined with portraits of Washington and Lincoln, letters from Bernard Shaw, Joseph Conrad, and other famous authors all in thin black frames, all exactly alike. These walls hold so many memories, voices that speak from my babyhood forward. It is bleak outside and the cold grayness brings back a memory of me at three skating in the back meadow on a small patch of ice while Nana watched. The red carpet seems an endless path with bits of my past battling for space to be heard. I see Puck ahead of me, hugging my mother, but she is far away. They are both far away.

My mother says, "Hello, darling. Your father died just a few minutes ago. I was with him. You can go over to him, if you want." She wipes her reddened eyes with a hankie. Later, she uses one of my father's very large silk handkerchiefs.

She does not reach out for me, nor I for her. We finished our deception of devotion that last night before school in Switzerland, when I asked her why she bothered to have children if she was just going to send them away at every turn. She could not answer. Ever since I can remember, I have been accused of being "Hard-Hearted Hanna" by my mother.

I notice she has lipstick on, and her hair is all in place. She is already dressed in a black knit suit with pearls about her neck. My father lies on his back in the hospital bed, eyes closed, motionless, covered in white sheet and blanket. His face has no color. My hand reaches out and I stroke his cheek with the back of my fingers, then most gently run my fingertips along his lips. They are very dry, but his skin is soft. Bill Madden must have shaved him already this morning. As I touch his skin and run my fingers over his face, I am aware I could not do this if my father were alive.

A sob erupts through my body. I gasp for air. My hands jerk out of control and my whole body shakes. Someone takes my arm above the elbow, pulls me from his bedside. It is my mother, pulling me away to follow her into her bathroom. Big as a bedroom, it is, all white, with two standing sinks and an extra-long bathtub. Embroidered rugs from India cover the white tile floor.

"Here, darling, take this phenobarbital. It will make you feel better.

Dr. Galbraith got the pills for me for just this occasion," she says, placing a small white pill in the palm of my right hand.

I do as she says and swallow the pill before she can hand me a glass of water. My mother looks alarmed. The taste is bitter.

Later, Bill Madden came to my room to tell me he was leaving. His job was done. "No, I never stay for the funeral. It is too hard on me." He gave me his phone number and a warm hug. Then he was gone. He had made me laugh so many times when I really wanted to cry.

I sat on the sofa as I had before my father died and picked up the knitting where I had left off. But I never completed that sock.

I ventured out after a little while to see if Nelson had come back, but his room was empty. I walked along down the hall to the curving open staircase. Two men, one taller and far slimmer than his chubby cohort, climbed the stairs. Both were dressed in dark suits. When they were parallel in my view across the railing, I noticed they were rubbing their hands almost as if they were washing them. Aha! I thought. I know who they are. They are Beenie and Divine, the undertakers, who will embalm my father. Tillie came to my room to deliver a message from my mother. "Go downstairs now and be at the door to greet guests." It never occurred to me to say I couldn't or wouldn't. I was just fourteen and glad to be needed, to be trusted with a job. I changed into my new clothes. I wore stockings and new black high heels and a gold charm bracelet. My long brown hair was modeled into a pageboy.

Admiral Luis de Florez, my father's flying buddy, and the inventor of a fast all-in-one book-printing machine, as well as several survival gadgets for downed naval pilots at sea during World War II, stopped his gray car over by the bare Japanese maple. "The Admiral" always brought laughter with him. Now his short legs swung out from behind the wheel and touched down on the gravel-topped asphalt drive. I let out a cry of delight from just outside the front door and ran to him with wide-open arms. The fact that he was a foot shorter than I didn't matter. His arms encircled me. He held me close against his barrel chest, reached up on tiptoes to give me a kiss on each cheek. His waxed mustache tickled. Memories of him singing by the fireplace to a group of rather staid bridge friends of my mother flashed through my mind. The song begins:

> *Oh dear, what can the matter be*
> *Five old ladies*
> *Locked in the lavatory!*
> *They were there*
> *From Monday till Saturday*
> *And nobody knew they were there.*
>
> *The first old lady*
> *Was Madeleine Keller*
> *She fell all the way*
> *From here to the cellar*
> *And nobody knew she was there. . . .*

This man loved us all. He took my hands in his, kissed them quickly, and said, "Let's go."

"Come see Dad. He looks like himself, but asleep," I said, though I realized I'd never seen him sleeping. We held hands as we walked across the circular driveway, through the heavy iron-and-glass door, down the front hall, and through the arched doorway into the library. My father lay beneath his portrait in the ivory satin–lined bronze coffin. He was dressed in his gray slacks and his favorite tweed jacket. He looked frozen.

The routine of greeting and viewing went on all afternoon. "Thank you for coming. Would you like to see my father? The undertakers have done a wonderful job. Let me show you into the library, where he lies below his portrait." I stood by the coffin with each guest for a minute or so, answered questions, or just stood quietly by. I showed them through his office, then into the living room, where Tony and his helper, tall Margaret, were serving tea and drinks. I made sure the guests were comfortable and then went back to my post by the front door. People came in waves, stayed awhile, then said, "I am so sorry," as they left.

Aunt Virginia and Uncle Uzal drove up. I ran to greet them as they got out of their car. "Oh, I am so glad you are here," I said as I hugged Aunt Virginia. She held me tight to her. Uncle Uzal kissed me on the cheek and pulled me aside. He told Aunt Virginia to go on in. He put down the two suitcases he had lifted out of the trunk, raised his head, and said, "I must talk to you, Neltje. I know it is a very sad and difficult time, but I know it will get too hectic in the house. Dearie, there just won't be money like there has been. You need to know that. So when you go shopping with your mother and she says, 'Get both dresses and the third one, too. It looked lovely on you,' you reply, 'I only want that one.' Do you understand what I am saying? It is up to you to help your mother economize, because money will be tight for a number of years." He paused. I looked at him in incomprehension. Why was he talking to me like that today? I remained silent. "Don't say anything to anybody about our talk. You're savvy. You know what I am talking about." I was scared. I could not think about money and controlling my mother's spending. What did he expect of me? My mind whirled. I told myself to think about it later. He picked up the suitcases and we walked across the drive to the front door.

The Runyons, the Beecrofts, the Brownells, most all of the Garden City people, and half the New York office came to say how sorry they were and ask what they could do, how they could help. When darkness fell, I was relieved of greeting duties and watched the last of the visitors disappear down the drive.

Harriet and Angus MacGregor, who had worked for my mother when she lived in New Jersey, had come earlier in the day to help prepare food, run errands, and serve meals. They collected the dirty glasses and teacups. Later, I found them at the big round table in the help's dining room, having their supper. There were more than a dozen staff members, laughing and crying at stories and telling tall tales about my father. I loved listening to their memories of my family and the parts each one played. I was comfortable there.

That night there were cocktails, then dinner, then raucous laughter, giggling, and nervous fun in the library. My mother lay on the blue brocade sofa, sipping brandy, staring at my father's coffin and his portrait on the wall above. She was dressed in one of her long hostess gowns of dark green velvet with gold embroidered edging. Aunts and uncles, cousins and other family, and good friends were spread about the paneled room in chairs or sat on the Tree of Life carpet my father loved so much. Nobody sat in his chair. He used to fondle the cocker spaniels, Foolish and Jocko, after dinner every night in that chair. That is what I remembered most, before alcohol took over his life. He was with us in our minds in the midst of our hilarity. Only when Puck and I got silly and sang a song did his face leave me for a little while.

Why we decided at this time, grief-struck as we were, to show off our uncertain singing and acting abilities, I'll never know. With fur stoles and coats swiped from the hall sofa around our shoulders, we came sashaying into the library, swinging our hips in unison. We sang as we peeled off the furs from our shoulders and threw them on the floor:

> *So, take back your mink*
> *To from whence it came*
> *And tell 'em to Hollanderize it*
> *For some other dame . . .*

I don't know who wrote the song. It was popular the previous year and I think came from a Broadway hit. There was less crying, and tension melted. Someone read bits of "The Emperor's New Clothes," by Hans Christian Andersen, from a small green leather volume with gold embossing. Jollity and laughter drew us together and for a moment made us feel as one.

John Sengstack, who had been responsible for Doubleday & Company's accounting and was a close friend of my father's, pulled me over to where he was pouring himself Old Fitzgerald on the rocks, his usual drink. I sat on a chair by my father in his casket. John Sengstack stood with his feet spread wide apart just above me. He looked down on me. "I want to tell you about money, what you will have, how to use it. Be smart. Dammit. Not like other stupid women, who just fritter money away on stuff, just stuff like handbags and shoes. Stuff they don't really need," he went on. "Women have too goddamned much money. They have no idea of the true value of money. You will have money. Use it well, dammit," he repeated. The vehement tenor of his voice and his obvious prejudice against women frightened me. I listened; let it wash over me. *Drunk talk,* I thought, and put the problem in a closet.

The funeral two days later was a huge affair. My mother, Nelson, and I sat in the back of the first black limousine. My brother had hidden out in his room since getting home from school. My mother was dressed all in black and wore pearls around her neck, as she had since my father died. Now a black veil, heavy enough to keep her face from view, was lifted only when she drew on her cigarette. We—Nelson, Pucky, Madeleine, who had flown in from California, and I—all had been given phenobarbital "to get through the day."

Much talk had gone into the flowers on the casket, the flowers by the choir, and the flowers on the altar of the cathedral in Garden City. And what hymns we should have. We, as a family, never went to church. "Fight the Good Fight" and "Onward, Christian Soldiers" were thought to be appropriate. And "Abide with Me" was one of my mother's favorites. We settled on them because they were the least God-involved hymns, except for the last one, and they were musically rousing and familiar to everyone.

We entered the pew from the side. I looked out at the mass of people stretching all the way to the rear of the cathedral. For whatever reason, it did not matter to me that all those people had come to say good-bye to my father. Most of them knew him from working in the company. But none of it seemed to matter. This was a play involving others, not me.

I watched the choirboy in front of me singing "Fight the Good Fight with All Your Might," his face cherublike, young and tender. WHAT AM I MEANT TO FEEL NOW? I FEEL NOTHING. THE PILL. BECAUSE OF THE PILL, I CANNOT FEEL.

Then the pallbearers stood by the coffin, which was blanketed in white camellias. They slowly walked the coffin down the aisle. My mother rose, followed by Nelson, who gave her his arm to hold on to. They moved out into the main aisle, turned, and followed my father in his coffin down the aisle while the choir and congregation sang "Onward, Christian Soldiers." I stepped out into the aisle along with Puck, who was on my left side. A surge of anger pumped through me. I loathed this formality and knew my father would have loathed it, too. This ceremony had nothing to do with him. Everything was chosen to make an impression on the audience. It was theater. I couldn't bear facing a thousand faces. I weaved off balance, stumbled; my legs and feet searched for stability. Pucky tried to catch my arm so I would get back in line or to keep me from falling; I didn't know which. I had stumbled like a drunk out of control. I knew clearly I did not want to be touched.

EIGHT

The Tipping Scale

In the summer of 1950, my mother took all of us—Pucky, my cousins Tommy and Sue McCarter, Nelson, and me—to California to visit Madeleine, her husband, Doug, and their daughter, Maggie, my mother's first grandchild. It was a year and a half since my father had died, yet I still felt him alive in my life. My mother was to placate Irving Stone and restaurateur Trader Vic with her charm, then visit Polly Adler, the famous madam with a functioning house of ill repute in Sausalito, near San Francisco. This errand for Doubleday & Company was promoted by Ken McCormick, editor in chief of the company, when he found out she was going to California. She was thrilled to have the job.

In Los Angeles we drove out to visit Irving Stone, the author of several bestsellers for Doubleday. The company had just reissued Stone's book *Lust for Life: The Biographical Novel of Vincent van Gogh*. It was a hot number-one bestseller. Literary societies, libraries, private clubs, bookstores, socialites, and social climbers all gave parties for Stone. Bookstores rolled out royal carpets for autograph parties. There were lunches with book critics and interviews with *The New Yorker* and *Time* magazine. However, the author was not pleased with the advertising and promotion for *The Passionate Journey*, his fictional biography of the American artist John Noble, which was not doing well. His book was getting "insufficient attention," he said. "I make a lot of money for Doubleday and I've earned the right to be treated with the best."

"I am so sorry you are upset with the treatment Doubleday is providing you," my mother said in sympathetic tones. The company did not want Stone hunting for a new publisher. This had been explained to us before we left the Bel-Air, a swank hotel where movie stars stayed, drank in the bar, and swam in the pool. That was the draw for us kids. I was fifteen, Nelson was sixteen, Sue eighteen, and Tommy almost twenty. Tommy was the only semiadult among us, but we would let him have that sliver of superiority. We spent the whole afternoon listening to Stone's unhappy complaints and my mother's conciliatory replies, except for a fast climb down rocky paths to the beach and the ocean, the never-ending ribbon of blue. We skipped stones, waded in the foamy water. I stuffed shells in my skirt pocket. The next day, we went to San Francisco by train along the dramatic coastline. I watched surfers riding the waves, bathers stretched out tanning on the beaches. Babies played in the sand with bright-colored pails. I loved feeling the open space, colors, textures, and the mixture of lives that was going on. The scene gave me hope, its clarity yet in my mind sixty-five years later.

My sister Madeleine and her family lived in Belvedere, a small town across the Golden Gate Bridge from the city. We stayed in nearby Sausalito at the Alta Mira Hotel, a strange place, with no sign of guests or staff during daylight hours but a den of drinkers in the dim, smoky night light of the bar. Evenings after dinner in the city we went out to nightclubs, where we listened to jazz, or a bar with a risqué routine. I felt very grown up. When we got back to the hotel, my mother lined us up. As we approached the darkened bar she called out the command "Eyes front." She did not want us to see the entwined bodies on the furniture and floor in the almost totally unlit bar, where soft music floated about in the smoky air. Of course, we tried even harder to see what was happening in the "den of sin." A sign nailed to the wall in each bedroom included two important items: "No guests are to visit other guests' bedrooms" and "No playing of musical instruments before 10:00 in the morning or after 9:00 at night."

We went places en masse, Doug and Madeleine included, which made us a force of eight before adding friends for our meals. Mrs. Dimond, Doug's mother, was a charming and intelligent woman, who enriched all of us with personal histories of people and events in San Francisco. In addition, she regaled us with stories of her youth in Charleston, South Carolina, near Yemassee, so intriguing to me. She was regal in demeanor and always presented herself impeccably dressed. I liked her quiet manner. She treated me as an adult, included me when talking with others, and remained sober. I could not say that about my mother. Her mood swings due to drink were confusing and often painful. She needed a target for her anger and I was the one most often available.

We made a business visit to Trader Vic's, where I had my first drink, a Mai Tai. It was delicious. I ordered a second one as my mother conversed with Trader Vic about his recently published cookbook. He, too, wanted more promotion on radio and in the press. He was getting ready to leave as the second round of drinks arrived. "That ain't soda pop, kids," he said as he lifted his big frame off the black leather banquette beside me. We spent the rest of the evening at the best jazz bar in town, where Madeleine used to work as a cocktail waitress, until she was fired for dancing on tabletops while on duty. Madeleine had her zany side. She was a very bright, well-read woman, who loved jazz, booze, and painting. She was a serious student of Clifford Still's at the San Francisco Art Institute and was often included in exhibitions of contemporary California artists. At one point, she became an active Communist. She liked fresh orange juice served in a silver container on a bed of ice when staying at the Ritz on my mother's account, which didn't fit the Communist charter.

On Tuesday afternoon, the day before we were to fly home, we went to visit Polly Adler at her house in Sausalito. Madeleine would have nothing to do with "that awful woman," and Puck had gone back to her job writing at *Theatre Arts* magazine in New York. The house was Victorian in style, painted light gray, with white trim. A covered porch stretched across the front, overlooking San Francisco Bay and the city. Sailboats tacked through the waters in zigzag lines, searching out a breeze. Miss Adler was the famous madam, powerful enough in political ways to keep her house, although illegal, open and flourishing. Doubleday & Company wanted the opportunity to publish her memoir. In editor Ken McCormick's words to my mother, "She needed sweetening, to be petted, or maybe *bedazzled* is a better word."

Miss Adler had a definite elegance. She met my mother, hand outstretched. "What can I do for you, Mrs. Doubleday? You are a most attractive woman."

My mother employed every bit of her charms to "pet, woo, and bedazzle" Miss Adler.

Miss Adler asked my mother, "Do you work at Doubleday?"

"No, I just give the occasional party, a lunch or dinner at Barberries, my home on Long Island, usually for a big book coming out, a special author. I visit authors when traveling if it is suggested that I could be helpful, like my meeting with you. Often authors become friends. Sometimes writers need a touch of encouragement, some comforting support from the company."

Sue, Tommy, Nelson, and I went by the water, watching the small boats tacking in the wind and farther out in the bay, a tanker and a tugboat heading together into harbor. When we returned to the tabled area at the back of the house, my mother and Miss Adler were deep in conversation. They were telling each other stories, each trying to outdo the other in a merry contest, like jousting.

My mother said we had to go. "Good-bye, Mrs. Doubleday. I have enjoyed meeting you. And all you kids, too." On the return walk to the hotel, my mother told us that Miss Adler had agreed to talk with Doubleday when her manuscript was a little further along.

My mother was very proud of the Doubleday name. She liked saying, in a commanding voice, "I am Mrs. Nelson Doubleday," to impress, as she had at Trader Vic's a few nights before as soon as she walked in the door, or to get service in Doubleday bookstores. I watched her pounding her cane, declaring, "I am Mrs. Nelson Doubleday," to anyone around, because there was no salesman in the area and she wanted help. I felt embarrassed by her attitude of hauty grandeur. I hated being treated differently just because my father had created a famous publishing house, along with his merchandising ideas: creating book clubs and bookstores that were so very successful. "More books to more people" was his credo. I was just a young girl trying to be myself, but I wasn't sure who that was.

"Were you satisfied with the meeting?" I asked when we were alone.

"I think so. You know, darling, I love doing what I can for the company. It was my life when your father was alive and it will be so until Nelson becomes president of the company. That's what we have to do as Doubledays." There was a silent pause before she went on, almost as if she were talking to herself. "But I am not really a Doubleday. My connection is just through marriage. You and Nelson are the real Doubledays," she said with sadness. She was to repeat this regret often. I had understood, as far back as I could remember, that Nelson would be president of Doubleday. There was never any mention of my having a life. What did it mean to be a Doubleday if you were a female? I had no idea of working in the company; the concept had never entered anyone's mind. So I was no threat. In my teenage years, I feared I would have no place in the outside world except as a society matron, married with children and helping my husband.

Life at Barberries was veiled with sadness most of the time unless we had guests. When Puck came down on a weekend, she brought friends, among them Tica Madrigal, a very funny Spanish teacher from Mexico. We lay about the guest room being girlie, playing the purity test about sex. Mike Lipton was an actor who came often, as did the Touring Players, a group of actors who traveled the East Coast, producing plays in various towns and cities. Liz Blake and Peg Murray were the creators of the Touring Players. Leora Dana, a Barnard friend of Puck's, was a well-known actress who came for a Sunday-Monday visit when the theater was dark. She brought her boyfriend, John Sargent. I came along the red-carpeted hall to go downstairs, when there they were, John and Leora on the second step in passionate embrace. I didn't know where to go or what to do. They were befuddled, as well. Later, John Sargent became Puck's guest, then my mother's guest as extra man at dinner parties or on author weekends. An equal number of men and women at the table were essential to my mother. She enjoyed the publishing gossip that John provided with humor and flair.

Jon Schueler, an artist friend of Madeleine's, came with Puck for Thanksgiving in 1950. Eight of us played lawn bowls on Saturday in a blustery, cold wind. I was home from Miss Porter's School with a concussion. I had been in a minor car wreck with Peter Stehli in early September and had a concussion from getting my head stuck in the jockey box of his Volkswagen when the car, out of control, hit an Anchor fence post. Peter Stehli was bringing me home from a dance at the Creek Club on Labor Day weekend. I kept saying I had headaches or vision problems, which had the slimmest attachment to truth, but it did get the doctor to say I couldn't go back to school until after Christmas. Jon Schueler became a regular visitor of my mother's. He and John Sargent were often around when I was home on vacation over the next few years. I took long walks with Schueler, sharing tales of woe and complex relationships, plain daily living messes that needed analyzing and help. I was afraid of the last. Dark corners lurked, mean thoughts.

My mother's social life usually was connected to the company's business. Not so when Eddie McIlvain and Tom Evans came for a stay at Barberries. "The boys," as my mother called them, were old-time bachelor friends, fun and funny, full of humorous stories, boisterously told by Eddie McIlvain and with genteel formality by Tom Evans. They were "old shoe" comfortable, a saying Puck gave them. They were friends of my father and his first wife, Patty. Together, they told the story of not being able to tell the two Mrs. Doubledays apart at a dance. The boys had solved the identity problem by never calling either Mrs. Doubleday by her first name. My mother would never allow me to meet the first Mrs. Doubleday, even on the day she came to visit my father to say good-bye just before he died. I longed to meet her, talk with her, find out what my father had been like when they were together, and felt cross at not being allowed to do so.

I doubt my mother ever told the boys the truth about how devastated and lonely she was or how hard she was struggling to pave the way for Nelson to become president of the company. But I watched her night after night weeping on the library sofa, where she lay in the same position, staring at my father's portrait. Raoul Fleischmann, cofounder of *The New Yorker*, often came for weekends in the summer, less in winter. He brought intelligence, wit, and literary gossip into our home; his presence was one of friendship for us all.

I thought of my father often, remembered him in gaiety at a dance he gave for Madeleine's friend Mary Blackwell when she was "coming out" or getting married, I don't remember which. The dance was held in the living room, before the decorator, Sally Lockwood, filled it with satin and French furniture. My father stood there smiling in a tuxedo. I wanted to dance, my toes in my black patent-leather shoes on top of his shoes. An idea I said nothing about, but I drank in his delight at the merriment around him. He'd had that same look when he was playing baseball for some company team years ago, when I was no more than six or seven. He was so big and so tall. He hit the pitch way into the outfield and got to second base. He was hit home by a friend, and he capered like a kid. "Hi, daughter. Come give your old dad a hug." I raced into his arms and he lifted me high off the ground. I wrapped my arms around his neck, nuzzled my nose into his shoulder. I have sentimental memories of his holding me close, or just of me enjoying watching him so caught up in passion, playing ball, tennis, planning a new area in the gardens with Mr. Evert, the landscape architect, or a new merchandise idea for the bookstore. His mind never stopped in the days before alcohol brought him down. Everything at full bore, that was his way for whatever he was doing. Oddly, I have no memory of my mother ever holding me or playing with me, other than at card games.

Daphne du Maurier came to visit. My mother and Daphne had been writing letters to each other ever since they met, when Daphne was being sued by an Argentinian writer who said the story of *Rebecca* was stolen from her book. My mother and Daphne had become close friends, in a way my mother wasn't with her bridge and backgammon ladies. I liked Daphne. She always spent time with Nelson and me in the playroom, where we lay about listening to music. Bing Crosby singing "Don't Fence Me In" was my favorite. Daphne listened to our worries about our mother's loneliness and her drinking. She had been drinking too much since way before my father died. I hadn't taken it in till after he died. She was drunk most every night now. She picked fights mostly with Nelson, because he didn't stay home at night to be with her. She had asked Bob Paine, Nelson's godfather, to talk to him. "Make him heel" was her expression, I think.

Daphne was staying with my mother again in the autumn of 1951. It was November, after Thanksgiving. My mother invited Gertrude Lawrence, who could come because it was a Monday night and Broadway was black. Gertrude was playing opposite Yul Brynner in *The King and I.* My mother wanted to have "a lovely dinner for Daphne."

John Sargent drove Gertrude Lawrence, Ken McCormick, and Lee Barker, a Doubleday editor, out from the city for my mother's dinner party. It was snowing hard. My mother started drinking cocktails at six with Daphne. Puck, who, like me, did not drink, and my boyfriend, Tony d'Almeida, whom I had met at a dance and who drank with care, watched my mother getting sloshed. Dinner was to be served at seven-thirty, but the city group lost its way in the snowstorm and did not arrive till ten past nine.

My mother, a gracious if tipsy hostess, gave everyone a drink before going in to dinner. Gertrude Lawrence changed into a stunning golden outfit that was far more glamorous than my mother's regal red-and-black velvet hostess gown. During dinner, at the impeccably set mahogany table, lighted by dozens of candles in silver candelabra, Gertrude told stories about theater life in New York and London, sparing no one. Her tales were delicious and funny. She entranced us with her wit, her dramatic gestures, and her grand delivery. She even told stories on herself, in a playful voice with almost childlike innocence. I was fascinated by how she could capture everyone's attention and keep them focused solely on her.

My mother, at the head of the table in her regal gown, a choker of warm, glistening pearls about her neck, with earrings to match, appeared small, even delicate from my distant end of the table. Tony d'Almeida and I were sitting "below the salt." My mother had met her match in Gertrude. Undeterred, she began a slurry account of the machinations and intrigues perpetrated by Machiavelli. Her head bobbed from time to time and her right hand waved above her head and then stopped. She looked at it as though it belonged to someone else and quickly brought it down to her lap. Her passion for this Italian scoundrel seemed sexual in intensity. His brilliant use of power and how ruthlessly he formed his decisions seemed to energize her. She kept losing the point she intended to make, until someone rescued the situation by reminding her of what she was saying.

Puck escorted my mother from the table before dessert was served. When everyone else had finished their crème brûlée, I got up from the table and said, "Let's go into the library for coffee and liqueurs." I was acting like my mother, trained to keep guests occupied.

As I passed the staircase on the way to the library, Puck called to me from the top of the stairs. "Come up, Neltje." It was an order.

"What gives? Where's our mother?" I asked.

"Go to her, she wants you," she said, pointing down the hall toward my mother's room. Puck turned and went quickly down the stairs. I called to her, wanting more. . . . She never answered.

How odd, I thought. That was not like Puck at all, and my mother rarely wanted me. Her bed was turned down, but she was not in the room. I became frightened. I passed her mirrored closets and the mahogany writing desk with spindly legs.

The lights were on in her all-white bathroom. I almost stepped on her before I saw her lying on the floor at my feet. Her eyes were closed. I thought, My God. She is dead. I called out "Ma, Ma" in a loud voice. I knelt down beside her, shook her shoulder. "Ma. Ma. Wake up, Ma. Wake up."

Her eyes were half-open, but her pupils were hardly visible. I slapped her hands, which lay limp in mine. I slapped her face. She winced a bit. Her eyes closed. "Oh no! Wake up, wake up, Ma." My mother had passed out on her bathroom floor, and Puck had left me, at fifteen years old, to cope.

I finally pulled my mother to a sitting position and placed my knees and lower legs firmly against her back so she could not slump down on the floor again. I took her beneath her arms and lifted her to her feet. She was upright, a rag doll unsteady on her feet. We spent several minutes not moving, she holding on to the sink, me with my arms around her, holding her up.

We walked slowly to her bed. Her five-foot-four frame leaned into my five-foot-nine one, making it difficult to hold her. She began to sob. "I am so lonely, so lonely. I miss Nelson. Help me." I was busy getting her out of her clothes and into her nightgown with as few tangles as possible. I made sympathetic sighs and *hmmmmm* sounds. "I understand. It is hard," I muttered.

"Oh, darling, what am I to do? Daphne loves me and wants to make love with me. What should I do?" my mother slurred as I slipped her feet under the covers. She lay back on her pillows, still crying. She asked again, "What should I do?" I handed her Kleenex, then wiped her tear-smeared face, which seemed so small and so innocent at that moment. I pulled the covers up to her chin.

"Do what you want to," I softly replied, and left the room.

Daphne would be going back to England in a few days. Was my mother so distraught with loneliness that she would move to England to be with Daphne? I didn't know what to think. I had no one to talk to. Was my mother really a lesbian? What would that mean to our family? I was scared. Scared that my mother, the only family figure I had, could be so out of control. What should I do now? Is it my job to take care of her? In the end I did nothing, never mentioned the incident to her, and I doubt she remembered.

I ran down the stairs to get to the library in time to serve liqueurs to the guests. Not one person asked after my mother. Puck never said a word to me, even later, when no one was around.

Over time, years really, my mother subtly told me what was expected of a woman, what a man wanted when he married.

"Learn to be the power behind the throne, help boost men's egos, and never confront them directly with your desires. Be clever. Take no credit for an idea. Let it always come from him, even if the suggestion was yours. Marrying for love is not always necessary for a happy life; mind and ambition are more important than the body. It is a woman's job to be the source of interest in a conversation. Bring up ideas about books you have read or something in the newspaper—I suppose sports, if you are pushed to it—and use your charms, darling. With authors, ask them about what they 'are in the midst of.' It is a good phrase that covers lots of territory without being specific, or tell them what you enjoyed in their book. Always read the book before meeting the author. Use your charms on everyone, women, too, for they are the competition. Think of something of interest that will capture the attention of a dinner partner, and at any party, rescue a man standing off alone, by himself. He is usually fearfully shy. Sometimes you do get a grouch who wants to be left alone, but rarely. And be kind to a lonely-looking woman as well. You never know when it might be you."

These were lessons my mother told me from the time I was ten, and they expanded in their intensity after my father died. I remember being eight years old, standing out by the swing set. I had just been told to go to my room for insulting my mother. I said to myself, I will give up who I am, what I want, and do as you want me to be. I will behave as you wish because I have no power and I am tired of being punished for telling my truth. I watched how my mother behaved. When I was fifteen, my head spun with her certainties for my future: dances, society, and marriage. I wanted nothing to do with the Machiavellian plotting, the secrecy, and what I considered the underhandedness of how she maneuvered in her life with the company and Nelson, but particularly when it spilled into mine. "Why the conniving secrecy about who knows what you are planning or thinking? If you don't want anyone to know, tell no one.

That seems academic to me. And ask directly for what you want," I said to my mother.

She replied, "That course would alienate men and bring failure in business or any personal relationship." Oh, you poor boys spoiled from birth on, I thought, but it took me until I was well into my thirties to realize I did not have to continue that course, by which time I had a son of my own. Fiery anger began in my belly against egotistical, spoiled males and, in particular, against my arrogant brother and my mother, who had carefully, lovingly created him.

Society balls in New York now captured my mother's attention: all four of them—the Mets, the Gets, the Holls, and the Cols. She wanted me to "come out" in society, which was, in fact, a meat market. This was her way of planning for my future, as she planned for Nelson's by politicking for him to take over the firm one day. Debutantes were dressed up in tulle, with bare shoulders, perfume, and a ready smile, a possible tasty morsel for marriage. I did it and found out I was no longer scared to dance with boys. Would-be partners were not going to molest or hurt me. This was a significant change, a relief. With gardenias in my hair and silver slippers on my toes, I danced and danced and danced. I was popular, fortunately, and spent four years happily swirling in a dream world of rhythms, smiling at each boy, whether I felt like it or not. He may have had bad breath and been stupid, but still I smiled. For a half hour, or maybe more, I would sit out and talk with the boys who really interested me. Most boys were ordinary, perfectly nice but boring. I was interested in the bruised and the lame, where life had already intervened. I could make a difference in their lives, even for a brief moment.

The debutante rules of behavior I had already learned, but I needed to think more for myself, evaluate what was meaningful to me besides having a beautiful time dancing and being popular. I had danced for the hell of it, not to find a husband. I had to start growing up. At sixteen, I was confident; at seventeen, I was scared and felt I knew nothing. I did not think of life partners nor envision who I would become. I took one day at a time. At home, I simply tried to survive and be kind. I had had serious boyfriends and happy-go-lucky, empty-headed dancing-fool boyfriends. First I would have one kind, then the other. Serious ones lasted longest. Now what? Do I really want to be a nurse? I had thought so since spending time with my father when his lung collapsed. No, not really. Then why continue the sham? I have to get my mother into the city to make sure she has a life in the wintertime. And I don't know what I really want to do with my life. Holding on to being a nurse gives me a sense of security, mild though it may be. I have to get away from my mother.

I saw little of Nelson by the time I was seventeen, as he was busy being in love with Flossie McKim, a funny redhead who was to become his wife. She went to Miss Porter's a year ahead of me, and we had always liked each other. After we were both married, Nelson and I would have dinner or go to a movie, meet at Barberries for lunch on a weekend, but the closeness we had shared as young children waned. As we grew older, we became people of very different interests and lifestyles. Nelson stayed with the Piping Rock Club friends of his youth, playing golf, yachting, being a great party giver after graduating from Princeton and doing his stint in the ROTC Air Force. Sadly, I had nothing to say to him anymore, as I was critical of that lifestyle. It seemed petty and pointless. Eventually, when he was working at Doubleday, his drinking gathered momentum and, like our father's, his practical jokes became more unkind and unfunny. I was an easy known target.

The pact of love with him, the trusting belief I had had that he would not hurt me ever, withered. My growing independence and demands to be treated fairly fiscally in the family business caused outrage in him and in my mother, as well. I didn't want a job; I did want a fair value for the company stock. Nelson developed a superior attitude toward me and, as my trustee, stopped my income because I was not staying within his acceptable social path. Eventually, I wanted him removed as trustee from all trusts I had an interest in because he was using his voting power of Doubleday shares for his benefit alone, while treating my sisters and me with mean-spirited arrogance. He increased his financial enhancement by lowering the price of the stock, then buying it up. I took him to court.

NINE

My God, What Have I Done?

I met John Sargent again, in our driveway the day before my father died. My father was in a coma by then. It was Monday, January 10, 1949.

In the years following the funeral, my mother asked John to fill in as her extra man for business lunches and dinners, and on social evenings. John was a junior editor now, no longer in advertising, which pleased him. He was very well read, amusing, and comically witty. His manners were impeccable when he wasn't drunk, and he knew enough to send flowers the next day if his behavior had faltered. My mother enjoyed talking business with him long into the night, plotting ways for her to gain power in the workings of Doubleday & Company. Her goal was specific and focused: to ensure the presidency of the firm for Nelson. In the meantime, she did her best to undermine her business enemies: the president of Doubleday, Doug Black, and Aunt Dorothy Babcock, my father's sister, who had demanded a dividend even while my father was alive, so her stock in the company would produce some income. My father believed in pouring profits back into the company. But that was all very well for him, because John Sengstack, board member and tax expert, had set a policy that the company would pay my father's considerable expenses, all of them, instead of a salary. (Aunt Dorothy had no such arrangement, of course.) Over cocktails before dinner, or brandy after, my mother responded with avid interest and delight to scraps of publishing gossip from John. Book publishing thrived on gossip as much back then as it does today.

I stayed at my godmother's apartment in the city for dance nights during winter and spring vacations. On a Saturday afternoon in late December, John called me at Aunt Al's. It was 1951 and I was seventeen, home on vacation from Miss Porter's School. The Get Together Dance, the last dance of the season, was to take place that night at the Pierre Hotel in New York City. John had been at the house over the past weekend, attending my mother's dinner for an English author.

He and I had spent many evenings over the years coping with my mother when she had had too much to drink, listening to her teary stories of being slighted or not having the control she wanted in the company, the same pains hashed over again and again. We giggled privately over some of the most embarrassing situations, never mentioning them in my mother's presence. Watching parents, mine or those belonging to others—in fact, adults of any age—getting drunk was an ordinary experience for me. Nearly everyone drank too much at our big summer lunches or fancy winter dinners, and I often watched guests behaving stupidly or becoming maudlin, sometimes both. My father had been the same. I had seen him behave in an outrageously mean manner, abusively rude to my mother, to Nelson, to me, or to anyone close by, when drunk. When growing up, I never knew whether what was said when my parents had been drinking would be remembered. Promises made were so often forgotten. I learned not to trust at a young age.

John and I had taken a long walk on Sunday after lunch, reminisced about the ghastly night with Gertrude Lawrence and Daphne du Maurier. He was smoking a cigar as we walked in the cold air, both of us wrapped in thick woolens. We talked about books, my wanting to be a nurse, his passion for Mozart and Verdi.

When he called me, I was excited to hear his voice and curious about why he would be calling. He never had before. With no preliminary chitchat, he said, "I want to go to the dance with you tonight. Do you have an extra ticket?"

I was stunned. "No, I don't have an extra, John. I'm sorry," I replied, suspecting he wanted to meet someone else at the party. Could he want to be with me? My heart jumped a beat, then collapsed. No, it couldn't be me, could it?

He went on: "Well, how can I get in?"

"Let me see what I can do, John, and I'll call you back," I told him, wanting time to think. He gave me his phone number and we hung up. The entire call had taken less than two minutes.

I already knew what I was going to do when on the phone with John. I would call off Winston Fowlkes, a school chum of Nelson's whom I had asked to join me. Most puzzling to me was what John was plotting. He had never shown any interest in me other than displaying routine jolly kindness toward me as Puck's younger sister, or Ellen Doubleday's daughter. We would chat in the library before my mother came down for cocktails before dinner. I always felt John looked down on me because I was young. I wondered if he was using me as a decoy. Damn, my heart was thumping. I wanted to be with John. Why? What is this excitement? I was only seventeen.

Twenty minutes later, I called John back. "Why don't you meet me at the Pierre ballroom entrance at ten? I may be late, as I have no control over the time my friend's dinner party will end. It is majorly rude to quit the table."

"I'll be there," he said, and hung up. His voice sent electricity right through me from heart to toes and back again. I took a bath and lay down on the bed to read for a half hour but kept going over the few words of my conversation with John. I looked for signs of affection and beyond but saw none. We had never even had an "older brother" kind of date, not even for the movies on a boring winter weekend.

John was at the Pierre ballroom entrance when I arrived. Very little was said. We danced around the highly polished floor to Lester Lanin's music, he in a tuxedo, me in a low-cut, virtually strapless evening dress, the bodice ornamented with crystal drops and sequins, the swinging bouffant skirt of dusty pink tulle. My other date (I always took two boys to the dance) was there, but I have no memory of even who it was. I danced with lots of boys that night, not really boyfriends, just buddies.

"Who are all these boys that keep cutting in? Are they all your boyfriends?" John inquired. His sharp-edged tone was close to threatening.

I figured he was huffy because I was popular, cut in on regularly. John was not used to seeing me at dances. He saw me at my home, at events that were connected to business, with one boyfriend maybe over a year's time.

We danced and danced. In between, he vanished; I never saw him standing on the sidelines. Where is he? But there was my old boyfriend, who was at Harvard now. We sat for a long time at a table with a pink tablecloth. I drank a Coke. We caught up on our lives, both so pleased to stay friends. John found me, invited me to dance. I got up, hugged my ex-love, and smiled up at John as he took my hand. It was close to midnight; the band was playing a Strauss waltz. We stepped on the dance floor, waited a second, facing each other in dance position, then began the liquid motions of the Vienna Waltz.

He bent his head down close to my ear. "Marry me?"

A question? A statement? I was not sure which. My throat tightened. I said, "Oh yes."

John held me close while we twirled and twirled.

I was used to boys or men saying odd things at night and not remembering them in the morning. Alcohol was usually the reason, but sometimes it was just stud bravura. John had been drinking. I could tell by how he held himself rigidly correct, and how the pupils of his eyes floated upward. But I had felt a wildness running through me when I was near him or even thought about him. I could think of nothing else.

In the cab on the way home, we could not get enough of each other. In the night, I questioned what was happening. I didn't really know him at all. He was an adult. I was a child, not yet eighteen. And we had never even kissed till that night. The situation felt weird. Would he remember? Would or should I back away? Should I just wait and see? What should I do?

The following night at dinner at the "21" Club, John gave me a gold charm for my bracelet, a small book with three pages. The first had the previous day's date engraved on it, the date of our engagement. I was so surprised at his thoughtfulness that I could only mumble trivialities. "I am touched, so touched, John. Thank you. I can wear it always." And I kissed him quickly on the cheek, not a passionate kiss like in the cab.

"The following page is for the date of our wedding," John said as he sipped his martini, recovering from my public display of intimacy. "And the opposite page for the births of our children."

That was it: the words *births of our children*. Those words zinged into me, piercing. This moment would decide my future. Yes or no? My God, what have I done?

The following day, I left for the winter term of my senior year. The train departed Penn Station at 1:30 P.M. We would have no more time together. I hadn't packed yet.

We wrote each other daily all winter. We weren't to see each other until I was home again for spring vacation, but Puck came to the rescue by bringing John up to Farmington for a weekend in February. Bless Puck. She pretty much stayed in her room, giving us privacy for serious necking and snuggling. John was more intimately verbal in letters than he could be in person. But I knew that he felt the passion, lust, and love for me I needed.

In March 1952, during my spring vacation, John told my mother that he and I would marry the following spring. She reacted with fury. I was not sure I knew all the pieces yet, but certainly jealousy on many levels was obvious. John had often been a dinner partner, weekend guest, and her confidant concerning her position in the company and her determination to sweep the path clear for Nelson's achieving the presidency of Doubleday. These events and murmurings had taken place almost since my father died, or at least for two years. Looking back on it, I can see where she could have felt that John had gone behind her back. But did any pair of lovers ask parental permission before falling in love in 1952?

Maybe she didn't trust John, thinking him an opportunist. She was not alone. I thought of it, as well, and so did many others. Nelson was even crosser than my mother. He wanted his little sister to marry a buddy of his, live close by on Long Island, lunch and play golf at the Piping Rock Club, not rock the boat.

My mother's anger swelled. She took me on a cruise that summer, along with Nelson and his girlfriend, Flossie McKim, in an effort to break John and me up. We visited Iceland and the North Cape, the fjords of Norway, and Stockholm, Ireland, Scotland, and Denmark. We spent a week in London and a week in Paris. I had fun, not with the dates coerced to take me out in London by Daphne's children and husband at my mother's request, but with Peter McCarthy from St. Louis, who was on the *Caronia* with us in every fjord, on deck at sunrise only occasionally. I learned how to drink with Peter every night after dinner in the rear bar of the ship, learned about hangovers, too. He was in Paris for two nights when we first got there. When he left for home, he passed me on to his buddies, all freshmen at Ivy League colleges, rebels in some way. I learned from them, too. I was not yet eighteen, sophisticated, yet still young, wanting to have a good time with people my age. Had my mother been a different sort of woman, had she suggested I live at Barnard, where I was going to college in the fall, give myself some space, my story might have been different.

I felt I had to get away from her. Nothing I did pleased her. This had always been true. I scraped my knee; she buffed her fingernails. I upset her with my straightforward way of speaking, calling it like it is, not mincing around in vagaries. No emotional situation was discussed at our house except tears from my mother when she felt left out or did not get her way. It was the mid-twentieth century, but mincing Edwardian and Victorian sensibilities ruled.

Her plan, I think, had always been for me to marry and mimic the lifestyle she had chosen. I was not her; I had different desires. The irony is, I jumped into that pot all by myself.

But first, I felt responsible to get her into an apartment in New York, so she could have a social life. Her card-playing and dinner-party friends all moved into the city before Thanksgiving and stayed until early May, when they returned to their estates on Long Island. I knew money was tight, but she found an apartment that the top decorator in the city turned into a space suitable for formal functions, each chair and sofa covered in elegant white fabrics. It was not a cozy home for suppers, family or otherwise. By the time John and I were to announce our engagement formally at the end of January 1953, I was exhausted from fending off my mother's rages every night when I got home from having dinner with John and a friend, or from a meal I cooked at his apartment. His mother, Dagmar Wetmore Sargent, and his father, Charles Sprague Sargent Jr., also lived in the city. We had dinners with them and John's brother Charlie, who lived across the street from my mother's on Ninety-first Street and Park Avenue. There also were evenings when we went to a movie, had a drink and a hamburger, then went to our respective homes and to bed by nine.

I think my mother was maddened most by losing control, given her interests in life, her heroes and heroines: Machiavelli, Elizabeth I, and Catherine the Great. She wished she had been all of them. It is reasonable that she even felt outwitted, which would have been cause to bring out the army, more or less what she did. We did not like each other; we were built of such different cloth, had different interests, liked different kinds of people, books, furnishings, food, and different basics of ethics and morals. I loved her, and all my life I wanted her to love me. She couldn't, not wouldn't. But I did not like her. And I ended up feeling the same way about Nelson.

She became obsessed in her attempt to destroy my relationship with John. The more she tried, the more determined I was to marry him. I was in love with him.

When they talked business in the library until well past midnight, their discussions never included me. My thoughts or opinions were never asked for. I sat in the library and listened. I did not complain. I was used to being excluded from those kinds of conversations as I was growing up. But I felt differently now. I was getting married. I was beginning to feel adult, at least at certain moments. The way I behaved now was the behavior of a good business wife, trained to refrain from voicing an opinion but to listen carefully for possible future questioning. The roller coaster of my emotions exhausted me. I probably would have backed out of the marriage if I hadn't been so scared of being alone, or, worse, having to live with my mother. At moments I loved John with a clear passion. Other times, when he put me down even in small ways, I thought myself nuts to be engaged to him.

Puck, my ally and confidante of the past, was not happy we were to marry. She would not say why, which hurt. So I lost her and had no one I could talk to. I hadn't faced why I wanted to marry John. What was it that had pulled me to him? For me, our love and eventual happiness was complicated by the family business, where John worked, and my mother's determined goal to make Nelson president of the company.

One night in early January 1953, just shortly before our engagement was to be announced, my friend Jon Schueler phoned to invite me to dinner. We set the date for when I knew John Sargent would be in Chicago. There was no rule about not seeing other men, but I felt it. I also ignored it. I liked Schueler as a friend. I wanted to be with him. We had had many long talks over the past four years at Barberries, some gloomy, some funny, many insightful. Schueler, as he liked to be called, was well into his thirties and had two daughters in California. I found him intensely passionate about everything: painting, people, books, life. He was also easygoing, with none of the performance of the society I was accustomed to.

I, the privileged, rich eighteen-year-old girl from the North Shore of Long Island, set off for Schueler's loft on Broadway in SoHo, long before the area was gentrified. He had given me instructions—which subway to take, where to get off—and directions to the loft building. I had no experience of New York subways. I had traveled to Barnard by bus and was used to taking taxis for shopping or movies, or any other social activity. However, I did not want to let Schueler know this or that I was scared of riding the subway. The subway was dangerous, according to my mother, who said, "Only the help or people like them travel on subways. They are not for our kind." I did not want Schueler to think of me as a spoiled young girl.

I found the subway stairs and hoped I did not look too dressy. At Fourteenth Street, I changed to a local from an express train, then watched each stop nervously until I got off at the Spring Street station. It was seven o'clock and dark. Because of the hour, there was little light from any storefront. Only two people passed by as I walked to Broadway. I found the battered blue steel door of Schueler's building, the buzzer and intercom button. I had never seen any entry like this, no building without a doorman, ever. "Just not safe," my mother had said. Schueler answered when I buzzed, told me to take the elevator to the third floor, where the steel door was now unlocked. When he opened the door to his loft and stood with arms open before me, we hugged. I felt such relief, I wanted to bury my head in his shoulder and cry.

Schueler said, "Hi, baby." All women were addressed as "baby" in Schueler lingo. He took my winter coat and stood nearby without a word. I knew he was giving me time to acclimate, to absorb his space, so entirely opposite from my home. I was still so nervous from the subway ride and the walk in the dark, unknown, and dicey area that I could not register thoughts or words.

A stack of canvases leaned against the wall at the right, and racks of stacked and stored painted canvases, two sections high, lined the left wall. Before me towers of painted canvases, face to the floor, rested atop drop cloths, allowing less than a quarter of the entire space for Schueler to use as living space. A wooden table with three odd chairs, a bed, and an orange crate as a bedside table were almost all there was of furnishings. On the crate, a fusty old lamp gave off a sallow light; a tatty comfortable chair was scrunched up close by. A line of white metal cabinets, bottoms only, separated the kitchen stove and garbage can from the main living space.

Schueler offered me wine, and I accepted gladly. I felt so awkward.

This lifestyle—seemingly messy and piecemeal, with secondhand furnishings—was foreign to me. "Furnishings define a person," my mother had always said, intending me, perhaps, to use her statement as a yardstick of success. Is Schueler broke? I wondered. Does he have enough money to feed himself, to live? These questions flipped quickly through my mind while I asked him, "Have you seen Puck recently? I haven't." I faced ceiling-high windows, twelve or sixteen feet high, when I sat at the table. They looked dirty, but I couldn't tell if it was just night darkness or dirt. Paintings were propped everywhere, in every available bit of space. The one on the easel was not all that large, but it was intense—dark greens, purple, and black, with an area of a creamy light in the top left corner. It was painted with a palette knife, thick short strokes of color, layer upon layer, creating a rich textured surface that made me feel that I was in a dense forest, scary but safe. I looked at it for a long time. Schueler never asked me what I thought, and I was glad, because I could not have defined my feelings.

Schueler had prepared spaghetti with a garlicky tomato sauce, bread, and a salad. He presented the food with a quiet pride. We ate in comfortable silence for a few moments before he began talking about his work, about the possibility of an exhibition of his paintings at the Stable Gallery.

"How wonderful. Aren't you thrilled? When will you know for sure?" I rattled off questions, excited for him.

"I should hear within the month, and the exhibition may be a year, year and a half later. I like Eleanor Ward, the gallery owner, and trust her. Her gallery is the best for us Abstract Expressionists and I am elated that she likes my work."

Schueler had been a navigator in the U.S. Army Air Corps during World War II. He had a breakdown and was hospitalized in England for a time. His association with England, flying, and a woman he met there became inspirations for his work that would last him a lifetime. He loved jazz and loved playing it. "What instrument is that? Do you play a cello?" I queried in disbelief, pointing at a large brown canvas-covered musical instrument tucked in the corner.

"No, baby, that's my bass. I play bass weekends with pickup bands at jazz joints around town. Playing jazz is immediate, like painting, in the moment," he said, smiling at me.

I saw myself sitting in a smoky bar listening to him play, as if I were his wife or live-in girlfriend. Would I be able to sit in bars every time he played without getting bored? Could I do that? Wait. What was I doing, thinking like this? Being with Schueler? As girlfriend or wife? I was unbalanced. I had no idea where these questions came from. I had never thought of Schueler as anything but Puck's friend. But why was I here alone, in his studio? Don't ask if you are not willing to turn over the wheelbarrow and spill, I said to myself as I responded to Schueler's description of jazz and painting.

"In the moment, yes, I understand that 'in the moment' feeling. I have felt it often. But I am ridiculed by my family for being impulsive, not thinking things through when I respond to intuitive imagination. I feel wide-open alive when it is rolling, happy to be in unknown territory," I said quizzically, because although I felt a kindred spirit, I wanted confirmation.

We were walking around the studio, stopping to look at the paintings. Sometimes I could only see bits of color, many of them somber. I instinctively liked the brighter multicolored ones, which felt less troubled. Schueler took my hand.

"Don't let anyone put you down. And not when your imagination is rolling. That is what it is to be an artist, baby." Schueler looked me in the eye as he spoke. With Schueler I could be free. That flash opened a gate inside me and terrified me.

At dinner the gap in our ages suddenly made me shy and silent. Schueler's lifestyle had stunned me, made me feel unsure of myself. The forks and knives we ate with did not match and the large gray-painted table had ugly, thickly carved legs.

"Schueler, where did you find this massive table with the less than beautiful carved legs?" I asked with a giggle.

"It was given to me by an old girlfriend who was moving out of the city." He laughed. "I use it as a drawing table and eat on my lap in that comfortable chair," he answered.

I had never known of anyone living this way. Could I be a painter and live this way? With Schueler? On my own? What was I thinking? I was marrying John Sargent. Inside me, a door closed.

After dinner he asked me to sit on the bed next to him. He had something he wanted to say to me before I got married. More opinions of my being too young to marry, I thought, and began to internally put up a wall, keeping him out. I would listen, be polite, then take my leave.

I said, "Sure, but let's do the dishes first."

"Leave them. I'll do them later, or in the morning,"

We were squared off on the bed, legs tucked beneath us. "Please, Neltje, don't marry John Sargent. He is a stuffed shirt, first of all. But most important, honey, he really wants you only for your money, your social position, and your business connections. I have watched him out at Oyster Bay. Don't be fooled by his looks, his elegance, and his way with words. He will hurt you. Stay. Oh, please stay. Stay and marry me. I love you, and I will treat you well."

Schueler held my hand, looked into my eyes. His touch was gentle, felt caring and undemanding. I was too scared to say yes. The lifestyle was too different, the switch with no family support too unthinkable. And I did not love him in that way. Was it just my imagination supplanting myself in another's life that had opened my insides, let me breathe? I said no as kindly as possible, my mind drowned in confusion.

I took a cab back to my mother's apartment because it was after ten and I was too scared of . . .

In so many ways I was more comfortable with Schueler than I was with proper John Sargent. We laughed and talked, admittedly mostly about him, but I was interested in what he talked about. There would be no drunken evenings with my mother talking about the company. Schueler hardly ever drank, and with Schueler, ideas were paramount. I let myself into the apartment, passed by the formal living room, furnished in white, and went down the hall to my gray-blue bedroom, the same color as my room at Barberries.

Schueler's bid for my love touched me. He had spoken with a passion for me, more than I had ever heard from John Sargent.

In bed that night, I went over all that Schueler had said and knew in my gut he was right. Our marriage was a business deal; each of us would get what we needed. John Sargent had a great family name and no money, but he acted like he did. We spoke the same language. And he made me aware of every cell in my body. Does a girl really want more at eighteen?

For days after that evening with Schueler, while coping with wedding plans, I was tweaked by the free-spiritedness of Schueler's life, yet far too fearful to risk jumping into his basket. I did not like my reasons for choosing John Sargent. I did not like me. I hid my messed-up search for truth from everyone amid my greatest performance, the loving bride-to-be.

John and I got married on May 16, 1953. I was eighteen and he would be twenty-eight in late June. My mother chose the date because the azaleas and rhododendrons that lined the driveway of our home on Long Island would be in full bloom. She even insisted that the gardeners place dry ice around the base of the azalea bushes to maintain perfect blossoms, if necessary, and she ensured that our wedding did not interfere with Nelson's final exams at Princeton. I was personally paying for this wedding but was not allowed to say how many people or even who should be invited, nor allowed to interfere with any of the arrangements. I abdicated my powers early on to avoid a fight, leaving John and my mother to sort it out. I wrote thank-you notes for silver pitchers, silver picture frames, silver ashtrays, silver nut dishes, silver salt and pepper cellars, silver toast racks and gravy spoons, all spread out with their accompanying cards on white linen—covered tables that lined the upstairs hall. These presents on display came from the hundreds of invited guests, most of whom I did not know: John's family and their friends, his publishing friends, his business associates, his society friends. The list for my mother was comparable; Nelson's and my sisters' friends had been invited, and a friend or two of mine from college, as well as a pack of them from Miss Porter's. I sat in the sun at the far end of the terrace, writing thank-you notes, took breathers to wander about the lawn, look over the woods out to Oyster Bay. I stopped thinking of anything except the physicality of the day of the wedding.

My mother was furious when she found me getting a tan. She told me to go in the house immediately, and said it was indecent and lewd for a bride to have a suntan at her wedding.

TEN

From This Day Forward

The day of the wedding began with a crystal clear sky, a sun to warm the spring air, and my wild excitement with every breath I took. We each had twelve attendants at the ceremony, bridesmaids and ushers. The gardens, beautiful in full blossom, with no dry ice, were bedazzling; everyone said so. Inside the house, all tables were adorned with magnificent bouquets, as was every table in the tent on the lawn facing the bay. A picture-perfect setting.

The receiving line was in the living room. My mother's mother, whom I called "Grandma," slipped me a small antique purse. It was packed full of bills in all denominations, as well as some change. She patted my arm. "In case you don't like it, dear," she said sweetly. John and I whooped with laughter and hugged her portly frame.

On our honeymoon in Bermuda, in a cottage all our own, apart from the main club, I was alternatively scared I had nothing of mental interest to delight or charm John and enthralled by experimenting with the sensations of his touch and my touch of him, laughing or wanting to cry.

Years later, John and I talked about our different agendas for marriage, but at that time we were both far too intimidated. At dinner, John and I sat opposite each other, with white tablecloth, crystal glasses, and a dinner candle between us. Our eyes met; we smiled but could find no subject to discuss. The mealtimes passed awkwardly for the first few nights. I could not, would not, consider that I had made a huge mistake, but it occurred to me John was thinking the same. What have I gotten myself into? Had I chosen a life of performance, a lifestyle I had wanted to flee? I avoided thinking by lying in the sun on our terrace, reading a novel while John plunged playfully in the sea with another woman. Would he always want another?

Nelson had been grumpy anytime he was around John over the past year, snapping, losing his temper over foolish issues like "Whose car shall we use to go to the movies, yours or mine?" The reason was probably male competition with a brother-in-law not of his own choosing, plus the loss of a close relationship with me. Our life together, the bond that had cemented us against the world, was ending. Nothing between us was there to replace it. And Nelson was getting a business competitor. But I did not think of that until much later.

John and I returned from our honeymoon to our dream apartment at 14 Sutton Place South, with two bedrooms and bathrooms, a living room, a tiny dining area, and a kitchen. It was filled with wedding presents and my clothes, all put away by the ever-faithful Tillie. The living room windows faced south, with an open view of the East River, which was peppered with tugs and barges, occasional sightseeing boats, and yachts.

I was ashamed to admit I had never held a vacuum cleaner, dust mop, or even a rag. I had cooked and I had washed dishes, made my bed at school, and washed out my underwear. I had not polished silverware, never mind silver nut dishes, candlesticks, ashtrays, or serving dishes or utensils. I had never pressed a man's suit. I was too proud to let on until forced to. "Something is wrong with the floor in the kitchen, John. It's all sticky. What's wrong with the linoleum, do you suppose?"

"Have you cleaned or mopped the floor? That might be the answer."

Oh, shame. I felt young, stupid, and spoiled. At Barberries, I had seen the kitchen maid clear the kitchen worktable and counter after lunch and at night. I had watched Tony, the butler, vacuum the library, living room, halls, and dining room early in the morning, but I had never seen the floors in the pantry or kitchen mopped.

I hated housekeeping, but I kept this to myself. We were busy inviting friends over for drinks or supper, so my wizardry with vacuum cleaner, dust mop, and dust rag were essential to the projection of myself as a good housewife.

The fact that I had an income-producing trust fund irritated John when he was either drunk or edgy, or both. I felt ashamed of my income, because what had I ever done to earn it? Since early childhood I had been told that "no one will marry you for your blue eyes." My father had explained, "That's why you'll have a trust and will get only the income. When you reach thirty, you will get a quarter of the capital. Nelson, because he is a boy, will get the entire principal when he reaches thirty." The unfairness registered with me as one more unkindness, but I didn't really understand then, when I was six or eight. I knew, even as I married John, how men controlled women financially, calling it "protection." But that was really a euphemism for domination.

I learned to cook, liked the creativity of the work, which was not true of dusting, washing clothes, or ironing. Eventually, I became a good and inventive cook. A year later we got two standard poodle puppies. One ate my wallet but left the twenty-dollar bill and my driver's license. Another ate the veal scaloppine I had left out on the kitchen table while I greeted our guest. We had to take John's crippled and aged uncle out to dinner. John never got upset at these moments, and I was grateful. I always felt at fault.

We gave and went to a stream of publishing parties, which included our young friends in the business: Jan Appleton, one of John's old school buddies, who worked for Harper; Tom Guinzburg, whose father ran Viking; Mike Canfield, who married Lee Bouvier, a schoolmate of mine, who found herself my superior just because she was, but not in French class, where I was a freshman and she a junior. We had sat next to each other. Cass Canfield, Jason Epstein, Tim Seldes, the list goes on. We were one of the few married couples, and our life together rolled smoothly from day to day. We went from event to event or spent evenings at home reading. Daytimes were the hardest for me. I was lonely and bored. I needed a job. I was suffering from performing, not speaking out. But I didn't dare tell John how insecure, shy, and frightened I felt. He would be bored with me. Without being aware of it, I was following my mother's instructions about how a wife should act and be.

In summer we spent weekends with John's parents at their farm in South Shaftsbury, Vermont; visited Bobby Goelet, John's friend from the

Brook Club, for a weekend at his mother's house in Newport, Rhode Island, which included a dance at the Newport Yacht Club. I forgot to pack John's cummerbund. A scene ensued. Another weekend we spent at the Pierponts' in Far Hills, New Jersey, where we attended a black-tie dinner. These elegant visits made me uncomfortable—more performance. I stayed up late reading; John snored even worse than Nana. I slept most of the day, getting up in time to fix supper. My friends, away at college during the school year, were busy playing or working in the summertime. Few wanted to visit, as they were occupied with new loves or wishing they were, or getting together with their college friends. I stopped my college career when we married and I had no skills to take on a serious job.

Deedee Knapp, an old friend from Miss Porter's, called to find out Peter Stehli's phone number. Nelson was in Georgia. He would have Peter's address. Peter was also doing his ROTC stint with the Air Force, but they were not at the same base. I was glad not to be in college; my life was more interesting but less youthful.

"Come have lunch with me?" I asked Deedee.

She came into the city, and we hugged, laughed, ate hamburgers at the local pub, and went to a movie—a normal vacation day of the past. I loved Deedee; her observations about people were usually right on, and there wasn't a grain of malice in her barrel. She became an Episcopal minister much, much later.

As he'd hoped, in spring of 1954, Schueler had an exhibition at the Stable Gallery, run by Eleanor Ward, one of the first gallery owners to be a proponent of early Abstract Expressionism. His thickly painted, textured canvases, rich in purples, blues, pinks, deep pinks, all pushing against one another, were paintings of emotional depth. Someone at the opening was flip and thought himself funny, joking, "What could one possibly see in this *mélange de couleurs*?" The jokester's fake French accent oozed out of his patrician mouth as he displayed false teeth and bad manners. Schueler overheard and laughed at the inanity. It was that ability to take himself less than seriously at such moments that attracted me to him. John Sargent was a touch on the pompous, "stuffed shirt" style too often. And here I was, still comparing!

Schueler's colors blended like a late-evening sky, sometimes hot, sometimes mellowing to a soft grayness, on large canvases, one almost as big as the wall it hung on, maybe eight feet long by five feet high. That measurement was huge for the time. I saw and felt energy and strength in these paintings, but I was unable to articulate even to myself how or why they enraptured or frightened me. There was no vocabulary for Abstract Expressionism; no critiques had yet been made by art pundits. Maybe I didn't have to know what I felt. Could that be?

In early December 1953, Ted Roethke came to stay with us for three days, the first overnight guest in our apartment. Ted was one of John's authors, a well-known poet who taught at Bennington College. He behaved in an "other than normal fashion" at times, I was told. This bear of a man walked in the door, gave me a hug that I felt for quite a time. John got a bear hug as well, but they were the same height and John was a big man. Ted dropped his backpack, got out a whiskey bottle, handed it to John, and said, "Get me a drink, just a little ice." He looked down at me. "You are a pretty one, did you know?"

Ted strode into the hall, on to our bedroom, and into the den, where I had made up the pull-out bed for him. This room immediately appeared much too small. I watched from the hall, frozen in place, not by fear, but from awe of this animal-man tearing through my home as though it were his. All our furniture seemed wrong-sized and staid. The coffee table in front of the yellow sofa that John's aunt Molly gave us as a wedding present, a butler's tray table, a copy of an old one, seemed part of a stage set. I had thought it all looked perfect until this moment. The upholstered chairs on each side of the fireplace were like those in the story of the three bears: small, too small, much too small. Ted paced the living room and called out to John in the kitchen, "Where the hell is that drink?"

We went out to dinner at a nearby steak house on First Avenue. The two men rambled on with memories and book quotes as they downed drink after drink, wine, and finally brandy. They were both plastered at the meal's end. Ted went off to a bar. I thought John would pass out before reaching home, a block and a half away.

At two-thirty in the morning, Ted stood in our bedroom doorway. He had turned on the bright overhead light, exposing our separate naked bodies, twisted sheets, and discarded clothes.

"I can't sleep, John. Help me."

John got up with a moan, dressed, and called a friend from work who had blockbuster sleeping pills. When he got back home, he gave them to

Ted with a drink of water and came back to bed without a word to me. The pills did not work. John fell asleep, but I heard Ted pacing. He walked back and forth in the adjoining room, bumped into furniture, then went out of the room to the front hall, where a floorboard squeaked; a hush ensued. He was in the carpeted living room. In my mind, I was a movie camera that followed three feet behind and above him. And like him, I was sweepingly critical of the staid bourgeois atmosphere in my house. *Zip*, like that, I become outside of myself, other.

Ted had a girlfriend, Beatrice O'Connell, whom he wanted us to meet. She had been a student of his at Bennington. It was Tuesday. Snow had been falling since late the night before. The streets and sidewalks were buried in snow, and by midafternoon a brittle wind swept through the streets, the avenues, and crosswalks. Travel by foot, bus, or cab would be a misery.

I heard Ted's key in the door. He held a large package of something wrapped in butcher paper in front of him like a platter. Carefully now, with his right thumb and forefinger, he peeled back the paper. A siren wailed close by. We turned to the window. Ted unfolded all four sides of the paper with precision. A porterhouse steak three inches thick, about twenty-four inches long, and almost as wide lay on the butcher paper in his hands. He held the meat up to my face in a ceremonial gesture, like a little kid with a surprise for Mom. He grinned and said, "Don't put it in the refrigerator. Leave it out, by the sink. But leave the paper on. Now, let's have a drink." It was 4:15.

John came home about six, thankfully. I had been edgy, alone in the apartment with Ted. After a while he had gone to get more whiskey and hadn't come back. John brought home two bottles of French Burgundy for this special dinner. Ted returned, but in a black humor. He and John talked briefly before his girlfriend arrived right at seven o'clock. Beatrice, a stunningly beautiful young woman of mixed race, slim and long-legged, walked into the apartment like a model, her posture regal. We had drinks and some cheese in the living room before the meal, but conversation limped awkwardly. I felt young and so unknowing.

When it was time to get the broiler going, Ted told me he was afraid of lighting the broiler with a match. He was afraid of fire. I found this touching. He needed my help. I was afraid of lighting the broiler myself, but Ted never knew, nor John.

At the table the enormous steak sat in front of Ted on a carving board with a platter beneath. Ted was very drunk by this time; his words slurred and he made little sense talking about rhyming and nonrhyming poetry. He carved the meat with panache, but his glee had gone. Plates were passed, potatoes, bread, and salad added, and we began to eat. Desultory conversation took place, with awkward periods of silence. The meal was delicious, the beef perfectly cooked.

After uttering a couple of tangled and mostly incoherent sentences, Ted picked up the carving knife, stood up, faced Beatrice, and, with a loop of his arm, placed the knifepoint on the tip of her nose. Then, in a whirlwind motion, he pointed around the table to include John and me and himself. "We," he commanded in a rasping tone. "We are the aristocracy. You," he said, swinging the knife back to Beatrice's throat. "You are the daughter of a SLAVE."

Beatrice pushed back her chair, found her coat in the bedroom, and left without a word. They were to marry within the year.

I fled to the kitchen. A short while later, I was at the sink soaking dishes when I sensed someone behind me. I turned to face Ted, moving across the space between us. He carried the carving knife in his right hand. He was ranting about the position of Negroes in America, incoherently angry at their diminishment, the cruelty and injustice of segregation, a subject he then polluted with garbage talk about the nothingness of Negroes. But what about your girlfriend Beatrice? She is part Negro, after all, I thought, but didn't dare say. I was scared, bone-jiggling scared.

"The damn lazy Negroes who do nothing to help themselves. Why should our WHITE tax money go to them? They don't deserve a damn thing." Ted came closer, the knife pointed now at my belly. Soapsuds slid down my arms, uplifted in defense. He pressed me back into the sink so far, my rear end was in the water. He held me there as words streamed from his mouth.

"Why are any of us dumb enough to wear—white guilt—over the stupid, lazy, lazy, good-for-nothing Negroes? Not a talented one in the whole bunch, not a writer, not a decent poet. What do you think?" Ted's sweaty face was inches from mine. I could see the pores in his nose and jowly cheeks.

Ted whipped the knife up to my neck, pressed the point into my flesh, the soft gully at the base of my neck. I screamed.

I was still frightened the following night, nervous, wondering when Ted would show up. I did not want to be in the apartment alone when he came back. John thought I was overreacting; he thought the past evening an amusing entertainment. I wondered how much he remembered, but said nothing. We were home alone, eating leftovers. I wanted John to feel and be protective of me. Am I being a silly young girl, full of romantic illusions that a husband would and should feel protective of someone he loves? Dare I say so?

I let the matter slide. John had already said I was a killjoy for not really drinking. I drank a Dubonnet before dinner, but rarely anything more. I hated the way alcohol made me feel, like clouds floating into my head at eye level, separating my brain from my body, everything, every thought fuzzy. The publishing world was juiced up with parties, cocktails, dinners, black-tie events, and the schmoozy drinks, just with friends in the business. I knew John drank too much. I thought I could live with it because I was so used to dealing with people who were drunk. I knew how to be a bland nothing when around a drunk. I felt pity, a real sadness that John wanted to anesthetize himself. Is it always going to be this way? Oh! Please no.

The next winter, I enrolled in a volunteer nursing program at the Y, training to be a candy striper. My training involved class time, learning simple triage and how to deliver a baby. Then I was sent to St. Clare's Hospital, on the West Side. I got up earlier than John, took the crosstown bus on Fifty-seventh Street to Seventh Avenue, walked down a few blocks, bought coffee and doughnuts, and woke up Puck at her apartment on Seventh Avenue and Fifty-third Street. We had time to swap stories and giggle before I went on to St. Clare's, where I spent the day doing assorted jobs for patients in the wards—bed making, bedpan cleaning, washing patients, and dressing them in fresh hospital gowns. We were not allowed to smoke anywhere in the hospital for the whole day. I was caught by the nuns in the bathroom puffing on a cigarette. Bad girl. Bad girl. After graduating, I volunteered at the James Ewing Hospital for Cancer for the next couple of years, involved in everything from being a hairdresser to doing research with one of the doctors. I was always terrified I would be asked to deliver a baby, because I walked to work and my coat covered my apprentice uniform; only my white stockings and shoes showed. But I did feel better about myself having a volunteer job.

We bought a tipsy house in the Catskill Mountains for under five thousand dollars. We couldn't believe all we got for so little money, only a two-and-a-half-hour drive from midtown. Not much acreage, but six bedrooms and four baths, with no window or doorway tilting at the same angle, a summer home in the WASP hideaway called Onteora Park. The McAlloneys persuaded us that it would be a great place for kids when we had them. They were old friends of John's who had a place a few houses down the road. Our house had two big stone fireplaces, one in the living room, one in the dining room. They provided the only heat in the house on frosty mornings or howling windy nights, and there were lots of both. Beds, mattresses, and bureaus as well as odd tables and chairs came with the house. Some went directly to the dump, but I had trouble deleting what had a history in the house. I tried to imagine the lives of those who had gone before. What were they like? Young, with families? Older, with grown children? Or middle-aged couples?

The house was near the town of Tannersville, a community with many Jews and Armenians. Jews ran large, old, decrepit wooden clapboard hotels. Armenians ran the grocery store and other village stores. There was a time in this town when the hotels were packed with Jewish families who spent the entire summer: grandparents, aunts and uncles, cousins, children difficult to assign to a family because there were so many. To buy our house, we had to join the Onteora Club, which was a restricted community from Jews, blacks, Armenians, in fact anyone but WASPs. I was uncomfortable with this exclusivity and rarely spent time at the club with the women and their babes by the pool in the mornings and at the lake in the afternoon. I enjoyed the facilities at other times, thus avoiding everyone. Their intolerant attitudes toward others not of their social class bothered me.

I stole a framed poem with a slur against Jews off the wall in the club bar. I did not tell John about it till the scandal of the theft passed. John didn't seem to mind the rules and regulations about who could be your guest and who could not. He called me "intolerant of the intolerant." On weekends and during his vacation, he played tennis in the mornings and golf in the afternoons with the well-dressed club types that I avoided.

Early on they had to check us out, so they invited us to their cocktail parties and played the "Do you know" game and "What school did you attend?" We were the new kids on the block. I loved the rugged landscape, the trees, rocks, and sky above, the merchants in town. I performed for the folks in the park.

And I liked fixing up this creaky old house. I worked with a carpenter, who put on a deck surrounding the living room, which became our nesting place every sunny weekend. I painted every bedroom and bath, the kitchen, living room, and dining room. I bought gay, bright-colored cotton curtains for all the rooms, cut the lengths to fit each window, sewed up the hems by hand. I did a lousy job. No curtain matched its mate in length. Oh well. But I felt I had been a responsible wife and saved money. This was only a summer house.

And I made a flagstone patio on the sloping land below from a huge stone by the kitchen. I was so proud at being able to pry large pieces of flagstone out of a boulder with a five-foot steel crowbar. I jammed the blade into a crack in the rock and lifted, jammed, and lifted until a slab of stone broke free. Then I had to carry it down and place it carefully to blend with the pieces of flagstone already in place, and grout the newly laid stone with sand. I liked this physical work, creating a space, the melding of shapes that became a whole, larger than the sum of its parts. Many years later, I would think it very like planning a garden with flowers, shrubs, and trees, as my father had done, or painting a large painting, as I do.

Almost every weekend, we had guests. Most were publishing people; occasionally family. My mother and Puck came at separate times, and the senior Sargents came over from their farm in Vermont. Nelson had married Flossie McKim and they were at an air base in Texas, fulfilling his ROTC commitment. I learned to be a good cook. Being Dutch stubborn and Irish difficult, I went to cooking school at the Y in New York City just to learn how to make hollandaise sauce, nothing else. If you can read, you can cook, I reasoned. I hated housekeeping, almost had a nervous breakdown watching the ad for Pledge on TV where the lady looked so happy polishing the dining table. I felt a total wimpy failure because I was bored to burial by dashing about the apartment with a dust cloth, singing any song from *The Sound of Music*.

John was a genial host, happy to shake up the cocktails and pass the

Brie cheese or peanuts, but any regular housework was not part of his vocabulary. I never saw my father cope, either, with any home chore except at the drink tray and in the gardens giving directions. Men just didn't do that in my world.

John was made head of Garden City Publishing, a division of the parent company Doubleday Doran, which was a big promotion from junior editor. I was proud of him, and knew way in the back of my brain the training of John to pave the way for Nelson had begun. John would be president of the company someday. He complained three or four times over the winter of 1955 that because of his new responsibilities, he was dealing with division heads, all of whom had some Doubleday stock, and he, having no stock, felt awkward. He felt he would be at the mercy of those who had stock because they had more say. Other division heads had either bought from or been given stock by my father when he was head of the company. I felt for John, mostly because my mother and John Sengstack, my trustee, often treated John in a dismissive way. There were the haves and the have-nots, and the line of demarcation was clearly identified by my mother. I thought once he had some stock, John would feel more secure, maybe not need to drink so much, and maybe he could love me more openly with a caress, a loving touch on the shoulder, or a kiss on the back of my neck, not just the occasional bunch of roses. I gave him a chunk of shares that I owned outright.

Both my mother and John Sengstack, the family adviser on all financial decisions, trustee of all family trusts, member of the board of directors of Doubleday, were furious. "How dare you give Doubleday stock to a non-Doubleday?" I was told in many ways. You would have thought I had brought the company to bankruptcy, my family as well. And I was furious, in turn, for being told who I could give stock to and who not. I let them rant and said nothing. None of their business what I did with what I owned. What was in trust I could not touch, but "Was John Sargent not family?" I asked. I got no answer. Eventually I became bored, frustrated, and drained by all the long-night sessions with my mother weeping about the company and the threat of who would inherit what shares, and when. It became her life's work, this maneuvering and manipulating to ensure Nelson the presidency. I was also red-hot angry that all her attention went to Nelson and no thought or consideration was given to me after the twirling debutante phase. I felt I didn't matter at all.

Even before my father died, Doubleday stock was tightly held by all sides of the Doubleday family. Control held by the major stockholder was the issue. Whoever held the control ruled the company. Would they vote with the Babcock family or the Doubleday family? The stock had paid no dividends while my father was alive, but it had to after he died, or his wife and children would literally have been on the street. Aunt Dorothy got her dividend.

On our side of the family, we—my mother, Nelson, and me—held stock outright or in trust. My father's sister, Dorothy Babcock, her husband, Huntington, and their children, Dorothy and Sylvia, all owned stock outright and in trust. In fact, Sylvia's husband, Hank Taft, worked at Doubleday. Janet Doubleday, Russell Doubleday's widow, also owned stock, but this couple had no children. Russell Doubleday, a generation older than my father, had been a writer and eventually worked at Doubleday as an editor. He was the brother of my father's father, Frank Nelson Doubleday, the man who started the publishing company of Doubleday & McClure. Frank Nelson Doubleday, my grandfather, died before I was born.

Should Janet Doubleday leave all her stock to the Babcock children, Dorothy and Sylvia, then that family would have the votes to choose the president, and thereby run the company. This was the dragon my mother had to slay.

Weekend days and nights, over drinks and dinner, my mother, John Sengstack, and sometimes my husband as well, discussed ad infinitum how to protect our family investment, how to deal with the present president of Doubleday, Douglas Black, the Babcocks, and Janet Doubleday. The few other shareholders were insignificant. My mother never let the subject rest. I had heard all the ramifications about who had how many shares and what they might or might not do with them, and the threat to us as a family ever since the death of my father and the termination of the voting trust agreement, which my father had signed just before he died.

The president of the company, Doug Black, had been my father's lawyer, put in that responsible job by my father well before he became ill. By placing Black as president of the company, my father felt he had ensured Black's allegiance to our family fortune. But my father became a nonfunctioning drunk, allowing Black to gain personal power and side with Aunt Dorothy Babcock against my mother. The three of them had created a voting trust agreement, whereby any two of the three could vote together and block my father from making crazy, drunken business decisions. But when my father sobered up and was successfully operated on for lung cancer, Black and Babcock refused to nullify the voting trust agreement, which restricted my father's power in the company. They blocked his entry into his office in Garden City in August 1948 and stopped his income that same summer. My mother had had to confess her part in the voting trust agreement to my father when he came back from the Hartford Retreat, now of sound and sober mind. Any two could wrest control of the company from my father if they so desired.

And that is what Black and Babcock did. The fight to regain my father's position in the company as Chairman of the Board, his decision-making powers, his salary, and his expense account began in August 1948. "For once, will you fight with me, Ellen?" my father asked. My mother happily agreed to help. Having him sober, wanting her on his side, was such a relief. Ultimately, the voting trust agreement was nullified three days before my father died, in 1949. It was the eighth of January. My father could sign only an *X* for his name. He went into a coma right afterward and died on the eleventh of January. The negation, or nullification, of the voting trust agreement allowed my father to die knowing his family's financial future was secure.

As Machiavelli was someone my mother wished she could have been, she now hatched the plot to unravel and conquer. The Doubleday stock was the only stock any of us had, and as it was family-held, there was no market for shares. Their value was kept as low as possible for inheritance reasons after the death of my father and continued so until well after my mother died. The voting trust agreement was finally broken, but the question of who would side with whom still stirred the possibility of serious trouble. I ached for it all to be over. I was too young to be interested.

Janet Doubleday, Russell Doubleday's widow, was a budding artist in her later years. I liked her and her gentle ways. She made small drawings—sketches, really—copied from magazines, for she was too shy to ask someone to model. She didn't think her work was good enough. My mother wooed her with lunches solely to get Aunt Janet to leave the stock she owned to Nelson and me when she died. I attended one such lunch. My mother told Aunt Janet how "wonderful it will be for Nelson to run the firm. He is the only boy in the family and we do need to keep it in the family, don't we?"

Aunt Janet's reply was clever and fair. "Yes, it would be lovely to keep it in the family, but remember Hank Taft, Sylvia's husband, also works there." He could be a contender for the presidency.

My father led a life of "all expenses paid" by Doubleday & Company. Aunt Dorothy had stock but no dividends. She lived on the land next to my father's, saw his lavish publishing and family events, knew of his trips to Europe, and of his plantation in South Carolina. They got along well until she wanted her due. She demanded a dividend be declared. I didn't blame her, and said so. I thought she had a perfect right to a dividend. It was her inheritance as well. My father's attitude had been to put everything back into the company to make it bigger, more progressive, and ultimately far more valuable.

"Dorothy is a goddamned interfering woman. She has no right." That was my father's position. "No woman has any business running the company or having any control at all." He said this a year before he stopped drinking, on one of his bad nights, when I was home for the weekend. I was hurt by his vitriol and even more by my mother's lack of any comment other than "Ah, Nelson, please." But even at that age, I knew not to answer back to anyone drunk, so what could she do?

Soon after my father's death, my mother became a director of Doubleday & Company and remained so until she moved to Hawaii in 1965. This position gave her the prestige she'd always wanted in the business. I felt sorry that she used her mind for only one thing—to protect the company's stock for her son.

ELEVEN

Travel Makes Perfect

Life with John was rich with interesting, creative people, charming to brilliant or acid to scorpion-like. We had, the two of us, the beginning of a family, yet I felt hollow. My dreams of an intimate life were not satisfied. John was emotionally cut off, and I was too scared to force an issue or confess to feeling so insecure. And no matter how hard I tried for closeness between us, an easy sharing of the day's small events, or the painful moments so hard to share, John's response was always, "That takes years." I felt rebuffed and put down, as though I were a child asking for too much candy. I buried my longings.

In early May 1954, a year after we married, we were off on a long business trip to England and Europe on the *Queen Mary*. What a beautiful ship she was. All the rooms were paneled in wood, which, once we were at sea, creaked and groaned as the ship rolled. Looking out on the vast waters below the ship's rail, at the distant gray horizon, I felt both burdened and enthralled by the power of this body of water. When I was not transfixed by the sea, when I was not questioning the meaning of my life, I reclined on a wooden lounge chair on the promenade deck and read *Frenchman's Creek*. I had read it before, but I read it again, and *Rebecca* as well. We were going to visit Daphne du Maurier at Menabilly, her place on the Cornish coast. I looked forward to seeing her on her turf. I felt sure her landscape would look and feel like the settings in many of her novels.

The scene with my mother after the dinner party with Gertrude Lawrence, when my mother told me of Daphne's desires, never entered my mind. When I was fifteen, she had been fun to be with, had spent time with Nelson and me in the playroom, teaching me how to get up from a lying position on the floor with half a glass of water resting on my forehead without upsetting the glass. I was a party hit. But much more important was that while visiting my mother, she had taken time to befriend me.

Every night on board the *Queen Mary*, the orchestra played dance music and the floor became crowded with satins and silks, tuxedos, silver evening pumps or sandals, and, of course, dazzling jewelry. We waltzed, we rumbaed, we sambaed, and we flew around the floor, crashing into other couples, who, like us, were putting all their energies into a polka. When we caught our breath, we drank liqueurs and brandy with other zealots until midnight. It was a fairy-tale time. Yet John seemed removed. What was I doing wrong? Why didn't he want intimacy with me? Was I an inadequate lover? Was that the problem?

After ten days in London, where we lunched and dined with authors, British book agents, and publishers, we took the train down to Cornwall. Daphne hugged us at the train station. Her blue eyes were merry with excitement. She was anxious to show us her world in Cornwall. Daphne felt so passionately about her land, the sea, her studio, and her great house, Menabilly. As is true of old English houses, the rooms were large, high-ceilinged, and without central heating, which meant always being cold and always having to remember to shut the door behind you. We sat by the fire in cozy chairs, talking with Daphne about books, her children, my family, Greece, which she loved, and her friend Frank Price, the Doubleday representative in Paris, whom we were going to see the following week. While she wrote in the mornings, John and I walked the rim of the windblown cliff and gazed at the distant horizon. We stumbled and sometimes tumbled down a narrow, rocky path to the water's edge, where roiling waves expelled themselves on a narrow beach. The pounding of the sea, the wind, the seabirds cawing, all left me with a sense of wild freedom tinged with remorse. I couldn't tell you why the rocks, the crashing waves, the foam and spume planted a picture so clearly in my mind. I remember still the pungent and bitter smell of rotting fish and salt water, the sharpness of the wind on my face, and, high above, the sight of puffy white clouds in a cerulean sky.

After a weekend of too much food in Paris, we flew to Cannes, where Alan Searle, Mr. Maugham's secretary-companion, met us and drove us to Maugham's home, the Villa Mauresque in Cap Ferrat. Mr. Maugham and I were familiar with each other. He and John were friends from John's days as junior editor. I always felt shy around him, treading carefully so as not to arouse his sharp tongue. At the first meal, a lunch in the atrium, I lifted the elegantly folded napkin rolled into a peaked crown, only to send a hard-crusted French roll flying through the air, just missing the butler's head. It landed in a potted palm. That was not a good beginning.

Maugham had written me a letter when I got engaged to John, warning that "sex lasts only two years and always in marriage, there is a giver and a taker." Of course I thought it would be different with us, that John and I would come to adore each other and have romping good sex for years. During the meal, the entrée was passed for a second time. I felt I had to take some, as Maugham had extolled the cook, telling us how she "gathers herbs each morning up on the hill" for the day's seasonings. As I lifted a small portion of the cheese omelette off the tray, Maugham said sharply, "N-N-N-N-Neltje. A second serving is p-p-p-p-passed but is not meant to be taken." Silence followed as I struggled to return the now-slippery portion of omelette back onto the platter while the butler stood patiently at my left to receive it. No one spoke.

At dinner the following night, John told Maugham that we were going on to Spain to get the money due Doubleday from books sold but never paid for. By Spanish law at that time, no money could leave Spain. Alan began a story about how some years earlier he and Maugham had gone to Spain to spend the money that had accrued in that country from Maugham's book and story sales. "We stayed at the Ritz Hotel in Madrid, in the most elegant suite they had available"—Maugham nodded his head—"and we entertained lavishly with caviar, champagne, filet mignon, paellas, baked Alaska, and Grand Marnier soufflés for a number of dinner parties," said Alan. "The c-cost made me sleep badly. S-s-spending money, that much m-m-money, bothered me," confessed

Maugham, "even though the whole trip was planned to s-s-s-spend my royalties in S-Spain. I bought paintings, fine paintings, one a Rouault at a close-by fine-art gallery. At the end of our th-th-th-three-week stay, I c-c-c-c-came downstairs with my luggage and asked for my b-b-b-b-bill at the c-c-cashier's office. He told me to wait. Eventually the m-m-m-m-manager came out from his h-h-hidden office to say good-bye, a polite thing to do for a good c-c-c-customer. The manager took my hand and s-s-s-said, 'Mr. M-M-M-M-M-Maugham, it has been such an h-h-h-honor to have you as our g-g-g-guest. There will be no bill.'" A fine O. Henry story.

John and I had no such luck when we stayed at the Ritz Hotel in Madrid. The manager did come out of his office to ask if Mr. Sargent wished to pay Miss Doubleday's bill as well. Whoever was in charge of paying attention to those details had not noticed that on page twenty-six of my passport, it stated that Neltje Doubleday married John Sargent on May 16, 1953, and now was Neltje Sargent. John, with a whoop of laughter, said, "I wish I had known it was so easy when I was single." I knew now why the secretary whom John had summoned to the room one morning for dictation had given me such a condescending look. I was in bed in my nightgown. She thought I was what? Certainly not a wife.

We entertained and were entertained, sometimes most grandly, by Spanish book publishers. An affable young man stole a beautiful Piaget watch off my wrist as I looked up at the vaulted cathedral ceiling in Toledo. I had studied this cathedral in a history of art class I had taken with Sarah B. MacLennan at Miss Porter's School my junior year. I could hear this teacher's voice as I took in the intricacies of this Gothic cathedral, telling us girls about the refinements in architecture in the Gothic era over the far more simple and direct attributes of Romanesque architecture. Sun made the stained-glass windows sparkle, each bright color dancing with the adjoining color, creating a bedazzlement, a work of art so stunning as to force you to sit down, sit still, look, and then at last see.

John needed to find a way to get a fairly large amount of money out of Spain, money belonging to Doubleday and various authors who had never received royalties from their books published and sold in Spain. I offered to wear the money about my waist, in my bra, or in my pockets, or to sew it into the lining of my coat. My bra size was 32A. That offer was quickly deemed inadequate, and I agreed my sewing was really not to be trusted.

In the end, when we were in Barcelona, Mina Turner, the foreign rights officer of Doubleday, decided she would take the risk herself by putting the great number of peseta notes amid skirts and blouses in her suitcase. She was traveling to Paris by train, and the likelihood of her luggage being looked through was far less than for us, as we were traveling by air. I did bring back to the United States spicy books like *The Story of O* and *Lady Chatterley's Lover*, books that were banned and illegal to bring into the country. My disregard for laws made John nervous. He saw headlines about himself in the newspaper, BOOK PUBLISHER JAILED FOR BRINGING PORNOGRAPHY INTO THE UNITED STATES.

TWELVE

Oh My, Motherhood

John and I had been trying to have a baby since a year after we married. The result of many, many tests revealed there was no physical problem for either of us. But months went by, anxiety building when my period was due. If my period was late, the tension felt nail-on-the-blackboard tight. I became snappish and aloof, then depressed as the months mounted. I was convinced it was my fault. Neither of us talked about how we felt, the subject of some sexual inadequacy too frightening a subject for anyone brought up in the WASP culture of Victorian and Edwardian secrecy. I think the subject particularly difficult for men, whose virility is of prime importance. But then so is the ability to bear children important beyond measure, I thought but did not say.

In late winter of 1955, I got pregnant, but I had to spend the first three months of pregnancy in bed to make sure I didn't miscarry. I didn't give a damn! I was so happy. I couldn't take in what it was going to feel like being a mother. I knew I was spoiled, overly protected, and still very young, a twenty-year-old with a skin of sophistication.

I loved being pregnant, felt wonderfully well after the first trimester. Loneliness and depression vanished like mist in the sunlight. When the contractions started, I went straight to the hospital. My doctor looked at the X-ray of my spine—which had just been taken the day before—and said, "We must do a cesarean." The screws from the spinal fusion I had had the summer before my junior year at Miss Porter's stuck out far enough to be a threat to the baby's head in the birth canal.

I had tinkered with the house in the Catskills, spring and summer, created a nursery and looked for a larger apartment in the city, because I wanted six children. That number fell into my brain from I know not where. I found a big beautiful apartment with lots of bedrooms on the East River at Seventy-ninth Street. We agreed to buy it, put money down, and agreed we would move after the baby was born. John Sengstack thought it a good buy and agreed to put the money up for the purchase out of my trust. Without that, we could not have managed so big an investment.

Ellen was born on December 8, 1955, and how beautiful she was, chubby-cheeked, with a tiny mouth, clear blue-gray eyes, and long lashes that angled down like mine. I ran my finger along her cheek and barely touched the tip of her nose. She was cute, her fingers so perfect in their tininess, lying peacefully in my arms, toes all there. I was overcome with protective love. That I had carried her inside me while she grew to be this perfect human being reduced me to quiet tears. I was awed and a bit terrified. Would I be a good mother?

John was nervous in my hospital room, and I felt for him. He did not know what to say or how to express any feeling of love or tenderness. I had to think his nervousness was caused by this inability. I couldn't bear to think he could not feel something. Oh, I wish. My feelings were hurt for both of us and my anger followed. I cradled her in my arms and whispered, "It is you and me against the world, babe. They don't pay proper attention to us, those men. No, they don't. And they run the world." I bent over and nuzzled her neck.

I had hired my Nana to care for our baby because, even though she had made it clear when I was little that Nelson was her favorite, I could depend on her totally. I was afraid of hiring anyone for a job, cleaning woman, plumber, or even cabdriver, scared they would say no to helping me, or be difficult or nasty and would intimidate me. That I could find someone else did not register in my mind. I was frozen with the fear of being helpless. At times now, I am still foolishly intimidated and scared.

We got home with Ellen, Nana carrying her. John was looking overwhelmed, carrying a large white wicker basket with tall, luscious hot-pink and white roses and my small suitcase. He put the flowers in the living room and my suitcase in our bedroom. From the front hall in a somewhat panicky voice, John called out, "I'll go round the corner and get us some lunch while you ladies settle in." I heard the door bang.

While in the nursery with Nana, I watched how carefully yet firmly she laid Ellen down on her back in the white wicker bassinet. She unfolded the outer blankets yet left Ellen still tightly wrapped in a thinner blanket. Nana saw me looking at Ellen and said in an instructive voice, "Babies like to be tightly wrapped early on; it makes them feel secure, like they were in the womb." At a measured pace, Nana turned to unpacking the few things in Ellen's suitcase. I rummaged around among the baby booties, cute nightgowns, and a silver drinking mug with Ellen's full name, Ellen Sargent, inscribed on it. There were two fluffy bunnies, a teddy bear, and a really big Raggedy Ann doll.

"I'll take it all to my room for now and we'll sort it out later," I said to Nana as I walked out of the nursery. This had been John's dressing room, our TV room, and our study; until five days ago, it had contained a desk.

Now it was Nana's domain. When I left, Ellen was fast asleep. I loved the way she puckered her lips, turned her head to the right just a little, as though she were trying to hear what you said. Was she dreaming? I was thankful Nana was with us. I didn't know the first thing about how to take care of an infant. I stupidly hadn't bothered to read a book about it or ask questions of other mothers, such as John's sister. Oh, but then she would have known how ignorant I was. All this ran through my head before I got to my room with the baby presents. I was tired.

I put on the red silk pajamas John had given me for our wedding night and crawled into bed, snuggling down under the covers. I was hiding, yet at the same time part of me wanted to have Ellen nursing at my breast and no one else in the apartment. And I, too, wanted to be held and told "You'll be fine."

I got up five minutes later to see Ellen; I had to look at her and touch her right away. I shook my head. My emotions were so up and down, I didn't know what to think. The major part of me was scared of being a mom. I was not the person I had been three days ago, and I couldn't settle down. I walked down the short hallway to the nursery. I had named Ellen after my mother and Pucky, thinking my mother would be offended and angry if I didn't. Had it been a boy, John would have chosen the name. This was the way John thought name choosing should go, and I had agreed.

Nana was already warming up a bottle of formula. I quickly said I would nurse Ellen when she was hungry and to save the bottle for the two A.M. feeding. It took all my courage to take charge at that moment. I knew in my gut that if I didn't, Nana would take charge of me, too, and I would let her. I breast-fed Ellen every four hours for three months. Nana made me oatmeal to help my milk come, and I loaded up on vitamins to pass along. I felt trapped by this routine at times, resentful, then frightened at my feelings. Was I going to be a selfish mother? Like mine? What then?

Nana left at the beginning of June. Ellen was now seven months old. I felt far more secure caring for her than I had at the beginning. We had moved up to the apartment on Seventy-ninth, where the view was beautiful and a breeze blew off the river. The park was nearby, but even so, by July the heat in the city and the drive to and from our house in the Catskills were a chore with Ellen and all her stuff, special food and certain wines and liquors that were unavailable in Tannersville, and our dog, Gimpy Truman. Ellen and I moved up to the country for the rest of the summer. John would take his vacation up there in August. We were happy.

Ellen had a room across the hall from us in the Catskills, so I could hear her if she cried. For the first week alone with her, I slept poorly, one ear open for sounds of distress. There was a terrible thunderstorm one night, which terrified Ellen, the crashing thunder ricocheting off the hills, Ellen sobbing in her crib or on my shoulder in my bed. She stayed with me until the final hiccup and sigh, then silence. Some days I took her to the lake to paddle in the water, my hands holding her under her belly. She was not sitting up yet, which bothered John and our mothers, but I figured she'd look at the world from that perspective when she wanted. Ellen had been diagnosed with celiac disease, an inability to digest fats and carbohydrates, which created severe diarrhea, producing a stench that could fell a Trojan. Her diet was pared down to bananas, scraped apples, skimmed milk, scrambled eggs, and nonfatty strained baby food, like chicken and certain vegetables. Jell-O was the only dessert, with a meringue if I baked. No bread, no peanut butter or jelly, no butter or mayonnaise or cookies. None of the things babies and young children eat. It was a pain-in-the-ass diet for me to organize. Panic set in when there was no skimmed milk. Ellen couldn't tell me about any pain, but she was often restless.

At the end of the summer, we all returned to the city. I hired a young German girl to take care of Ellen, leaving me free to be the corporate wife, going to and giving parties. After all, I was trained for this. I enjoyed some of it, enjoyed meeting new and interesting people, escaping the tedium of child care. Oh God, I hate admitting this. I was going to be the perfect mother, happy to be with my children from infancy forward, but I was not that perfect mother. Babies bored me.

I became pregnant again before Christmas 1956 and was delighted, forgetting the boredom of babies. Motherly instinct comes with no sense of remembrance.

The following summer, in late July, we moved out to my mother's on Long Island. It was hot in the city and we had had to stay there the past month because I was to have my next baby at the beginning of August, again by cesarean section. Ellen had been out to my mother's with us in May and June over weekends, as well as the prior summer, so I felt she would be comfortable there with a nurse. The new nurse was knowledgeable about celiac disease. Do babies remember the prior year at that age? I didn't know but hoped so. Ellen was content with occasional attention from my mother, either in the pool or playing games the likes of patty-cake. John drove us and all our paraphernalia to my mother's in Oyster Bay in our blue station wagon. Gimpy went to a kennel because dogs and my mother were not a congenial pairing.

My mother had sold the big house shortly after both Nelson and I had married, and she now lived in a much smaller house with a pool and a gorgeous view of the bay on land at the far end of our original property. I was worried that Ellen would not take to the new baby nurse, Miss Schmidt, a German-Swiss woman whom I had interviewed in May. I would be with Ellen alone for just a few days. John had to be back in the city. On August 4, I picked the nurse up in the city. How would Ellen fare when I left her two days hence? She was so attached to me. I was afraid she would cry when I left for the hospital to have the baby, so I skipped out before she woke. I could not bear to hear her cry. Miss Schmidt seemed understanding. I hoped she would be loving with Ellen.

On August 6, 1957, Johnny, John Turner Sargent Jr., was born. He was the same length—twenty inches—and the same weight as Ellen— seven and a quarter pounds. I knew he would be fine. I checked his tiny toes and fingers, his soft cheeks and long eyelashes. His nose was a nubbin, no patriarchal Greek god nose like his father. He had a wispy curl, just a few hairs on the very top of his head, and a poochy mouth; his lips pursed up into a heart shape. He was adorable. I kissed his face, nuzzled his neck, and held him close. I felt relieved that I had given birth to a boy. You will be one to watch! I thought.

When I awoke the second time, my mother and John were sitting over by the window. "Hello," I said, and they both popped up. I could tell by looking at John, seeing the open pleasure on his face, that he was bursting with pride. I said to myself that the old adage "Every man wants to plant a tree, build a house, and have a son" was true. John told me much later he had felt that way. Was it a matter of having a male descendant to carry on the family name, like it was in centuries past? Or was it far more a male hormonal and psychological urge to create a male, a like gender to satisfy a hunger for companionship? I felt shut out, unnecessary, and a bit miffed. I had the baby, dammit, not you, I wanted to say, but didn't.

When we got home from the hospital, I gave Johnny to Miss Schmidt, who was at the door to welcome us. I followed her down the hall to make sure Johnny was content in the bassinet. I left him on his back, sleeping swaddled in two thin blankets.

Ellen must have heard my voice. She let out a scream, a heartbreaking, piercing scream. I ran to her door. She stood in her crib, arms outstretched to me, her beautiful face miserable with fear. She started dancing up and down on her toes, sobbing, as she reached out to me. I picked her up, wrapped my arms around her, and said in a soothing, soft voice over and over, "It's all right. I am here. It is all right, Ellen darling, I am here. I am so sorry. It's all right. Hush, baby, hush." I rocked her in my arms, rubbed her back, her neck, the back of her head, kissed her wet face while I cooed in her ear until her sobbing eased. She hiccupped and let out a sigh. I wiped her tears with my finger.

I had made a huge mistake, and I knew it when I did it. John and I had left my mother's house to go to the hospital in the city before Ellen woke up. I hadn't told her the night before that I would be leaving very early and would not see her when she awoke. She was not yet two years old. I so hated to make her cry; her tears made me feel guilty. That all mothers cause their children pain and have to live with it, I did not know. I felt I was a bad mother. I am haunted to this day by that image of Ellen in pajamas, screaming.

The new nurse knew a good deal about what those with celiac disease could eat. John's sister's children had the same disease, and it was thought that possibly it was genetic. I felt so sorry for the limited diet Ellen was on. Banana flakes, which I had never heard of, were now her favorite breakfast food. Miss Schmidt suggested them and the doctor okayed them. Ellen was such a bright and happy child, with bouncy golden hair and a sweet smile. She charmed her father and every man in the park, in the grocery store, or at the garage. All the elevator operators and doormen stopped working to say hello.

Johnny was full of mischief almost from the beginning. When he was less than two years old, in the early morning, before I was up, he would call from his crib, telling Ellen, who now slept in a bed near him, to go to the kitchen and steal crackers and cookies for both of them. And of course she did. They were both on the celiac diet now. Starchy treats played havoc with their digestive systems. My pleadings not to do this at five in the morning were ignored, circumvented by big eyes and adorable smiles. And I couldn't get mad at either of them. I thought them clever. Discipline did not come naturally to me because I thought like a child, and often still do.

At the end of summer in 1958, a very large, twelve-bedroom and seven-bath house with fourteen acres of land came on the market for $25,000. It had been owned by a club member who had died several years previously, and his wife before him. Their only child, a daughter, had no interest in the property she had inherited. The house came fully furnished and including everything: sheets, towels, pots, pans, and dishes. We bought it the next day. What pleased me most was that the property was not part of Onteora Park itself, meaning we could sell it on the open market, not just to a suitable club member. We could not do that with our well-loved rickety house. We had to find a buyer suitable to the club's board of directors, which, fortunately, happened quite quickly.

I was sad to see the rickety house go to another. I had worked hard to create a fun spot for us, our kids, guests, and friends. We had entertained so many so often and so well.

When Ellen and Johnny were small, I stayed on schedule, taking them to and from the park in the city, while on weekends and school holidays we wandered the woods, the meadows, and around the beaver pond on our new property in the mountains. We collected bunchberries at a certain time of the year, or bits of bark and leaves, odd-shaped stones, or wildflowers to save and savor on the porch. Ellen loved to make flower arrangements for her father on summer weekends, picking multicolored sweet peas, which smelled heavenly, from the garden. Every season, we meandered down by the beaver pond to admire the skeletal frames of ash and maple trees now dead, their trunks drowned, thanks to the beavers. On a misty gray day in spring or fall, the pond and surrounding lands held a touch of melancholy magic. I often went there by myself to drink in the energy that came from the open waters, naked trees, dark and dramatic against a wide sky. I found a certain peace in that landscape.

In the vegetable garden, Ellen and Johnny learned how to pick currants for our cook and housekeeper, Mrs. Humphrey. The job was a delicate one of plucking, with just the right firmness of pressure between thumb and fingertips, and the precise pull, to get the fruit off a branch and into a bowl. A misjudgment of tension could bathe clothing in the bright red juice, a stain forever on a favorite sweater. Mrs. Humphrey made delicious spiced currant jam from bowl after bowl of currants. We gave small jars of her jams away at Christmas to only the cherished.

THIRTEEN

A Wallaroo in Revenge

At a publishing event in early May 1957, I sat next to Ivan Sanderson, who was being honored for his big book of wild animal photographs; a copy of it was on every table for guests to admire. He operated a zoo in Dover, New Jersey. His animals were often leased out for television shows or special scenes in a play, or for a store promotional. He was a tall man, with kind eyes, straight dark hair, and large hands, so much larger than mine. I noted his hands when he reached for his water glass. John came over and stood behind us, listening to us chat about animal wiliness, and interrupted. "Be careful, Ivan; my wife is hopelessly emotional about animals," he said in a derisive tone, ending with a "ho-ho." John drifted away. The awkward silence felt unbearable. I wanted to flee, embarrassed and ashamed that John would put me down like that in public. I could think of nothing to say.

Ivan asked, "What animals do you like best, elephants, the big cats, or the quirky ones, like kangaroos?"

I turned to a photo of the sometimes crazily dignified, yet oddball-looking animals that bounced across the desert of Australia with super-speed.

I asked Ivan if he had a kangaroo or wallaby at his zoo. "It's not for television," I told him. The upshot at the end of the evening and a few telephone calls later was my purchase of a wallaroo, a bit smaller than the housebroken wallaby that we had discussed, but that one was on a job and unavailable for some time. I arranged with Ivan and John's secretary to have the wallaroo delivered to John at his office. Timing was vital. Three days later, Mike, one of Ivan's assistants, stepped into John's office. "Are you John Sargent?" Mike asked.

John said, "Indeed I am."

"Here," Mike said. He pulled his left hand out from behind his back, handed John a leash, and slipped away. At the end of the leash, a frightened wallaroo did cartwheels right there in the middle of John's brand-new blue carpet. "Hey. Hey, come back, now. Come back," John howled.

In a few moments, Ivan came down the corridor, out of hiding. John stared at Ivan in disbelief until Virginia, John's secretary, guffawed with laughter. She just couldn't keep it in. Then everyone laughed. I heard that John's laugh had an edge of fear to it when he learned I had bought the wallaroo and that it was going home with him in a cab that evening.

The wallaroo took our twenty-five-foot-long living room in two jumps, back and forth, back and forth, while the men drank cocktails and murmured to one another. I sat in the chair by the fireplace, holding Ellen, now eighteen months old. I was seven months pregnant with my next child. I smoked a cigarette and smiled with satisfaction. I gave Ellen to her father and got up to find the dogs. I would bring one dog in at a time to meet the wallaroo, now named Peaches. The new puppy immediately hid under my chair. A dog belonging to John's niece, which we were caring for while she had a baby, was far more interested in the possibility of food, but Gimpy Truman, my standard poodle, went for Peaches in midair with his mouth wide open, getting only a mouthful of the wallaroo's very fine gray fur. A now-terrified Peaches bounced from one end of the living room to the other. Ivan said we must get Peaches to her place, an unused upstairs pantry with a linoleum floor. She was not yet housetrained.

With Ellen once again on my lap, I watched three fully clothed men in business attire try to corner Peaches. The trick was to get her at the base of her tail so she could not kick you with her savagely powerful legs. At one point, from the safety of my chair, I watched a cornered Peaches sail over the bent bodies of my cousin Henry Tift, John Sargent, and Ivan Sanderson, their three good-size posteriors all in a line. The backdrop was of cranes in flight on a gold Chinese screen.

Peaches's visit with us came to an end because John did not want me to retire to the upstairs pantry after dinner every night to train her. I wanted her to trust me enough to eat out of my hand. She ate root vegetables, hamburger twice a week, and enjoyed jelly beans on Sunday. I asked for them at my local delicatessen, saying they were for my wallaroo, "a kind of kangaroo, you know?" The man at the counter bagged the jelly beans, took my money, and handed me the bag and change without a word. Typical New York "heard it all."

My biggest worry was that Peaches might jump off the terrace onto the East River Drive, creating her own demise and a spectacular multi-car crash. You would have to be very high or very drunk to accept for real a flying wallaroo. John thought the whole adventure was nonsense. The more he voiced negativity, the more my Dutch and Irish heritage surfaced. Eventually I had to let Peaches return to the zoo without a trip to the park with Ellen in a stroller and without a visit to a bank, my dream to bring humor to stodgy bankers.

A new business associate and friend of John's, Wolfgang Foges, was an Austrian by birth. He lived in London now with his German wife, Kathrin, and young son, Peter. Earlier, Peter's parents had been forced to flee from Nazi Germany. Their escape had been dicey. Wolf told me the story of their trip once and never mentioned it again. As he was a voluble man who talked as compulsively as he ate, I knew enough not to bring up the subject at any later date, but I reflected on their flight, and the stamp of such a horror from time to time. I thought of how hard it must have been for Wolf to establish himself in business in England. The *v*'s and *w*'s in his speech never changed.

Wolf usually wore a blue suit or a sports jacket and gray pants. His jacket, shirt, or tie had food stains by midmorning, even crumbs from the last meal he'd eaten. He looked untidy—his heavy body crumpled. I thought him fragile, this big man.

His publishing business, Aldus Books, created educational books for children. When Africa first opened up to foreigners, Wolf had meetings in Ghana with Kwame Nkrumah, one of the early businessmen to recognize the importance of a viable market in Africa. Because he was always trying out new ideas, Wolf was fascinating to be around. His creative mind never rested. He was a brilliant, sometimes conniving, untidily dressed man who needed to create, bored by the follow-up of details that made a project work. He had a team of women in his office in London who took care of the pedantic nuts and bolts of the business. A portion of Aldus Books was eventually sold to Garden City Publishing, the division of Doubleday that John now ran.

"Wolfy," as we affectionately called him, dined with us at least twice during the workweek in the city and spent many weekends with us in the Catskills during his stay in America. We were to travel in England, Europe, and Russia, working on projects together. Quite often when he was traveling elsewhere in the States, he would phone in, like a child calling home for reassurance. He hated the "huge steaks" that were served to him in the American Midwest and begged to come to us when he got back to New York.

He wanted to create a book series for children, using people famous in their field as authors: Bertrand Russell for philosophy, James Fisher for ornithology, Lancelot Hogben for zoology and other sciences, Hans Erni or Oskar Kokoschka for painting, and so on. It was decided by Wolf and John that John and I had to go to Europe to help pitch the idea to these renowned people.

Our first meeting was with Bertrand Russell at his apartment in London for tea. The living room walls were painted a soft shell color, emanating a warm glow in the approaching darkness. It was mid-April 1959. Russell's wife was a tall, handsome woman who had been an English instructor at Bryn Mawr. She was now serving me lemon pound cake with my tea, because that was "what Russell liked." He affirmed Wolf's proposal that he write a large picture book giving an overall view of philosophy for young readers. Wolf's book series with Doubleday as a partner was confirmed that night, and we celebrated.

Next, we traveled out in the country to meet Lancelot Hogben, a scientist of some renown, who had taught at a number of different universities. He was a conscientious objector during World War I and had been imprisoned. That was all I was told.

When we got off the M1, Wolfy told me to get in the car with Hogben when we met him at a crossroads by a certain field, and added, "Neltje, soften him up." He and John would follow in the chauffeur-driven automobile. John said nothing. When I got into Hogben's car, it was obvious he had been enjoying a toddy or two before our arrival. He was, in fact, drunk, dangerously so. We sped off to the west on a not-so-well-paved road.

The car was tiny, as only British or European cars can be. I was close to five ten and had to fold myself up into a knee-touch-nose position, head bent forward, arms tucked in like a fledgling's wings. We careened over the paved highway for a short spurt, then onto a rutted country road through bleak gray and twiggy fields, bumping and bouncing. Hogben had been a handsome man in the past. He was now wrinkled and seedy-looking, scrunched into this tiny car, driving more off the road than on. He made a lascivious remark about my body and grabbed for my breasts. When I blocked him with my arm, he jerked the wheel hard to the left, sending the car humping off the rutted, muddy road and into a soft field, where we came to a stop. We had to be pulled out by the chauffeur in the hired car, after a lot of grinding wheels and swearwords. I whispered to John what had happened to me in the car. John only thought it was pretty funny.

We came to a house, a wife, and eventually a meal. Hogben, although drunk, became excited by Wolf's idea. He was enthusiastic and as the day passed he became almost sober. I pretended, as I had all my childhood, that nothing had happened in his car. Hogben signed on. I was angry and felt used in this game of "catch an author if you can."

We left in the waning light to visit the ornithologist James Fisher. John and I knew Fisher in New York and had had him to dinner many times at East End Avenue. He was a pleasantly cheery man, an easygoing weekend guest in the Catskills, as well. James fit into family life, having a bundle of children himself. He loved walking in the woods and tramping in the soggy earth around the beaver pond no matter what the weather, sometimes with me and the kids, and sometimes alone. He was a big, broad-shouldered man with a massive nest of unruly hair. His wit was very quiet indeed, humor a second thought perhaps, and his eyes sparkled with delight and curiosity. He, too, said yes to the book proposal. During and after dinner, the men talked about how the need to educate children in a broader, more sophisticated way was globally significant. I fell asleep on the sofa after dinner in the Fishers' living room, from relief more than exhaustion.

While we were cleaning up before dinner, I had told John again about Hogben's groping me while driving. I hoped for a caring remark. John just laughed again and said he didn't think Hogben "had it in him." I was livid and disgusted at John's disregard for me and felt hurt that he thought my being groped was amusing. I was bait, and what a pretty bit of fish I was. Didn't matter the way other men treated me. I wanted John to be protective of me, to not want me hurt. Years later, I was to learn he was unable to feel emotional attachment with women or men or his children. I don't know what happened to him in his youth to cause this detachment. It is only now, many decades later, that I can feel a sadness and not rage toward him.

I phoned Ellen and Johnny when we got back to London to hear their voices and know they were fine. I worried that by our taking this long trip, they would feel abandoned, as I had, and I felt guilty for enjoying the stimulating people we had visited. A young German girl, Berta, who had been with us for quite some time, was caring for them now, along with Emma, our Finnish cook, who helped out with meals, cleaning, and advice. As they chattered on about their day in Central Park, I felt I was a bad mother. I wanted to travel, meet new people, see, taste, and listen to innovative ideas, watch them become realities. This made me feel alive. Ellen was going to a birthday party the next day. What should she wear? Berta asked. I reminded Berta to take meringues to the party so that Ellen would have something to eat while the others had birthday cake. Did she have a present to take? Saying good-bye was a relief. I didn't want to feel guilty anymore.

Two days later, we left for Germany. Wolf was in charge of all arrangements for the European part of this trip. As we flew over the English Channel, he talked about the publishing meeting that he had set up with Willy Droemer, of Bertelsmann, in Baden-Baden. Droemer was going to be there on holiday with his wife, but what most excited Wolf and then John, too, was the description of the restaurants where we were going to eat. "Only the best, John, not the fanciest, but the best," said Wolf. The two men described one fantasy dish after another: a breast of pheasant accompanied by pâté, stuffed prunes, and a light brandy sauce, or *steak au poivre*, with asparagus hollandaise and potato soufflé. Wolf had a detailed list of the restaurants in Munich, which dishes each considered their specialty. He was busy telling John all the possibilities through-out our flight. I tried to read.

In Munich we stayed in a remodeled old hotel. A feature of our large, modern marble bathroom was warm perfumed air that was released when you sat on the toilet. I spent quite some time testing how heavy you had to be to set the mechanism in motion. It made me laugh.

John and I also had a round king-size-plus bed, which was very dis-orienting. The bed sat on an eight-inch-high platform with a curtain that could be drawn. I giggled, thinking of a movie set: Heroine with sultry brown eyes and cascading auburn hair puckers her full lips and with closed eyes reaches out to her lover, et cetera. I had no idea how they made a bed with no corners.

In Switzerland, we were to see Hans Erni, whom I had never heard of, and Oskar Kokoschka, whom I did know of as a painter and con-temporary of Picasso's. Wolf would say, "Maybe we'll have . . ." or "I think the lamb shanks would be perfect at this lovely inn I know." He salivated as he talked, spitting onto his dark blue sports jacket, then wip-ing it off as he spoke in an easy rhythmic way. After dinner he and John lit up large Cuban cigars. They were like two young townies out in the big city: drinking brandy, sloshing it about in big globe brandy glasses, smoking cigars after licking the ends before lighting up, just like men did in the movies. The cigar ends became a bit mushy, but neither one clamped down with his jaw, or talked through his teeth like a gangster. I found them both somehow sweet, given their taste for gastronomic pleasures and the other Lucullan delights in life.

In Baden-Baden, Wolf got in touch with Willy Droemer, the acquisi-tions officer of Bertelsmann. Bertelsmann had the biggest book club in the world; for this company to sign on would be a coup that would en-sure production. Hours were spent plotting what to say, what inflection to use, who would do the talking, when the presentation should be made, over a meal or at a business meeting.

"No, the best thing is an early meeting the next day. A straight business meeting, not involving wives and food," said Wolf.

The elaborate planning was like a theatrical production, a moment-by-moment rehearsal of possible outcomes, the pluses lined up like ducks in a shooting gallery. The response hinged on what? No one knew.

At nine sharp on the first morning in Baden-Baden, I was taken to the world-famous baths at Baden-Baden by Wolf and John. "It's your treat for being charming and engaging on this trip," said Wolf, but I knew he just wanted to slip back into my good graces. I was angry with Wolf. He had invited hundreds—authors, publishers, columnists, magazine editors and their wives—to a cocktail party in Munich "in honor of Mr. and Mrs. John Sargent," with "Mrs. Sargent née Doubleday" printed below. I hated being tagged as the boss's daughter, the heiress. I felt it set me apart from everyone. I hated the hoopla that went with my family name. It embarrassed me, put me in a family cage where I didn't fit. I have never paid attention to family genealogy, the accomplishments of ancestors, because I have always been more interested in what I do in the universe around me. The one exception is Abner Doubleday, the general who ordered the first cannonball shot from Fort Sumter, on April 12, 1861. That shot started the Civil War. He was the supposed inventor of baseball, a myth I have been told now by some.

John bought me a ticket for a massage, a flimsy bit of paper, like a grocery receipt.

The baths were in an imposing stately building, set on an incline, with the rich green of the Black Forest as a backdrop. I was standing in the front hall with my ticket in hand when Wolf, clearly agitated, grabbed my arm. "There is Willy Droemer's wife, getting in the elevator." In a rush of words, he said, "Quick, quick. Run after her. Talk to her in the baths. Find out what Willy is thinking." But the elevator doors slid shut just as I got there. I watched the needle above the elevator point to three. That was where Willy's wife was getting off. I had noticed she was alone in the elevator before the doors closed. I looked at my massage ticket. It said fourth floor. I was home free, out of a spy job.

On the fourth floor, a uniformed attendant took my hand, showed me into a small curtained dressing room, and made motions for me to undress. I was lithe, with small breasts and a good figure, but nudity in a public place was a new experience. I felt shy and vulnerable. I was given a towel and paper slippers. I had never been in a steam room and did not want to be in one now. I had no idea what I should do or how to avert my eyes from the large naked female bodies that lay on the upper benches inhaling a fog of hot air that clung like a cloud to the ceiling.

A big-breasted, overweight woman came through the door. Her gray hair frizzed, her eyes dancing, she was ready to meet her maker in this hellhole. With a kind smile, she asked me if I spoke English, and in that split half second, she became my new best friend and mentor. She offered help, and I said, "Oh, yes, please." She was my guide through the steam rooms, the big pools, the sandy-bottomed pools, some only a foot deep, where you lay down, letting the water pumped from opposite ends float over your body. It was a tricky business finding room to lie down quickly without stepping on a floating breast belonging to one of the large women on either side. To get out of that pool required the agility and speed of a frog.

Next came the part where my entire body was to be scrubbed with a brush such as I might use on a stubborn stain on the kitchen floor. The thick-armed attendant who bent over me, brush in hand, could have thrown the discus across the English Channel. I was very close to tears. Ultimately, I felt raw and abused, but clean. After the scrubbing, I entered a room with a very large pool, where women were actually swimming. I was pushed toward the showers at the end of the pool and to the right. All the showers were occupied, but I saw no harm in joining a woman under a shower at the nearest end, as there had been endless close contact through every phase of this venture. My shower mate did not think so. She smacked me across my cheek. Now, without towel or slippers, all lost along the way, my cheek smarting, I waited for a shower. I still had my ticket for a massage, soggy and crumpled but readable. I abandoned the idea of a swim and headed for the floor desk. "Ya," I could have a massage. When I left the baths, I felt humorless.

We met with Droemer, who liked the idea of the children's book series. Adoption by the German book club market meant the project could go forward. Rights in the French, Italian, and Spanish markets would follow. Germany was the big win.

After the meeting, John, because of his long legs, sat in the front of a dark gray chauffeur-driven car; Wolf and I were in the back. The men chatted together about the book business, what and where the next meal would be. They sounded like schoolboys drooling over their baseball cards. How could they think of food right after downing a three-course lunch with wine? I was left to daydream as I watched the countryside pass by, the small towns, and the open fields beginning to ripen. Men plowed fields. Women beat rugs on a wire in their yard, or some flayed them out the window, ridding rugs of dried mud and winter smells. You could see the dust cloud. Household chores, how I hated them!

My thoughts turned to Ellen and Johnny. I wondered what they were doing. Were they missing me? One part of my brain condemned me for leaving them. The other part declared a self-righteous sense of pleasure in my travels. Did Ellen and Johnny feel that black loneliness? Could I make up for any damage? Would they tell me?

We arrived at Kokoschka's studio on Lake Geneva in the failing light of late afternoon. The setting was postcard-perfect—expansive water, worn chunks of aged stones, a backdrop of imposing Alpine mountains, plus the famed Château de Chillon.

Kokoschka was in his studio, painting a watercolor of a pink rose, one stem in a glass jar. With quiet pride, he told us it was the first rose of the year. He had picked it from his garden that morning. Pleasure was visible in his eyes and the crinkled lines in his face. The studio, a wooden building with wide barn doors, sat up a small incline from the main house. A woodstove heated the space on cold days. Every bit of wall space I could see was taken up with various-size canvases leaning against the wall, some paintings visible, most turned to the walls. They were stacked three- to ten-deep. Paint spattered the wood floor and turpentine scented the air. Immediately, I felt comfortable. I wanted to sit in the middle of all these paintings and look at them one by one, by myself. Then I wanted to be able to talk with Oskar Kokoschka about how he painted them, what he was thinking or feeling, but I was too shy to say how I felt. I wanted so much to see the painting against the wall close by. I became speechless, in awe of this tall and thin, messy gray-haired man. He was dressed in paint-spattered blue-and-gray-striped coveralls. His bony hands and long fingers gestured toward the dancing watercolor of his first rose of the year while he talked about painting and his rose garden. Could we sit on the floor and talk with him? I wondered. I wanted to know how he decided what to paint. Was it a fluke of the moment, an instant passion, or a considered subject? What did he feel when he began a painting? Was it different each time? What did *abstract* mean to him? Did he miss a painting when it sold? Would he do another like it? But I stayed quiet.

Later, at the house, we spent a cozy evening by the fire with Kokoschka and his wife. The business conversation did not go well; he said he was too busy painting to spend time on a children's book. I was surprised at his tone of voice; it was a bit sharp.

Wolf bought the watercolor of the rose Kokoschka had just finished. He wanted the artist to write: "For Neltje and John" and the date on it. Kokoschka did as Wolf asked, using his brush like a pen. He wrote with graceful ease. An assistant wrapped the painting. While this was being done, Kokoschka asked me if I would do something for him. "Of course I will," I replied.

"The others won't, but I know you will. I want some publicity in the United States. Picasso, you know, he and I are about the same age. I am a better painter, but he gets all the publicity. It is not right. Help me. You know how to do this. Do it for me."

Kokoschka's words rolled out of him with intensity. I sensed they could not be contained. His jealousy of Picasso ran deep. I said nothing of my conversation to John or to Wolf.

I still have this tender and happy watercolor. It is a reminder of that day, and the power of his passion to paint, to be heard in the world. I felt Kokoschka a kindred spirit driven by passion, but I had yet to find my voice. Being a good hostess or corporate wife was not enough.

We drove on to visit Hans Erni. His studio, a guarded sanctuary, was part of a very large modern house, where his wife protected him. She was lovely-looking, thin and lithe, and her walk flowed like a dancer's. We went through a ten-foot-high-by-four-foot-wide shiny black door into the studio. Later in life, I would see many doors of this size in galleries and museums, but back then I was wide-eyed. We looked at a few prints in sleek white cabinet drawers that his wife pulled out. The sterile feel of the space felt clinical rather than creative, a direct opposite to Kokoschka's studio. We went through another equally large shiny black door to the inner work studio, which was spotless. Two images hung on one wall of the studio, but I have no memory of them other than a fluid quality of black lines that conveyed no passion to me.

Hans Erni was not a tall man, but sturdy, like a workman. He had dark hair, a firm handshake, and he looked me in the eye, which I admired.

Erni found the layouts of the proposed books impressive and liked the concept of educating kids early in new ways. He was busy but thought he could participate if it would not take up too much of his time. He wanted layout control. Wolf agreed. From what I gathered, much of the text could be created at Aldus, with final control being placed in the hands of each artist, scientist, or philosopher.

Wolf and John complimented each other at dinner that night at each course. I thought about Kokoschka.

In the car on our way to the Zurich airport the following morning, I thought about the artists I had met, their different personalities and approaches to art, and revisited their studios in my mind. I had felt a sense of belonging, a kinship in Kokoschka's studio, as well as a very strong sense of the passion that drove the man. Years later when I created my studio, I remembered the feeling I had had in Kokoschka's studio, how thoroughly comfortable and aware I had felt. I wanted to feel that sense of easy comfort in my space. I often think of Kokoschka when facing a blank canvas.

FOURTEEN

Stretched to Breaking

In the final days of November 1961, John was in London, on his way to Moscow. He would be traveling with Lord and Lady Boyd Orr, Wolf Foges, and Douglas Black, president of Doubleday. His mission was to get Khrushchev's memoir for Doubleday to publish. The Soviet leader had let it be known that he was considering Doubleday as his American publisher. John and the others were to meet with Khrushchev himself, the date to be solidified once they arrived in Moscow. While in Moscow, John planned to meet with two or three Russian authors and scientists. He had gone to Washington weeks before to review with our State Department and the Russian State Department all possible interviews or contacts he might have while in the Soviet Union.

Lord Boyd Orr, a friend of Wolf's, was very friendly with higher-up government officials in the Soviet Union, including Khrushchev. Boyd Orr's life work had been planning how to feed the ever-growing world population, a subject of great concern to the Russians. It was really only through Boyd Orr and his connections with the Soviet government that this trip was made possible. I was jealous. I thought it would be fascinating to see Moscow, be in that city, experience walking the streets, watching people, talking with them, eating Russian foods and seeing what was in the stores: clothes, bedding, and home furnishings. What were their apartments like, old-fashioned or sleek modern? What was available as far as foods in the average grocery store? Were fresh fruits and vegetables available? We heard only what the media told us. I wanted to see for myself.

But I was to remain in New York to be hostess for a dinner in our apartment of over a hundred, in honor of the Duke of Bedford, the first Saturday in December. This party had been planned in celebration of the publication of his book. Guests had been invited a month earlier. My mother-in-law, Dagmar Sargent, bless her, invited me to go shopping for a "smashing" dress to wear for the event. I was delighted. I felt frumpy. I had nothing of suitable elegance in my closet. We met at eleven by the perfume counter at Bergdorf's on a Tuesday, the week before the dinner was to be held. I was there on schedule because "Mother" was punctual, always. You could count on her like Greenwich Mean Time. I tried on only two long dresses before I found the perfect one, the one that made me feel elegant, sexy, and a tad bit naughty. The dress was strapless and formfitting, made of the palest green lace over cream satin, with a tuck under my behind, and at my feet, a kick pleat of material to allow space for dancing. I felt voluptuous and regal at the same time. SO THERE, JOHN SARGENT!

John phoned me from London on November 28. The president of Doubleday, Doug Black, was taking his daughter Gina on the trip to Moscow, so I could go after all. Did I still want to? he asked. Absolutely. But I had to be in London in forty-eight hours. Visas and tickets to Moscow would be ready when I got there. John's secretary, Virginia Clough, would get my airline ticket to me the next morning for the flight to London, leaving Idlewild Airport that night. I put the telephone receiver down in its cradle and let out a whoop of joy. Scenes of Moscow danced in my head. Oh, thank you, thank you, gods and goddesses of travel.

I called my mother and asked her to play hostess for the dinner. My mother was thrilled. I gave her the name of the caterers, sent her the guest list by hand, and danced my way into the shower to wash my hair. My mother would love to be "in the swim of things" again. She could talk all night long to the duke about how his book would speak to the American lust for English royalty that was so prevalent in the States, plus the river of interest from Anglophiles, myself included.

I could go to Moscow at such short notice because Ellen and Johnny had Annie, a young English girl who had been with us for two years. I still felt pangs of worry. I loved getting away, having the opportunity to stretch my brain and enrich my life by going on trips, but would the kids feel abandoned, think that I had deserted them to please myself? I wouldn't be home to eat supper with them every night, or watch a cartoon and read to them at bedtime. Guilt and delight were dancing partners in this pageant of anxiety.

Padget, a six-foot-four gay black man, a would-be actor, would also be there. He had been with us now for two years as well, and he loved to help the kids. He earned a livelihood by being our cook, butler when needed, maid, child minder, and my friend. He would make the dinner for the Duke of Bedford swing with the proper dash of elegance, and he would be in his glory. He would also be around to answer any questions my mother might have, and to announce each guest on arrival in the big upstairs living room.

It was November 30, 1961, when I landed in London. I took a deep breath, and we took off for Moscow the next morning in a Russian plane, no flourishes. This was just over a year after Khrushchev had slammed his shoe down at the United Nations General Assembly over comments made by the Philippine delegate and British prime minister. Our group of American and British businesspeople was one of the earliest to get into the Soviet Union, as the Cold War was at its height. Would Khrushchev show up? He was said to be boar hunting in Siberia. Would we get his memoir, a signed contract?

We were met, even before going through customs, by our translator, guide, and government agent, all wrapped into two bodies, one male, one female. They were to be with us wherever we went, watch what we did, whom we talked to, what we bought, and what we said to one another or to others. We stayed at the Metropole Hotel, in suites with heavy, dark upholstered furniture and the usual bug to capture our conversations. We ate chicken Kiev and bullet peas day after day. Strawberry jam from Georgia was a big hit. The men consumed quantities of wine and vodka; whiskey was outrageously expensive. We waited for a call from Khrushchev's office. As John's wife, there was little for me to do but go to meetings with the men, sit quietly, and try to be charming in a few sentences. We visited writers, scientists, and some diplomats while we waited. Evenings, we ate huge meals at regional restaurants, and we endlessly talked over what Khrushchev possibly was thinking and how we could get to him.

I liked Lady Boyd Orr. She was a Scot with a soft burr, even though she had been in England most of her life. She effervesced kindness and a dancing wit. She wore a brown fur hat at all times, and her smile crinkled the lines of her face. Lord Boyd Orr called her "Wee One."

Dinner at the Georgian restaurant was a special delight. The restaurant was situated half below street level. It had ocher-painted adobe walls that gave it a cavelike atmosphere. The restaurant was jam-packed with men and women talking in strong voices over the orchestra, which was playing what sounded something like our square dance music or the Virginia reel. We ate delicious, rich country food, drank Georgian wine, and watched the surrounding patrons laugh and sing their country songs in their own dialects and dance reels together, whooping it up to a high pitch. Then they included us, making us part of their party. You didn't need to speak the language to dance a polka.

Khrushchev, we were told once more, was still boar hunting in Siberia. There would be no meeting. He had been jerking our chain. So much for his book about conquering the Russian proletariat, ruling the educational and economic machine, and bringing the United States to its knees. We were free to travel with our interpreters. I wanted to go east to see the glories of the Silk Road. Ultimately, we had a brief visit to Tashkent.

Due to a wild snowstorm during our flight to Tashkent, we were forced to land and spend the night at the airport in Sverdlovsk, the place where Gary Powers's U-2 spy plane had been downed. Even before we arrived with a full planeload, the airport was out of food and packed with people huddled on the floor in open areas and hallways, anywhere space was available. Those in our group of nine were each given a room with a double bed. I was grateful, but in the morning, picking my way through even more tightly packed sleeping bodies on the floor brought on a shower of guilt. As we descended the curved, open staircase, the upturned faces of those in cramped quarters on the cold tile floor looked on us with envy.

The city of Tashkent promised a sense of the romantic past, including Marco Polo and Genghis Khan, and I looked forward to narrow cobbled streets and small shops, the smell of baking bread. The city had undergone a laborious renovation by the Soviets and lost much of its mystery and charm. Heavy cement government buildings had altered the scenic streets and squares, the quiet neighborhoods of homes and shops. These new buildings were proudly displayed by our Soviet guide, Gilda, who was always with us.

Snow was deep, mounded along the sidewalks and canal ways, making travel on foot treacherous. I was saved from sliding into a canal on the way to a jewelry shop. John's arms caught me in my heavy fur coat, a purchase made in Norway on the North Cape cruise with my mother when I was seventeen (the trip meant to destroy my relationship with John). He didn't even drop his cigar. Stores had very little to sell. I found two or three hand-wrought silver bracelets and a beautifully made silver teapot with matching creamer and sugar bowl. The shop owner, an old man, wore a heavy dark blue wool coat, a hat, and brown gloves. He was apologetic and looked furtively at Gilda. He could say little, nor could we.

I wanted to be away on an adventure, to take the train back to Moscow by myself. I wanted to feel the breadth of this country, how people lived, in what kind of houses, made of what material. Would they be painted bright colors to offset the white of winter? All I needed was my toothbrush, a couple of books to read, and a few rubles so I could get something to eat. I would feel daring traveling on my own. Would I be too afraid? Could I do it? I was not allowed. I didn't have the guts to insist at that time.

In Moscow, we Christmas-shopped for caviar and bought it in one- and two-pound tins, the contents of which I separated into two- to four-ounce glass jars in London on our way home. They would make great Christmas presents. We also bought good vodka at the foreigners' store for a couple of the cabdrivers who had been good to us. It was unavailable to them.

During a short stroll on the last afternoon, John took the cigar out of his mouth to say a few words to me. We were walking in a tunnel under a wide street. When he put the cigar back in his mouth, the moist end was frozen. No wonder all the press photos of people in Moscow during the winter show human forms bundled in depressing dark clothes, their heads, mouths, and noses buried in wool, with only their eyes visible. The searing cold can damage the lining of the nose and the lungs if the face is not protected. I wore long winter underwear beneath a wool suit and sweater every day, and a Persian lamb coat, a wool hat, gloves, and a scarf when outside. The only color of wool coat available in the stores was dark blue, so everyone looked alike.

When we got home, the children were bouncing off the walls, excited because it was Christmastime, which meant round after round of cocktails, luncheons, and dinners with John's family and mine and mountains of presents for Ellen and Johnny to open. Far too much of everything—food, family, and feelings. One family was noisy, the other drunk. Christmas was a family ordeal that I did not look forward to this year. Not so the kids. They took in every event with wild and crazy delight, ripping through paper and ribbon. They had missed me, but they were fine.

We spent our winter weekends in the big new house. We filled it with guests almost every weekend, wanting to show it off, or was it a way to avoid being alone? I muttered to John every so often that I wanted a home life. He avoided the issue, never responded. It was the same conversation I had always had, begging for intimacy and a full family life with the children. I felt worn-out from being on show, pretending our life together was perfect, worn-out from being the perfect wife.

I took no great joy in decorating the tree in the Catskills house or taking the kids to the Christmas feasts at both grandmothers' homes. I felt dead inside.

Years earlier, I had taken on the job of modernizing this old four-story house in an easy, comfortable way. I turned the basement kitchen into a playroom for Ellen and Johnny, and made a modern kitchen out of the past owners' study next to the dining room. The rest was a job of painting the walls, changing the furnishings a bit, or just adding new chintz bedspreads and colorful curtains to the many bedrooms and windowed baths. The heating and hot-water systems were in good shape, allowing us to spend fall and winter weekends and vacation times in the mountains, which had become important to both John and me. It was the landscape that fed me. For John, it was the skiing and the ability to entertain generously on weekends during the gray months of winter. Occasionally on summer weekends, we made picnic lunches of cucumber sandwiches on well-buttered thin white bread, or perhaps some pâté and crackers, or shrimp with seafood sauce, watermelon, and wine. We drove down to the Jewett valley with our guests, found wide, flat rocks, almost room-size, to sit on in the riverbed. The sound of the gently running water and the surrounding silence filled me with a sense of belonging, which I took with me back to the city.

In the fall, the kids and I tortured city hunters by letting the air out of their tires. Some of these hunters could not tell a deer from a cow. Once we could stay in the mountains all winter, we were able to skate and ski and sled down the hill in the meadow. John skied with the children on all but the wettest and most windswept days. I skated or watched Ellen and Johnny whip around the arena, ankles turned inward to the point of almost touching the bumpy ice. I took long walks in the crisp air through the woods on snowshoes, sometimes as far as town, two miles downstream, as any bird can tell you. And in the spring, with carpenter and overseer Donald Thorpe's help and hard work to get the ground prepared, we all planted vegetables and flowers—carrots, tomatoes, lettuce, squashes, pink, magenta, and white cosmos, and a full palette of colored zinnias. We played in the mud and waited for the summer sun and other playmates.

During the winter, we had four to six guests most weekends. Mrs. Humphrey was unfazed by the numbers and managed delicious meals. One long New Year's weekend, we had fourteen guests when a big snowstorm hit, downing trees and power lines, taking out electricity for four days. We could not flush toilets, and there was no heat save for two large fireplaces. We fed these fires all night to keep the house warm enough that our hands and fingertips wouldn't freeze. Many, many trips to the woodpile on the porch, with an occasional tasting of our "Crown Jewel Eggnog," made for merriment and laughter. Sun shone brightly on the snow, made the white landscape sparkle. All roads were closed, so escape was not a choice. The kids, Annie, and I thought coping without light, heat, or water was a fun adventure. We became as inventive as we could in the face of the storm. But some of our guests became grumpy as hours, then days went by without the basics.

In the city, my life with John was still one of cocktail parties or dinners most nights of the week. I was not happy with this schedule and complained that I wanted a home life with Ellen and Johnny. I wanted to focus on being a good mother and having a family life unlike the one I had had. I wanted us to eat with the kids at least on the weekends, instead of them eating earlier in the kitchen. Our fights on this subject usually ended with me in tears and John smoking a cigar in his den.

FIFTEEN

Seam Split

The incessant business entertaining ended abruptly and for good after a dinner party for Bennett Cerf at our home on East End Avenue in 1962. He had been one of John's authors from the days when John ran Garden City Publishing. John was president of Doubleday now; Bennett was president of Random House, a well-known public speaker, and a TV personality on the panel show *What's My Line?* with Dorothy Kilgallen and others. We were at the dinner table, which was lit by twelve tall white candles in each of two silver candelabra. The glowing candles, reflected in the surrounding smoked mirrors, created an ethereal soft light. I heard snatches of different conversations interrupted by engaging laughter. The publishing guests were happy. I sat at the end of the table. Bennett sat on my right, as was customary for the guest of honor. He turned to me in the middle of dinner, bending his head down slightly, and said, "Neltje, I don't think you like me."

"I think you are a horse's ass," I replied, and turned to talk to the person on my left. I knew it was the end of the marriage. Cerf got caught in the crosshairs.

Ten days later, when we were at home alone on a weekend in the country, John and I had a fight, the same one we had had many times, only this time it was different. We both had had too much to drink that night. Maybe it was not the time to look seriously at what was wrong, but I could not contain it any longer. I said I wanted to live alone, as I had said other times, but this time I had to make it stick. I had blown the good business wife pretense when I took aim at Bennett Cerf at our dinner party. I gave no apology. That took all my courage and then some. I felt no closer to John—in fact, less close now than I had after the first year of marriage, despite his telling me intimacy took time. What was wrong with me that he kept so distant? What was wrong with him? He had rejected me sexually for several years. Each of us had found another. I couldn't continue living like that. I was fed up with pretending we were a happily married couple. Our problems were fundamental. The next morning, John asked, "Did you mean it last night when you said you wanted to live alone?" His tone was that of a simple inquiry.

"Yes, I did mean what I said," I replied quickly, surprised that he'd remembered last night's conversation. Our prior arguments had always fizzled out, with nobody saying anything the next day. Pretense. Pretense. And who is afraid of Virginia Woolf?

"I will leave this afternoon for the city, after I get my things packed."

I said, "Okay. That's fine."

He went to his dressing room, where he now slept, and began putting his things together. We stayed polite with each other. When his car disappeared down the driveway, I had to turn away, or tears would have drenched my clothes. I wanted him back, but on my terms, and that was never to be. Well after the kids were in bed, he phoned from the hotel where he was staying and said sadly, "No one knows where I am now."

"I know, John, but you can tell people in the morning. It's late now." It took all my resolve not to say, "Come home, we will work it out."

The long process of separation and divorce began. I was twenty-seven years old and had never lived alone or been totally responsible for every aspect of my life. My friend Geoffrey Hellman had told me, "Get out before ten years, or you won't." It was advice from his own experience, and I took it to heart. I had no idea how I was going to cope with two children aged seven and five, two large homes, and no structure, no center to my life, as my marriage and the business had been. I told John I didn't want money from him for child support, as I was the one who wanted the split, and I had enough money to care for the kids while we were separated. John and I agreed to go to the same psychiatrist, who was well known for taking couples, Smiley Blanton. I felt like a pious prig when I asked John how his sessions with Smiley were going. I thought in my most crazed moments that I was doing just fine. It was really John who had the problems.

John was the one to tell the kids we were splitting up. I couldn't. I would have burst into tears, not good in front of them, I thought. He said, "Daddy is moving out to another apartment, where you can come visit. Mommy and Daddy are going to live separately, not divorced, but living apart, trying to sort out their differences." The kids never knew the reason why until they were in their teens. I did not want to tear down the image they had of their father.

The most ordinary thing, like making out a grocery list, became a herculean task for me. Nothing clicked in my mind. I felt disoriented and frightened. I wept openly on the bus, walking along the street to the park, in the drugstore when picking up meds, or going up or down in the elevator. I cried because I was terrified that I couldn't cope. I missed John. I loved him. I had no sense of direction. That was the most humiliating of all. I cried less up in the country, where the wide mountain views fueled me and the dappled light in the woods, the stones, ferns, berries, and the trees, tall and strong even in gale winds, all stood beside me as allies. I didn't want anyone to see me. I had no idea of who I was. I had no core other than being a mother, and my maternal instinct wasn't strong enough to hold me together. I was holding on, barely surviving, wanting to hide from anything that even scented of responsibility. I could not concentrate enough to read and understand the mythology homework for the class I had signed up for at Barnard. Breakdown. I was having a nervous breakdown. I finally realized that was the problem. It took me over two years to become steady. I asked my psychiatrist at the end of the ordeal why hadn't he explained what was happening to me and why didn't he send me to an institution where I could have gotten daily help, instead of letting me struggle to be a mother and do it badly? His answer was, "You managed, didn't you?" For over two years, I went to that psychiatrist three times a week, took LSD under his guidance three times to get to the root of my problems. I was angry, boiling angry at men because of the man who had molested me when I was nine, at John for failing to love me, at my father for his misogyny. It took me a long time to recognize how mean and demeaning he had been to women. It was a different time, but even if women were chattels to their husbands all over the country, there were men who treated women fairly. My hero father, my drunk hero, how he had failed me.

I have children to care for. Forget it!
I am a baby inside, wanting to be cared for.
I can't. I can't. I can't. I can't.

Round and round went these thoughts in my brain. Terrified.

Eventually, I pulled out of that very dark place.

But my phone, which had always been busy, had ceased to ring. After all that entertaining I had done, only four people from the publishing world had nerve enough to contact me after my separation: Wolf Foges, Tim and Lee Seldes, and Adeliene Barker, Lee Barker's widow and a good friend. I felt so lost. Wolf told me what was new in his world and rarely mentioned John.

I had lunch with Adeliene, who said, "Neltje, you wouldn't have found a lover if that part of your marriage was good, would you?"

"No. No," I replied. "I think if sex works, the marriage works. John just had other desires. It killed me inside."

Tim and Lee asked me to a wedding at her family's place. It was a Saturday in September, sunny and a little crisp.

"Neltje, you look so beautiful," Lee said when I arrived.

"I see your kids are full of life, bouncing about as though they were the center of the whole world," I said to her, finding my voice. I talked with several writers from *The New Yorker*, a generous mixed bag of easygoing people who had become friends over the years, and with Tim, whose sardonic remarks always surprised and slightly frightened me.

But I left early because I was nervous, worried about the kids. I had hired a French governess over a year before, at John's insistence. He wanted the children to learn French because he had not had that opportunity as a child. I had, but was wary of what could go on when my back was turned. That night, I wanted to make sure Mademoiselle let Ellen and Johnny watch the special TV show I had promised them. I got home more than an hour early, to find Mademoiselle pulling Johnny by the ear from my bedroom, where they watched TV. She was not going to let him see the promised show. He was sobbing, screaming, "That's not fair, Mademoiselle. Mom promised us." Ellen was following Johnny, in her wrapper, also crying.

"Stop right now. Tell me why you are taking the children away from watching a show I promised they could see?"

"I thought it was their bedtime."

"*You* know better. I told you they could stay up late and watch that show." I fired her after I had the kids settled down, watching TV. I suggested she be gone within two hours. We were all relieved. At meals when the kids and I were eating a hamburger or chicken, her sharp French accent pierced the quiet: "How can you eat your brrrotherrrr?" Rolling *r*'s and accusatory tone now *gone*. I don't remember if I got someone else to help care for the kids or not.

I needed to move out of our huge apartment. I finally found an apartment with an interesting layout on two floors, which made it seem cozier, more like a house. It was at Eighty-fifth Street and Park Avenue. Ellen could walk to school straight east to Brearley, and Johnny could easily walk to Dalton. I had begun painting in oil on canvases, and could make the dining room part studio. It would work with Padget, too, room for us all.

I would reach thirty in October 1964. A quarter of the trust assets my father had created for me could be released to me. In September, just after the kids started school, Nelson called. He was genial at first. I hadn't heard from him since John and I had separated, but his tone had changed.

"Nelch, when your birthday comes up, I could turn over a quarter of the trust to you, but I think it would do better to leave it in the trust. I have done that with my share."

"Yes, Nelson, I understand, but you get all the assets of your trust, not a portion. That makes a difference. No, I want my share turned over to me."

"A-A-A-A-A-Ah, Nelch, come on. We need to keep it all together so we vote as a family. I am the sole trustee now that Ma has resigned."

"I know, Nelson. I want my quarter share. I am alone now and will have no child support until we get divorced."

"Have lunch with me, at least, so we can talk," he said, and we set up a date for the following week uptown, so I didn't have to dress up in fancy downtown clothes.

I wore a comfortable tweed suit and moccasins after painting all morning and met Nelson at a little French restaurant on Seventy-first Street and Lexington Avenue. He had obviously arrived early, for his martini glass was empty.

"Why do you wear those trashy-looking clothes, Neltje?" he said, not getting up from the table.

Oh boy. This was going to be a bad one. Nelson persisted with his position on my trust, and I was firm about mine. We had quiche and salad. I had coffee while he finished his wine. We had really nothing of consequence to say to each other; our lives were now so different. Nothing of the intimacy of childhood was left between us. He had been the love of my life once.

A week later, Nelson stopped my monthly income from my share of the trust. I hired a lawyer, who threatened to sue Nelson on my behalf. After conference calls with Nelson's lawyers and John Sengstack, we were unsuccessful. It took six months and lawyers' fees to get a check. Underlying his spiteful behavior was his need to control. He wanted to tell me how I should live. I thought he might have wanted to see me happy, finding a new life. But my departure from the Piping Rock Club set when I married still galled him. We were barely on speaking terms at the end.

My mother and John Sengstack, who had been my guiding business mentor and true friend at times, complained that I did not have the right attitude toward company business. Nelson did, too; he was already secretary of the company; John was president. I went to the stockholders' meetings and saw how the minority stockholders were treated. Only the big ones—Aunt Dorothy, Aunt Janet, my mother, and Nelson—were treated respectfully; the rest were given a polite but guarded greeting and then ignored. When I had met with John in the office two days before the stockholders' meeting, I happened to see a stack of printed minutes of the meeting that was yet to happen. What? I was burned. I brought it up at the meeting and was shushed by my mother. They never changed the stockholder minutes of that meeting to reflect anything I said, including the question "When will the company consider going public? Several stockholders need a more liquid financial investment than Doubleday stock affords. As we all know, the only buyer for Doubleday stock is the company itself, at a diminished price."

After I had a legal separation from John Sargent, I had a call from Jon Schueler, asking, "Would you have dinner with me?" I did often and

I modeled for him. There was nothing more than grateful friendship on my side, but he had a dreamy romantic fantasy about me. He called me in the Catskills on his way to Boston to marry his fourth wife, Mary. He was in a panic, felt trapped, he said. "I don't want to marry Mary tomorrow. I don't want to marry her. Help me."

I replied, "Schueler, you cannot back out now, that would be too cruel." She'd had her brother give her black satin sheets for the wedding night. "Get out of the marriage later if you want, but not now."

He did marry Mary, and he did get out later. I have often wondered about my advice.

Schueler invited me to go with him to Bob and Abby Friedman's for dinner, and I did so many times. Bob was a writer and collector of contemporary art, and Schueler's good friend. He was a precise, intelligent, and angry man, curious, well read, with an incisive wit that often flew out without consideration for others. He drank martinis, notable wines, smoked cigars and marijuana. He was deep into psilocybin and other hallucinatory drugs, which he felt freed his mind. He often referred to his friend Timothy Leary up at Harvard and took LSD and mushroom trips with him. I was slightly frightened of Bob. I sensed a threatening mean streak underneath polite servilities. His wife, dark-haired Abby, had the most glorious wide, sensuous mouth. When she smiled, her lips became fluid, dissolving with a delight that encompassed everyone around her. But her intense gaze was only for you. She cooked fabulous meals and became my caring friend. We played tennis and laughed a lot at the vagaries of the male species. The Friedmans' guests were always writers, painters, actors, dancers, musicians, or anyone involved in the arts. They lived in a house in Turtle Bay, next to Katharine Hepburn's, which impressed all of us, and they entertained often with warmth, good conversation, and an easy grace.

Schueler and I had become friends, good friends, who looked after each other in a quiet sort of manner. We talked endlessly about how we felt, or, rather, how he felt. I learned that what had been missing in my life was indeed possible: a man who could talk about his feelings. And if he could, so could I. My feelings were not "claptrap, overemotional nonsense," as John Sargent had referred to them. I felt a freedom with Schueler, an ease of being. Could it have something to do with our relationship being a friendship and not one of sexual desire, at least for me?

We went to museums, MoMA especially, exhibitions, sometimes

gallery openings of Schueler's friends and peers—Franz Kline, Jackson Pollock, Willem de Kooning, Cy Twombly, and others. Once we went to a party for Cy Twombly after an opening of his work. On the way up in the elevator, Schueler asked me what I thought about Twombly's work, difficult work for an untrained mind and eye. As we got out of the elevator, I said, "I think he is sort of a hoax. He paints just scribble marks, black bits on a white canvas." At that instant, the door opened.

"Hi, Cy. So good to see you," said Schueler.

Cy Twombly stood before me just inside the doorway, head bent down a little. He looked me in the eye. His face was wrinkled, but his eyes held mine with a wry kindness. Had he heard? Schueler just smiled at me, made no reference to my remark even later on. He was that way, nonjudgmental.

During the three years I was separated from John Sargent, I modeled nude for Schueler occasionally. He was painting a series of works exploring sex and sensuality, nude women alone, with other women, and with men. His canvases were all huge, six feet by eight feet or more, the figures often more than life-size. At that time, I wanted to free myself of sexual primness, a fear of my own sensuality. Betty Friedan's book *The Feminine Mystique* had just come out. Her views made women of every genre question their sexual selves. It was the beginning of the second wave of the women's movement. I read all kinds of books, searching for insights and answers. What I came to realize was that there truly were no blueprints, but there were layers of knowledge that spoke clearly on intuition, its scientific status proven. That fact freed me. I felt free to follow my own intuitive spirit.

I spent hours and hours weekly prowling into my past for answers not only to my behavior but to that of all those with whom I had had any sort of relationship. Granules of memory surfaced bit by bit, accompanied even more slowly by understanding. I started to regain an unadorned self. I remembered again saying to myself at eight years old, Give it up, Neltje. What I was giving up was trying to make adults understand my feelings. I said to myself, I'll do it your way. They told me my intuition was hooey. All right, I'll behave the way you want me to, not who I am, I decided that day. I was picking up the pieces of myself now.

The reality is, my mother did not want children; she was bored by them. No wonder she always blamed my father for not wanting us around. I think he did feel annoyed by the noise and chatter once he got hooked on booze. I remember going to a greenhouse, Bertanzel's on Route 25A, with him in my early days. He'd ask me if I liked this color azalea or that magenta one. He swam with me in the pool after his tennis game on Saturday mornings, but he had absolutely no patience with me on the tennis court. But he played with me. We went to see Frank Buck the snake man, who held a python around his neck, the snake's circumference too large to hold even in two hands. I was scared but fascinated. I wanted to do that . . . the impossible . . . the daring.

As the past became clearer, such as why John hadn't wanted me in bed, I gave up any thought of having a life with him. Had the sexual part of our marriage worked, at least some emotional intimacy would have been there. I was in love with him, and I had to get over it. He was not going to change because I wanted him to. Oh, foolish child. I had to give up daydreaming about life with John, face my angers, and be aware that I had certain reasons to be angry, which I had not known. As a child, I was put in the closet if I got angry. Now I needed a focus, a job away from the publishing business. Could I learn to draw professionally? It appeared to come easily. So does that make it a worthless talent? I lived in uncertainty.

Two weeks after taking LSD to help get to the root of my problems, I went to the Museum of Modern Art. The Tchelitchew "tree of life" painting, *Hide-and-Seek,* hung on the second floor. It mesmerized me. The infant heads at the ends of tree branches put me back in the loose, brain-floating effects of LSD. I stood there for many minutes, transfixed, and that image has surfaced in my mind over many, many years. I ended up in St. Patrick's Cathedral that day and came to in front of a wax figure of a priest. I don't believe in God or in any part of any religion. I was scared and fled.

I delighted in the expanding world of the painters and philosophers I met through Schueler. I listened to him talk about painting, not the craft, but the emotional and intellectual content that was the cornerstone of Abstract Expressionism. And about the spontaneity that fed that style of painting. All that sparked interest in me. It spoke to the importance of intuition, which validated the way I thought and felt. But when I met some of the painters at parties with Schueler, I had no idea of what to say, or even how to begin a conversation. They talked of automatic writing, surrealism, philosophies and theories about what it meant to be an artist, and the importance of the criteria by which painting was judged. There was cozy gossip about who had a show, who was leaving this or that gallery, and what Susan wore to her opening. It was a separate world. I was intimidated, and I told Schueler so. He just laughed quietly and said, "Never mind, babe. They love to hear themselves talk. They are trying to figure out their lives, vindicate themselves, I think, sometimes. We all need to babble to know."

"I don't understand their arguments, Schueler. Why not just paint?"

"It's not as easy as that if you make painting your life's work. There is more, always more." Only years later did I recognize how vital knowing form and other technical elements is to creating a painting. And how necessary it is to experience, before making the mark, the concentration centered within, letting the mind evaporate into the moment that allows spontaneity and creativity.

Two years after my separation from John Sargent, Ken Wilson of *Reader's Digest* and his wife, June, invited me to dinner and a play in Greenwich Village. They were entertaining a visiting writer for the *Digest*, who would be my escort that evening. "Is it all right now, Neltje?" asked Ken in his mild voice, which was almost impossible to hear over the phone.

"Yes indeed, Ken, I'd love it. What fun. Tell me the time."

"We will pick you up at five promptly and go straight to the Village. June has heard of a good new French restaurant she wants to try."

The stranger stood in the small entryway, dressed in a blue wool coat, his arms hanging loosely at his sides, a smile on his lips. He was tall, almost bald, his blondish hair hardly visible. His lower jaw was prominent. He was not handsome, but his smile was electric.

"I am your date, John Kings," he said.

We got in the cab with the Wilsons, and immediately the lively banter began. We teased June rather ruthlessly because she was being stuffy about the play we were to see, having read up on it. June had translated the book *Papillon* from the French, a heroic job that took someone with a highly trained mind and a code of rigid perseverance. I liked both Ken and June, but it was especially fun finding a mind in John Kings that traveled as fast as mine, with equal naughtiness.

Dating was an on-again, off-again affair with John Kings, who traveled back and forth between New York and London, where his wife and child were. I didn't like myself for being involved with another woman's husband. I had never intended to date a married man. But here I was, committing adultery in terms of English law, and, I think, U.S. as well, at that time. I asked for no commitment, and I could give none myself. I was afraid to ask John (why couldn't I find a lover with another first name?) how he saw our relationship now, or in the future. We just glided along from one visit to the next. My kids and I moved out of the large apartment on East End Avenue, Padget right beside us. We settled into the apartment on Eighty-fifth Street, a doorman building, a safety net.

When he was in this country, John Kings was happy to include my kids in daily events like meals, movies, walks in the park, or cherry-spitting contests on a weekend picnic in the Catskills. We had fun together, and I came to know what a sense of belonging felt like. We laughed, loved, kidded, ate, drank, spoiled the kids, and painted together and apart. I started remembering the paintings I saw in the Prado in Madrid, the subtle Corots in Paris, and the Monet water lilies here in the city at MoMA. I heard the voice of Miss MacLennan, my history of art teacher during my junior year at Miss Porter's, as she showed one slide after another of a particular artist while asking us what we saw and how one could identify the works of Masaccio. Lifted high by being loved, loving John Kings, made my sensual juices rip. John was bright, quick-witted, and amusing. He loved to dance, was good in bed, and he loved me. He had had three wives, so I knew him to be a restless man with a constant eye to windward. I had enjoyed a few lovers who were not married, but I knew hormonal pull. I had no idea of what kind of woman I would become. For now, I was happy, and my kids seemed happy—even though they really wanted their father to return, particularly Ellen. Johnny had said after John Sargent told the kids we had split, "Look at it this way, Ellen. We have two houses now, with two sets of toys. What could be better? They're the ones with problems, not us. Let them be. Let's go play." He was five years old.

In May 1964, on a Friday evening after John Kings had finished his workday at *Reader's Digest,* up the Hudson River, we set off for

Chincoteague, Virginia. In the morning, we lay together in bed, and on a warm sand beach, slurping up the sun in every pore. We watched the wild ponies of Chincoteague prance about as they grazed on the beach, cerulean sky above and infinite sea beyond. This weekend was ours alone for the first time. My kids had always been with us before. On the trip down, we talked sporadically. I was tense and mostly listened. With spaces of silence now, out in the open, I could talk about myself, in the present and past, my fear of being abandoned, how the landscape of the Catskills fed me. John said, "I use my charm to get out of situations. Don't let me do that."

We laughed at our idiosyncrasies and ate deviled crab sandwiches. John sketched in his life during World War II and after, why he had married and remarried. That was what happened in those days; lovers didn't have affairs as openly as they do now. We listened to the lapping water, inhaled the sea air, and made up dreams.

I started painting seriously. John Kings helped me buy art supplies and suggested I try painting with a palette knife. I began on a small canvas, a landscape in oil of a rounded hill I saw every time I was up in the Catskills. I watched Ellen and Johnny playing jacks on the wooden floor of the dining room/studio or just "hanging out," as they put it, curled up or stretched out flat on the living room rug. I drew them in charcoal with quick short strokes and lean lines. I was amazed that I could capture what I felt in seeing them. A photograph could provide the literal image, but I wanted essence. Quickly, my canvases became far too small. I needed freedom for large brushstrokes. In February, I created what I thought quite a beautiful painting of myself, in profile, melting into the woods behind, a strong lyrical work. The soft greens and yellows, creamy tan, blues, and a hint of purple and other pale shades, layered one atop another in small strokes using knives and brushes, created an atmosphere of mystery, the kind I had felt in the swamplands at Bonny Hall when I was very young. I was so joyful when I finished that painting. I had a voice. I had visually defined my feelings about myself and in some ways found myself. That sounds gooey, but I have no other words to describe the enlightenment I felt looking at that painting. My elation didn't last long, of course; self-criticism drove me down to dark places, where my effort seemed a foolish dream, and I could not paint for days.

John continued to encourage me from afar. "Paint. Do collages. Get wax or clay and let your fingers tell your story." He suggested I sculpt when I became so frustrated that I could not feel or define the depth of the people or landscape I was painting. Without that, my paintings felt flat and one-dimensional. I needed to learn how to create perspective. I had so much to learn. I kept hitting walls, changing venues, trying again, getting a bit further on, learning something every time I picked up a knife or brush.

Eventually I did get some wax and sculpted several pieces: a nude man standing, and a nude woman sitting, legs spread apart, head and body bent over with grief. John Kings encouraged me to have them cast in bronze, and we found a foundry on Long Island. I was so nervous the day we went there, worrying that someone would tell me my art was not worth messing with. The foundry men were, in fact, kind. They told me the lost-wax process involved making a resin mold of each piece, then they would burn out the wax, which had no metal armature at all. Once that was done, another resin mold would be made, just a bit smaller. Liquid bronze would be poured between the two molds, creating a sculpture. A month later, I could pick up my bronze sculptures. They would do the finishing color. Wow. The process seemed so easy from the foundry guys' description, swallowing my mind. These early sculptures became my stepping-stones, my foundation. I stroked them daily.

In the apartment, my dining room now served as my studio, with a full wall of plywood and Homasote mounting board to use for hanging canvases. I had built a large counter to the right to store paints, charcoal, papers, pens, and other artist paraphernalia. I was painting in oils then, so I had gallons of turpentine in aluminum cans, the odorless variety. I would use the top of a counter as a paint palette, which provided enough space to blend any number of shades and differing hues. I copied this example from Schueler's studio.

John came to the States when he could. I was still seeing a psychiatrist to find the source of so many of my anxieties, which seemed to multiply the more I dug. The pain of awareness, reversing what I had believed or felt, flattened me, sometimes for days. Dr. Blanton was a Southerner and a Freudian. His views did not blend with mine, and he didn't like John Kings and wanted me to end the affair. I told him, "But you're not the one who is alone, and I need somebody." There it was, *out*. I stayed with Dr. Smiley Blanton in the first years, hoping he could help me work out a life with John Sargent. Then I stayed because I had come this far with him and didn't want to break off and start anew with another psychiatrist and have to tell all those painful stories again.

As John Kings and I were quietly painting together, living on and off together, while the kids were going to school that winter of 1965, civil rights activists were planning a march from Selma to Montgomery, Alabama. Their purpose was twofold—first to "rectify voting injustices in Dallas County, Alabama, where half of the potential voting population was black, yet only 200 of 15,000 blacks were registered to vote in 1961"; second, to gain national attention through media exposure: newspaper, magazine, and especially television, hoping to cause voting procedures to change not only locally in Alabama but throughout the country. And it did happen.

On January 19, Sheriff Jim Clark was caught by the media "roughing up" Amelia Boynton, a civil rights activist and protester, during a voter-registration march to the Dallas County Courthouse. He was known to beat up on black protesters regardless of the news media's presence.

On February 18, during a march in Marion, Alabama, about thirty miles from Selma, around five hundred people marched from the Zion United Methodist Church to the Perry County jail to protest the arrest and jailing of civil rights worker James Orange. The police claimed the protesters were there to aid a jailbreak, and violence ensued. Protesters tried to return to the church. Three protesters, Jimmie Lee Jackson, his grandfather, and his mother, were pushed into a café behind the church. In an effort to protect his mother and grandfather from being beaten by the police, Jimmie Lee was slammed against a wall by police, then shot twice in the abdomen. He died eight days later, on February 26.

In protest of Jimmie Lee Jackson's murder, a march, organized by the local Southern Christian Leadership Conference (SCLC), took place on March 7, leaving from the Brown's Chapel headquarters for the voting-rights protest in Selma. Governor George Wallace of Alabama wanted the march stopped and sent state troopers to block the protesters' path on the bridge over the Alabama River at the edge of downtown. Sheriff Clark and his men, some just appointed for the day, stood behind the state troopers. When the marchers refused to turn back, the troopers unleashed tear gas and billy clubs. The nation watched unresisting protesters being beaten on national news that night. Some individuals praying by the roadside were chased into the river and beaten down into the water, young and old alike. Seventeen protesters were hospitalized with serious injuries; all were scarred for life. That is what I heard on the news and it was the fact that people praying at the roadside were being beaten and maimed by white men, state troopers and local police, coupled with all the other injustices of white people against blacks, that tipped the scale of outrage in my mind. It shouldn't happen and must be prevented from happening again in my country. This stinks of inhumanity, I thought.

For months, even years, Martin Luther King Jr. had been demanding "equality for the black people of the United States," and saying, "Let us register to vote like anyone else."

President Kennedy had been assassinated in November 1963. Tension sizzled in the cities, particularly in African-American neighborhoods, and especially in the summertime, when the temperature was unbearable. Black people rioted violently all over the country, in big cities and small towns. Martin Luther King had made his famous "I Have a Dream" speech in August 1963, calling for national action to end segregation. Black people were tired of being forced to the back of the bus and denied the right to vote.

Photos of the March 7 march, seen on TV and in magazines and newspapers, revealed hatred in the eyes of many police and state troopers as they used their billy clubs to pound on the marchers. Protest leaders were jailed. Martin Luther King vowed they would march again.

I was painting the afternoon of that march. The radio was on with the news that King was organizing a march in two days' time, on March 9, 1965. John Kings was sitting at the dining table, writing letters. He called across the room, "We should go down to Selma, join this march, don't you think?" His tone was conversational. "Yes," I replied immediately. "I think we should." I went on painting as we talked about organizing the trip south, the dental or doctor dates scheduled for the kids, how long we would be gone. Two nights and three days, I figured. Could Padget tend to Ellen and John? We mulled over all the possibilities and who had to be notified, until it was time to pick Ellen up at the bus stop. This decision seemed so easy and so right. There was no reason to question it. The kids would be taken care of if Padget agreed to help.

After dinner that night, we started making plans on how we would get to Selma. Where would we stay? I spoke with Padget, asked him to take Ellen and Johnny to doctors' appointments, make sure they got to school and to bed on time. He would meet them in the afternoon either at school or at the bus stop. He always fed them well, loved to tell stories, and was gentle but firm. He happily agreed to take care of Ellen and Johnny. I knew the kids would be safe.

As I thought about the march, I recalled that some protesters had been jailed after the last one. I hired a lawyer in Selma in case I was imprisoned there. While making these arrangements, I began to feel a new sense of power. I was acting on my beliefs. It was my right to do so. My psychiatrist, the president of the United States, my brother, and my husband all said, "No. Don't go."

There was a hotline with instructions on how to get to Birmingham, Alabama, where to stay, and where to meet for the march. We listed our names with the march organization and I got plane tickets. The hotline itself gave limited information. I wondered about the distance from Birmingham to Selma via back roads. How long would it take? What was the temperature and weather forecast for the area? There was no Internet at the time.

In Birmingham we were met by a man and woman, both in their thirties. A younger guy was meeting three other marchers over to the right in the airport lobby. We were told where to rent a car and where to stay, and given a map of how to get to Selma on the back roads. All the main roads into Selma were blocked by police barricades. I felt frightened. I understood the significance of why I was there, what I was doing, but my fears seemed to remove me from what was happening around me. Early the next morning, I dressed in my standby purple tweed suit and comfortable moccasins. I looked at the yellowish-tan color of their leather, hated the shade, and thought they wouldn't be of much use if we marched the whole distance to Montgomery. I will end up in bare feet. There was nothing I could do about it. My pockets and purse were full of goodies to nibble on.

In Selma, we congregated in an open field next to a white church. I was not a believer in any religion and worried that there would be a long sermon in the church, where I would be uncomfortable with the religious rhetoric. We waited for instructions. Many white people milled about with crowds of mostly young black boys. There was not much interaction between the two races. Eventually we were lined up eight abreast: two whites at each end and blacks in the middle. The young black boy who took my hand couldn't have been over fourteen.

Martin Luther King came out of the church with his entourage of about ten men, maybe fifteen, and walked down the wooden steps and onto the field. He stood before us, a man of peace with a mission. I was filled with admiration for him, and to this day can feel the power of his presence. We began the march with men, women, a few girls, and lots of black boys under the age of eighteen. Slowly, the wide belt of humans began to move, to march quietly, as instructed, with peace in our hearts. After a few blocks, we turned left to face the bridge. Phalanxes of police riot squads lined each side of the road on both sides of the bridge. Dignitaries like Governor Wallace, Jim Clark, and Bull Connor faced us across the river. King began walking across the bridge. They met halfway. We had no idea what was going to happen. I was scared. We waited. The dignitaries turned back across the river and King returned to the head of our line. We began to move, still uncertain, until we saw Governor Wallace, James Clark, and Bull Connor step aside, allowing us to pass.

Dr. James Reeb came from Wyoming (I later found out) to march and was severely beaten that day behind the scenes. I heard the wail of the ambulance passing by the drugstore where I was phoning Pucky to let her know it was over and that I was all right. Driving back to Birmingham, John and I saw an ambulance off to the right, in a half-wooded area tucked close against a tree. Men, maybe three or four, stood around the side. We didn't dare stop to investigate. I felt ashamed. Dr. Reeb died in the Birmingham hospital two days later.

I felt empowered to have taken part in an historic moment, to have done something my children could perhaps be proud of someday, and, more important, I acted on my beliefs against the wishes of powerful others. Up until that time, such action had been unthinkable, because women brought up as I had been did not do what the men in their lives told them not to do.

SIXTEEN

Moving On

I was ready to get a divorce. My lawyer and John Sargent's hashed out the intricacies, times of visits, et cetera—painful ideas to end a long relationship. Wyoming required only a two-month residence in order to get a divorce. I called my roommate from Miss Porter's, Martha Walker, now married to a Wyoming cowboy named Bobby Gibbs. She said they would love to have us stay for two months on their ranch on the Powder River.

John Kings, Ellen, Johnny, a friend of theirs, Kipper Williams, my standard poodle, Gimpy Truman, and I set off on an adventure driving cross-country to Wyoming. We would spend the summer on the ranch of my roommate from Miss Porter's. We were driving an early Dodge RV we'd dubbed "Maybelline," which provided beds for all of us, a bathroom with shower, and a full kitchen. I was fascinated that I could cook a turkey in the oven as John Kings drove down a highway at seventy miles an hour. I was ignorant of all camping life.

When I was young, I had seen the movie *The Long, Long Trailer*, with Lucille Ball and her husband, Desi Arnaz. Everything possible went wrong on their drive: Pots and pans flew out of cupboards, dishes crashed to the floor, the toilet got stopped up—and throughout these catastrophes, Lucille laughed and chatted with a hyper Desi. The audience laughed till they wept. In my fantasy, I could be Lucy, make my audience roll in laughter.

I gave a party so that my city friends could see the daring life I would be living on the road, driving in this huge vehicle. I wanted it to look casual, as if it were no big deal. But it was a huge deal to me, breaking away from the summer in the Catskills. And a divorce. I was moving forward with my life.

John parked the RV in front of the apartment house door and I gave tours to anyone who, even in simple politeness, asked about the interior. I had never seen a camper of any kind, so this spacious suite of beds and other accommodations was like a spaceship to me, a marvel. The party mood was half festive, half disbelieving. Brian and Sidney Urquhart thought it a grand adventure; not so my old friends Tim and Lee Seldes. They thought me quite mad. Who would want to be so uncomfortable, and for so long? Why not fly? The kids were excited. At six and eight, they were the perfect ages for a wild road trip and a summer on a working ranch. The only must-do was that we had to spend two months in Wyoming in order for me to get the divorce. I hadn't said much to Ellen and Johnny. I didn't want to get into a discussion of why I was doing whatever, particularly with Ellen, who missed her father. He was barely available when they visited, preoccupied with other engagements or a woman he was wooing. Ellen was just plain angry with me for disrupting what she thought a happy home, and I guess it had been for her. There was no consoling I could do.

We began our drive on the west side of the Hudson River, meandering our way upstate to Cooperstown. I was glad John drove us out of the city snarls, but then I wanted to have a try. He would not relinquish the wheel for another three days. I thought, Here we go again with the fragile male ego that I have always heard about. They want to do the male thing, drive, and be brave. Never interfere. I kept quiet and let John drive, but really I wanted to fight to take the wheel. I rented the vehicle. Now let me have my turn, DAMMIT! But I was fearful of losing him if I came on too strong, so I sat in the bucket seat up front next to the driver, and I stewed. The kids were busy at the table: Ellen, in the corner, read a book, John and Kipper Williams played war games with plastic camouflaged soldiers, and Gimpy lay under the table. From the outside, this looked like a serene family picture.

Our first stop was to see Cecily Symington, an old friend of my mother's. An outspoken, humorous woman, she had been a comfort to me when I had spent a lonely summer at a camp nearby when I was eight. She was also my godmother, and I thought her wonderful. I wanted her to meet my kids and John, and to take them all to the National Baseball Hall of Fame in Cooperstown, where baseball began in this country. That early childhood summer, I had refused to pay the twenty-five-cent admission because I was Abner Doubleday's great-great-niece. The lady in charge was taken aback by my claim and dithered about, but in the end, she let me through. I was so proud of my courage that day.

That summer of 1942 at Pathfinders Lodge was the second summer in a row I had been sent away to camp. The previous year, I was at camp in New Hampshire, until I was sent home with whooping cough. At Pathfinders I had been allowed to visit Aunt Cecily on occasional Sunday afternoons. She listened to my woes. Her humor somehow made them bearable. "Why should Nelson stay home and I get sent away? My mother keeps promising to come up, but she never does. It's just plain mean. She could come visit for two days without my dad feeling left out," I told her.

She tried to explain my mother's behavior. "You have to understand, your father wants your mother with him. She believes she needs to be with him; that is her place." I liked the way she did not make excuses but tried to help me understand. She became my mentor, although I rarely saw her during my teenage years.

We arrived late in the afternoon at Aunt Cecily's white clapboard house with its green shutters, perfect lush lawn, and flowering dogwood trees. White summer furniture was spread out on the lawn. We had a family picnic. I could tell John was nervous, because he told one story after another, not waiting for a response. The kids ran around chasing Gimpy, everyone relieved to be outdoors. Did Aunt Cecily like John? Would she say something positive about him or about me to my mother? I liked to think she would.

The following night, a kind gas station owner told John we could spend the night in his field instead of in the A&P parking lot. The field was rough, with muddy clumps, and John drove too far, until, with a metallic clunk, we came to a stop. We were stuck with a broken rear axle.

Here was my first opportunity to play Lucille, to make merry of such

a disaster. I forgot that fantasy as we trudged across the lumpy field
and a mile farther down the road to another gas station for help. We
needed a new axle. After three calls back and forth, the dealer agreed
to ship a new axle by bus at no cost. It was late Friday afternoon. Not
until the following Wednesday did we finally get back on the road. I
was impressed that John had gotten such a good deal. We had stayed in
Maybelline, our RV, and had spread collapsible chairs out in the field. I
had felt like a gypsy, and fortunately the kids thought our incarcera-
tion was fun. In the evenings, the camping out was an adventure. Who
could find the most bugs, spiders, or worms in a given time? Candy was
the prize. I baked brownies for supper and we told tales, ghost stories,
and horror stories in the dark and enjoyed feeling scared but safe.

We drove past Chicago, north toward the Canadian border. There was
a famous old hotel on Mackinac Island, at the tip end of Lake Huron.
It was grand, with its white linen tablecloths and waiters dressed in
cropped burgundy jackets with black satin lapels, the kind of formality
that had always made me uncomfortable—too like life at Oyster Bay.
We just had lunch and then pressed on south, taking a ferry across the
bay to Menomonee Falls. John and I stood at the rail, held hands, and
felt very lucky to be together. We had now driven by, been around, or
crossed all of the Great Lakes on this trip.

As soon as we got off the ferry, we stopped for gas. John strode across
the street to the mom-and-pop grocery store. The kids tumbled out, looking for candy and soda machines. The air was dusty and dry. Wind blew
across the baked earth in a swirling wide ring. My eyes stung. The elderly attendant took the gas nozzle out of the RV and placed it back in
the gas tank. "That will be thirty-eight dollars and seventy cents, boy.
Tell your pop when he gets back," he said to Johnny, who stood at the
pump drinking a Coke.

"That ain't my pop," Johnny said fiercely.

That phrase became an answer for everything that summer, which
made us all laugh. By laughing, we avoided a confrontation between
Johnny and John Kings. Johnny's jealousy and anger toward a possible stepdad was at times ready to blaze into an ugly scene. Growing up
with a single mom is hard for a boy, and I didn't have the presence of
mind, or the courage, to sit down and talk quietly with my son. He had
always been so easy to get along with. The new biting anger surprised

me. What effect was my relationship with John Kings having on my children? The stress of coping, being a mother, being a lover, and being alone most of the time weighed on me. What was my responsibility toward others? Just being a mom was so often overwhelming, particularly by five o'clock, gangrene hour.

We drove on to Wyoming, arriving at the turnoff for Martha and Bobby's ranch late of an afternoon. "John," I said, "let me drive now. I know the long, rough terrain here, and you—"

"No," he cut in. "What would they think of me if I let you drive in?"

Again I wanted to say, "They wouldn't give a damn, so let me do it," but I saw nothing was going to help change John's mind. His jaw was set, rigid. Ellen picked up on the tension and said, "John, let Mom drive. She does know this road because we visited here a couple of years ago and she drove in and out a number of times, and it's a really rough road, not an easy drive . . . not an easy drive."

"I can't" was all he grumbled in reply. But oh, I was so proud of Ellen for speaking up for me. I had envisioned impressing my old schoolmate Martha with being a tough hand at the wheel, not a wimpy Colony Club lady from Park Avenue in the big city. Another failed fantasy.

We spent a glorious summer on Martha and Bobby's ranch, which lay along the Powder River. That river was famous, known to be "a mile wide and an inch deep, too thick to drink, too thin to plow." On hot days, we all splashed about, sang songs, threw balls to one another, then flopped backward into the water. Martha made delicious biscuit and gravy breakfasts, and almost daily the smell of bacon and fresh-baked bread of some sort drifted across the yard from their house to where we stayed. The kids learned to ride horses, pitch hay, clean out stalls, and they cleared rocks from a field that would later become a hay field.

John and I lived in the ranch hand's trailer. It was well laid out, with comfortable furniture, good appliances, and air-conditioning. The kids stayed in the RV, without air-conditioning. They thought it unfair, and we agreed.

Martha had been my roommate for all four years at Miss Porter's. After graduation, we kept in touch, filling each other in on our so-opposite lives. She lived on a ranch in the far back hills of Recluse, Wyoming. I lived in a duplex penthouse overlooking the East River in New York City. We both had two small babies. I whined about the endless business dinners I had to give and attend. She wrote of carrying her three-year-old son, who had been kicked by a horse, three miles through deep snow to find a vehicle that could then get them to a doctor. I considered her realities far more significant than mine, closer to the bone.

I was still vacillating about going through with the divorce, still wanting John Sargent to be different, wanting him to want me. In my dream world, we walked into the sunset together as a family. I had considered a life apart often but had been too scared of coping alone. My whole world, friends and family, were involved with the publishing business. How could I survive with no family support, my old school friends scattered and deep into busy married lives? I had trouble admitting my marriage was a failure, just as my mother had predicted. I hated the idea that she was right. What effect would the finality of a divorce have on Ellen and Johnny? I was being selfish, I told myself. My doubts resurfaced and vanished.

We spent a good deal of our summer watching kid rodeos or going to one cowboy event or another. At the Little League rodeo in Gillette, Johnny got pitched off, but Kipper stayed on for the eight-second "bull ride." Actually, steer ride would have been more truthful. We were properly impressed and applauded madly. Johnny was red angry that he had not stayed on board for the allotted time. I had a tailgate talk with him about sportsmanship.

"Sometimes you just don't make it and someone else does, Johnny. Kipper is older than you by two years. That makes a big difference, because his muscles and coordination are much more developed than yours. He is stronger now than you. There will be a time when you may well be much stronger than Kipper. You did really well and I am proud of you for staying on board as long as you did. It is important for you to tell Kipper, 'Good job.' That is being a good sport. What do you think? Could you tell Kipper 'Good job'?" Johnny was growing up, facing new social problems, and he didn't like it one bit.

One day when we were in Sheridan, shopping, we decided to go on to the HF Bar Ranch, a dude ranch where the kids, Annie, their English companion, and I had spent a month three years earlier, a year before I separated from John Sargent. The kids remembered many things differently from the way I did, but the sunset rides, we all recalled. Ellen had become as one with her horse; Johnny had been off in his dreamland. We laughed, remembering how I had had to lead his horse with a rope.

They both remembered playing in the pool and where the dances were held in the log building up the hill, and where we ate in the big dining room in the main building. They didn't remember our cabin on the creek, with the rushing water right alongside. During the month we had spent there, I'd tried to decide whether to divorce their father that fall or give another year's try to make the marriage work. I had told John I was fed up with his cold shoulder and wanted out. But Ellen, Johnny, and Annie knew nothing of why we were there. That was two years before I asked John to leave. John had been made president of the company the winter after I got back from the West. I didn't have the heart to walk out on him as soon as he became president.

I remembered the chatter in the dining room at the ranch, how apart and scared I'd felt. Everyone was seated at long tables. We ate farm-style, with the potatoes, green beans, and sliced meat loaf already on the table when we sat down. Hot rolls and butter came with each meal. The other ranch dudes were dressed in designer blue jeans, smart white or print long-sleeved shirts, and colorful scarves about their necks. They looked put together, something I neither looked like nor felt. They were older, most of them, and had been coming to the HF Bar Ranch for years, some for generations.

We talked with Hank Horton, the owner, who had welcomed us with remembrances of our earlier visit. As we climbed into Maybelline, I gave a quick look under the table for Gimpy to let him out for a quick run. He was not there. I felt panic grip my throat. We had stopped at the A&P to get groceries for the week. Could he be there? We phoned. The workers had seen him sitting outside after they closed, but he was no longer there. We left and raced back to Sheridan.

Once there, the three kids and I got out and walked the quiet streets, calling for Gimpy, while John Kings drove Maybelline in a crisscross pattern from east to west, searching for him. I left bits of clothing—a glove or hat, one of Johnny's T-shirts—on the sidewalk in case Gimpy came by later. Nothing. We found no trace of him. I felt heartbroken and so guilty for not having checked to make sure he was in his usual resting spot beneath the table. John took us to the Four U Drive Inn on the north end of town so I could order supper for us while he drove on to the Trails End Motel, where we had stayed a few weeks earlier, to get us rooms for the night. It was almost dark.

Fifteen minutes later, John drove up, shut off the motor, and opened the door of Maybelline. There stood Gimpy Truman, tail wagging, at the top of the stairs. He had made his way back to the Trails End Motel, where John had found him patiently waiting on the grass near the door to the room where we had stayed two weeks earlier. Gimpy had never seen the way into downtown Sheridan from the Trails End Motel, so how did he find his way back to it?

John had been an editor and writer with *Reader's Digest,* but he had wanted to paint. Words came slickly easy to him. He wanted to prove himself as a painter.

The Gibbses gave John and me a bunkhouse cabin on their ranch, maybe eight by ten feet, to use as a studio. We had to paint one at a time; only one person could fit in the space—it was so small and the roof so low. We put our canvases on the rear log wall, hung on two or three nails, level with either the floor or the ceiling, but not both. There was a table for all our oil paints and a large piece of Plexiglas to use as a palette. We both used rags more than brushes, so we needed a big garbage can. But the squished-down size didn't matter to either of us. We were so pleased to have a work space. The bunkhouse had a low roof, barely high enough for John to stand upright. We did not care about that, either. I was painting thirty-by-forty-inch canvases, using oil paint and rags, the heel of my hand, paper towels, anything I could get ahold of, to create transparency in my paintings by layering thin washes of oil paint one on top of another with different intensities. I did not consider these paintings of my children, my mother, or John as portraits. My goal was to capture the emotion I felt and saw in them: a moment's essence. I was pleased that my skill was growing as I developed more confidence. John used the same technique, but he abstracted the landscape, and his work had sold quite well. My mind kept working for clarity. Our pattern of painting at different times meant one of us was always with the kids, so they didn't feel left out. I was glad of that.

The public in Wyoming did not respond to my work or to John's, which was too contemporary for them. We both had tried to exhibit our work in a large, popular restaurant, but the owner wanted traditional landscapes and portraits. There was no proper gallery in town at that time, just a few small works in gift stores, all traditional. So we had no show, but we would always carry some paintings in the RV when we went to town and would show them if anyone asked. We were pleased with our development, the space, the sun, and playing with the kids.

Meanwhile, there were thornier matters to deal with. I talked with Bobby Gibbs about the one thing that still bothered me, that was not settled to my satisfaction. I had given John Sargent a sizable chunk of Doubleday stock to boost his ego at a time when he felt outmaneuvered because he had no stock. Early in the spring, before we left for Wyoming, I walked with John after a lunch along the south side of Seventy-ninth Street between Madison and Park Avenue as a chill wind blew. I said, "John, the stock I gave you should go to our children."

He snapped back, "No. They are mine. I deserve them . . . for living with you. Besides, I may need them if I have another family." He looked straight ahead, took a puff of his cigar, and rolled the wet end in his lips.

My stomach flipped when he mentioned another family. I was stunned by his callousness and could not speak. My body became rigid. I flagged down a cab and fled home.

On hearing my story of what had happened, Bobby Gibbs advised, "Get that stock back. Fight for it. Don't let him intimidate you."

I did as Bobby said. I canceled divorce proceedings and prepared to fight to get the stock back for Ellen and Johnny.

All of us loved this country: the wildly varied landscape, from mountains to deep arroyos and on to the Powder River Breaks; the vast space and far horizons; the way of life; the light on the landscape, which altered the vision in seconds; and the play of light on the waters of Lake DeSmet and on the creeks that flowed clear, or that cast shadows on the rolling foothills of the Bighorn Mountains. The ever-changing light dazzled and delighted both John and me in different ways: The painting fed his mind, and I relished the intimate essence I found in the smallest cluster of twigs and stones or in the brilliant colorings of everything around us. We began talking about finding a ranch, a home here, somewhere near

Sheridan. I was certain my kids would love to live in this open environment. I didn't dare say anything until I was sure John Kings was coming with us. I couldn't do it alone. A week later, John and I began ranch hunting. It was the week before we were to go back to New York. I was ecstatic that John had, without any conversation of love or marriage, decided to become a part of our lives. There was a commitment. I had a love.

We found a ranch north of Sheridan with breathtaking views and a rushing creek, but it was too large and difficult to operate. I settled on a much smaller property with a simple stone house, sheep sheds, and a barnlike structure. Piney Creek bubbled alongside it on its way east, and the view enticed the eye the full length of the valley to the Bighorn Mountains. The house would need redoing, but we could live in a trailer adjacent to the barn, which had room enough for two studios if I had the space reworked during the winter. The price was fair and the four hundred–plus acres seemed more than enough land. I agreed to buy the ranch, and put a down payment in escrow.

Piney Creek valley was lush now in a summer flood of greens, the hay fields ripe and rippling in warm afternoon winds. The front range of the Bighorns lay in silhouette against the bluest sky. Each mountain of granite and the forested forms would change shape with the slightest shift of light later in the day. This view touched me in a way I did not fully understand. I would live here, my children would grow up here, and John Kings would join us. We would be a family. I would belong in a loving family. We would be together.

On August 28, 1965, we headed homeward to my apartment in New York. School would begin soon for both kids. As we approached the George Washington Bridge, I said to John, "I don't want to fight John Sargent for the stock. He might well make trouble about your living with us, or threaten to fight for the custody of Ellen and Johnny. I doubt he would, but I don't want to take the chance. Our summer was sweet. To end it in a custody battle for stock or children is more than I want to face. I'll get a divorce in Mexico."

A week later, I flew to the Texas border town of El Paso. I waited in the dreary brown hotel room for the divorce lawyer to phone me, as arranged by my lawyer in New York. Outdoors, the sun blazed a white heat. Indoors, the room's air conditioner made a gritty hum. I turned on the radio, then turned it off again. The Texas twang irritated me. I paced the worn tan carpet, tried to read a magazine, threw it on the bed, took out my journal from my small overnight bag, found a hotel pen, and sat at the glass-covered vanity table to write. The phone rang, a shrill sound. I allowed it to ring twice before I picked up the black receiver. I said hello with more bravura than I felt. The woman on the phone identified herself as my lawyer, Señora Sanchez. She said she would stop by the hotel at nine in the morning. Did I have my passport with me for the border crossing? she asked. I did. I placed the phone back in its cradle and wondered how many thousands of other women had done the same thing in rooms like this one all over town during the past decades.

I slept poorly, waking up several times during the night not knowing where I was. I could not remember my dreams, which troubled me. I thought they would be clear, a signal for my future life. Instead, I felt half-suffocated in muddy waters, fearful, not knowing why. I dressed quickly in black pants, an off-white shirt, and a bright scarf around my neck, a sweat rag if needed. I picked up my red shoulder bag from the bed. In the empty hallway, the click of the door shutting behind me sounded loud.

I went down for a breakfast of coffee and a doughnut at the nearby coffee shop. I felt separate from all I knew. My watch read 7:40 A.M. The small coffee shop was crowded—five businessmen in suits, a patrolman in uniform, three women nicely but plainly dressed. I sat at the last stool available. I hoped I would begin to feel I was doing the right thing. I was still bothered by breaking up a home. The coffee helped me feel alive, more ready to face the day. I had three cups in quick succession. I bought a newspaper on the way out.

"Mrs. Sargent?" Señora Almira Sanchez asked with the lilt of a question in her voice. She held out her hand with a flair of welcome. She was not as tall as me, a thickly set woman in a sensible gray skirt and white top. In the cab, she told me we would go right into the judge's chambers when we got to the courthouse. The procedure appeared so formalized and slick, worn from overuse. As I got out of the cab, the driver's eye caught mine in the mirror. "Good luck," he said in English with a half-smile. I returned his smile.

The steep stone steps up to the courthouse were indeed worn from centuries of footsteps climbing and descending. That image comforted me as I sat on a hard straight-backed chair outside the judge's chambers, waiting my turn. My lawyer seemed to know everyone. She moved from one desk to another, chatting quickly in Mexican Spanish, not the Castilian Spanish I had learned at Miss Porter's. Yet I understood her quite well, though she didn't know it.

A well-groomed man, followed by a woman crying into a white lace-edged hankie, came through the very tall door next to us. I was ushered into the judge's room, pushed toward his desk, and introduced to him by Señora Sanchez. He did not bother to rise from behind his desk or to extend his hand. He gave me a cursory nod. His dark-wood desk was vast. On each side of the rose blotter before him were stacks of papers a foot and a half high, which appeared to swamp the judge, a smallish man, with an overwhelming workload. It was a constructed scene, created to impress. As soon as Señora Sanchez and I sat opposite him, the two of them started a fast-paced conversation about how profitable divorce cases were; the price of each divorce varied according to the client's wealth, made known to them by the client's lawyers back in the States. As they chatted, I watched the pudgy judge move a paper from the pile on his right to the left side of his desk. He never bothered to look at it. He said in rapid-fire Spanish, "The papers are in order; all we do now is collect the money." Señora Sanchez turned to me. "I need a check for five thousand dollars made out to my law firm," she said, handing me a paper with the name of the firm in bold type at the head of the page. The judge chuckled. I didn't let them know I understood what they were saying; what advantage would it give me? I learned more staying quiet. I wrote the check, handed it to her as she rose from her chair. I got up as well, nodded to the judge, and followed Señora Sanchez out the very tall door. What a tawdry end to twelve years of married life. I was in shock and I felt cheated.

The years of effort in creating a loving environment at home, the striving to help John at work, from travel to those endless dinner parties, and the love I thought John Sargent and I shared, all was inhaled into the void. The tenderness that had once been there between us was gone. My heart was breaking for the life that had died.

SEVENTEEN

Ranch with a View

In November, John Kings got slapped with a court order to appear at the Old Bailey in London on charges of adultery. I was named as the adulteress. Apparently, we had been chased by detectives all the way to Wyoming that summer. I read no further. This cross-country hunt and this declaration of sinful behavior read like a Nathaniel Hawthorne novel of early Puritan days. More truthfully, I did not want to face the charge that my love for John Kings had taken something vital away from his wife and young daughter. I felt a traitor to women, two in particular, and that feeling of guilt stayed with me. I hadn't liked the tune when it was played on me.

I called my divorce lawyer, Bruce Hecker. He had listened to my vacillations over my divorce during two of the most miserable years I ever endured. John Kings talked with his lawyer in London. Hecker took the papers served and coped so that I did not have to appear to face John's wife in court. In the end, neither of us had to stand up in the Old Bailey.

Our life in my New York apartment continued, Ellen and Johnny back at school, Padget revitalized by the summer off, and John tortured by his abandonment of Tarka, his daughter, age three. He wanted to be the best father, but those were dreams. He had abandoned another daughter by his Australian wife, again when she was little. That picture was disturbing. John barely talked about his past, only in a surface "and then" way. I understood; John was a man who moved on. But our love for each other seemed strong and open. I was aware that the same thing could or would happen to me, but in the meantime, I said to myself, I'm holding on to what I've got.

He strengthened my confidence in my work as a painter, and in being a woman. I was considered a second-class citizen in my family. Women were servants to men. They enriched their husbands' lives with children, attentions to family, and support for every interest a husband might have, from charity to golf. A wife must be charming, witty, and give great dinner parties. I am talking about the fifties and the early sixties. If you didn't want to do that, there were not many opportunities open to women, certainly not those without the stamina or vision to fight the system.

John Kings and I spent weekends in the Catskills with my children, enjoying the riotous autumn colors, raking and kicking leaves. We talked and talked about moving to the ranch in Wyoming. What fun it would be to be able to ride over all those hills within sight of more hills, as far as the eye could see. I had done all the paperwork on the ranch, signed it, and put the down payment in escrow. I would take possession on January 1, 1966. Ellen and John, as he now wished to be called, no longer Johnny, were at school; my divorce was final, but John Kings's divorce was still in a state of limbo.

Another excitement came. My mother invited us all to spend Christmas with her in Hawaii. She had disapproved of John Kings when they first met in New York the winter before, but I could see her invitation as an opening for, perhaps, her acceptance of him. Ellen, John Jr., John, and I flew to Hawaii in December 1965. My mother lived on the island of Oahu, where she had a house with a swimming pool right on the coastline. The house was not big enough to bed down our tribe. She arranged for us to have an apartment with a view and the sound of ocean waves outside our windows. She also gave us a limited membership to the nearby beach club, which provided days of baking in the sun, swimming, and splashing in cool waters, as well as eating and drinking ourselves silly. We rented a car for day trips. I shopped for bathing suits and shirts for the wife of one of John's friends, who had a store in Bedford Hills, New York. We had dinner with my mother every evening. Ellen and John Jr. called her "GiGi," at her request. My mother didn't have an easy way of communicating with the kids. She had never been able to do so with any children that I knew of—too formal and judgmental, I think. She could be charming and generous with cash and presents, but to sit on the floor or at a table and play rummy or wrestle, teach the girls to knit, no, not possible. Beyond her capabilities. Her lack of interest in our lives had always bothered me. She praised Nelson for his astuteness in business or for his golf game; it didn't matter which. He was the focus of her life, certainly whenever she spoke to me.

And she was friends now with the once-traitorous John Sargent. "He is coming to visit me in February. I am so thrilled he will be here for a full week, and I am giving a dinner for him, with some big names. That will please him," she added, wiping her lips with a white damask napkin. John Sargent had been president for a few years now and would be moved into the chairman of the board slot as soon as Doug Black retired. John had been trained for the job, to hold it down till Nelson was ready to take over those responsibilities. It was working out as my mother had planned. She was happy.

She and I had never had an intimate conversation about my life with John Kings, my children, or my new life of painting. She made not even a passing remark asking how the children were surviving the divorce. When I told her I had bought a ranch in Wyoming, what it was like, and how we were moving there in the spring, when school got out, she asked, "Where will the children go to school?"

"They will go to a one-room schoolhouse in Ucross, just eight miles away. There will be about twenty kids in eight grades, taught by one teacher. The kids will get a more personal education than they have in the thirty-pupil classrooms at their private schools in the city." I was enthusiastic.

"You two are only thinking of yourselves," she said, pointing to John and me on the sofa. "The children will never be able to get into a good school later on. No private school of any consequence will accept them, nor will a decent college. What are you thinking of?"

My mother's response did not really surprise me. I knew that anything outside the world she lived in was always degraded. But it hurt anyway. I had to remember that anything I said would be repeated and possibly exaggerated in her conversations with John Sargent, who thought in the same manner. I wanted to avoid his belittling our lifestyle in Wyoming to Ellen and John Jr. A rebuttal was senseless. I disliked my mother's cozying up with John Sargent. It felt like a betrayal. But, in fact, it only mirrored what I had always known: Men were gods to her. Other women did not make the goddess slot; they were disliked.

During our visit, she had talked at every meal and at times late into the night about the company, the Doubleday stock, how much Aunt Dorothy had, how much Aunt Janet had, wondering what Aunt Janet would do with her stock when she died. Would she leave it to Aunt Dorothy's children, as well as to Nelson and me? That was the key. The cadence of the play never changed. Shakespeare would have admired the plot and maybe the characters.

Before leaving the islands, we had a two-day adventure on Molokai, at a time when there was only one motel, which had six rooms. The beds had sagging metal springs that creaked at the slightest body movement. Creepy-crawlies raced across the worn wooden floorboards and occasionally over our bedclothes. In the far distance, a thin line of dark gray defined the wide horizon that stretched across the rolling ocean before us.

The morning after our arrival, we trailed through the jungle of lush greens, listened to birds sounding the alarm when we invaded their environment. We searched for a waterfall that was marked on a small map the hotelier had given us. She was a cheery, nearly toothless old woman with dancing eyes and a lusty laugh. The children's morning glum humor broke apart when the innkeeper sat down at our table and began her wild stories, crossing animal and human life on her island, legends and reality mixing, becoming folklore. When we all got up, she took John Jr., age eight at the time, threw her arms about him, and held him tucked close against her breasts. She called him her lover and laughed to the sky above. His eyes, huge in horror, implored me to release him from his admirer immediately. I took his hand and said, "We are going now." She released him, sending a kiss as we got to the car. We had been laughing, all except for him. Once we left, he admitted the morning escapade was silly but not fun.

Down, down, down we climbed the rocky jungle hillside. In places, we slid in greasy mud or tripped over sharp stones uncovered by weather. It had rained hard the previous night. I had awakened to the rhythmic pounding of tropical raindrops thumping on the metal roof. John Kings, too, was awake. We lay in bed for a while nuzzling, talking about the ranch, the hike to the falls the next day, and our love, until we dropped off to sleep.

Now, as we hiked, huge tropical leaves and thick undergrowth drenched us as we passed by, tickling our bare arms and legs. Mosquitoes provided a keen and sometimes painful annoyance, altering the idyllic into a slapping contest. We finally came out of the dense foliage into an opening of knee-high vegetation, pliant greenery that bent or broke with each footstep. The air was moist and sweet-smelling. Below us, a stream wound through the light green foliage. Alongside the stream, huge trees, with wild hairdos of leaves, stood tall against a blue sky. The moisture in the air became a misty cloud. We saw the waterfalls, way to the left, the thrashing, crashing water cascading down the hillside in a roar. In the stream between us and the falls, seven women, bare as the day they were born, stood washing their brown bodies, their thick hair, and their colorful clothes. Another four women, closer to us, who were dressed, wore bright-colored sarongs, their breasts bare. Their shiny black hair hung to their waists. They glanced our way with little interest. A Gauguin painting lay before us, perfect in its simplicity.

We flew back to Oahu for a final visit with my mother. The day after, we were to leave for Wyoming to take possession of the ranch I'd bought. We again told her about the vast open spaces of Wyoming, the hills, the valleys that provided coziness to the wild terrain, and Piney Creek, which ran alongside the edge of the ranch, providing water for growing hay. It moved along past the thick willow banks, curling and twisting, eventually joining the Powder River, then the Yellowstone, flowing on to the Missouri and Mississippi rivers. We told her the Bighorn Mountains were older than the famous Tetons and, because of that, less sharp. But my mother had no interest. Half an hour after lunch, she left to play bridge. She was an avid and very good cardplayer. She did not return until late in the afternoon.

I became teary after she drove away, hurt that she would not even listen to the joy I had found in a new life. I wanted to lash out at this cold woman. Her love and focus fell on herself. My life, pleasures, and pains had always eluded her interest. A horrid thought crossed my mind. Was I doing the same thing with my children? The difference being that I included them in my life and did not ship them off to live with others at their young age. But still, I was dragging them along on my impulsive choices.

My mother dressed in a luxurious silk muumuu of pinks and gold for dinner that last night, with her sapphire-and-diamond bracelet, and pearl earrings to match the pearls about her neck. My mother had a beautiful face, even now. Her wrinkles, I thought, added to her expressions of mirth or outrage. Her intelligence, her charm, and her wit made her a very popular invitee for cocktails and dinner parties, even ones given by her nemesis, Clare Booth Luce. Mrs. Luce was considered the "hostess with the mostest," a position my mother angled to take away for herself.

Mary Flueger, my mother's best friend on the island, and Tom Vaughan, my mother's decorator, joined us. Mrs. Flueger also wore a silk muumuu, hers in shades of blue, and she, too, was adorned in jewels. While my kids were glued to the television, we sat on the patio in the low light, having cocktails.

"Your gardens and house look so beautiful," I told my mother. "And isn't it wonderful to have Hanna with you? Bless Hanna. She was always such a good cook. And Aagot, she takes such pride in your house and adores you. They both have been with you for so many years. And now you have a man who knows about gardening to take care of the place when you are back on Long Island, as well. It makes life easy, doesn't it?" I said, smiling. "I know you are always struggling to get good help."

Mary Flueger complimented me on the pretty peasant blouse and the dangling earrings I was wearing. "With your long dark hair, you look a bit like a Gypsy," she said. My mother did not comment on my remarks, but turned to John and asked him to make her another daiquiri. "And what will you do in Wyoming besides painting?" she asked as he passed by her, taking her glass to the bar inside. Over his shoulder, John replied, "Raise a herd of cattle."

As we sipped our drinks and nibbled on pâté, John began telling stories about *Reader's Digest* authors, some he had worked with, others from just hearsay gossip. They were funny tales, told out of school, which made them far more interesting, and John was a good storyteller. My mother loved to hear publishing gossip, particularly anything secretive about a celebrity. She laughed and chatted with John, reminisced about Maugham and his *"awful"* companion, Alan Searle. She continued on about her travels with Daphne du Maurier in Greece, which brought up Gertrude Lawrence and Irving Stone. My mother and John had a high old time swapping stories, each trying to outdo the other; both knew the game beyond the stories.

John Kings was a charmer. He knew how to flatter, he knew how to amuse, and his one-liners were truly funny. After more than a few cocktails, we were called to dinner.

"Bring the pâté, will you, darling?" my mother said as she passed by me. "And get the children to the table," she continued over her shoulder, taking Tom's arm. John, with a sidelong glance at me, took Mrs. Flueger by the arm, and I followed, hors d'oeuvres in hand.

I found Ellen and John Jr. on the floor together, watching television. I turned off the TV to cries of "No, not yet. I want . . ." They appeared rumpled and happy before I made them stand. I straightened John Jr.'s clean shorts and shirt and smoothed Ellen's wild hair, remembering how Nelson and I had been spruced up to be presented to my parents.

My mother became upset when I sat next to John at the table. "Husbands and wives do not sit next to each other at my table," she announced, sounding like a dowager duchess.

"I am not John's wife," I said, laughing. "And what does it matter?"

Oh dear, I am not her favorite child, I thought to myself, and I am going to pay for my last little quip. And pay I did. Later in the evening, she couldn't help herself from taking digs at my clothes and hair, and she needled me by telling me how "wonderful John Sargent is." I smiled and said nothing. I tried to keep my mind on Wyoming.

We left shortly after dinner, giving excuses that we needed time to pack and get the children to bed. We both thanked my mother for her thoughtfulness, and I told her I was so pleased that she had included John in her gift of this trip.

"Your generosity made our holiday time a superb treat," I told her as we hugged at the front door. The kids squirmed and looked bored. John hugged her and kissed her on the cheek. He thanked her for "a phenomenal adventure in the Hawaiian islands, from the beauty of your house to the primitive paradise of Molokai, all of it." I left with a sense of relief and a sense of failure. My mother never would like me. But then, I didn't like her. I just needed her love.

We arrived by plane in Sheridan, Wyoming, at three in the afternoon on New Year's Eve, 1965. From above as we came down, the hills and fields were covered in clean white snow, the shadowed valleys shaded from gray to black. We were to stay for a week at the Trails End Motel on the north end of town. The owners, Laural and Jean Kinnison, were the reason. We had become friends when we had stayed there the past summer. I would home-school both children here for the week, so they wouldn't get behind in their classwork.

By prearrangement, at nine on New Year's Day, I signed the papers and wrote a check for the ranch. "I am going to miss the old place, those trees around the house I kept watered, and all those beautiful hills. My horses will miss it, too," the seller, Windy Carlson, commented as we got up to leave the table at the title company. His wife, a gray-haired woman neatly dressed in country style, was teary-eyed. She held my hand in hers and told me to call if we had questions about anything.

"Nice to know ya," Windy said with a half-toothless grin as we shook hands on the sidewalk.

The ranch was mine, but I thought of it as ours. In the traditional way I was brought up, the man paid. But our relationship was not traditional. Even so, as we drove out to the ranch in our rented Jeep, I felt cross that I was paying for the ranch, the Jeep, and the meals. My crossness was not really fair. John and I had had a talk about money before we'd left New York, and I had agreed to pay all bills for two years to allow John time to be a painter, find a gallery, get established in the art world. After that, he was on his own. He had to find money to pay his child support for two daughters, one in Australia and a three-year-old in England—perhaps by doing some editorial or writing work for the *Digest*. John had done nothing that I knew of to earn money, other than the money he'd made from his exhibition in the gallery in New York the winter before.

"Why?" I wondered. Except—I knew his life had been a relay race between New York and London, then with the Hawaii trip and Wyoming the previous summer, what more could he have done?

Why did I promise to do things that I resented? Partly because it was the momentary flood of love, which still gets me in trouble, or a sensation within me that I can help support, alter, relieve, or make happen something in another's life. Forget mine. I pay little real attention to the nuances of what I do. I am still a rescuer at age eighty, just not such an ambitious one.

We barely fit in the Jeep with our bulky winter clothes. Packed snow, deep and rutted in places, covered the streets in town. Snow was piled high on each side of Route 14 as we traveled southeast to the ranch, the pavement snow-covered as well, with occasional patches of black ice that made driving slow and nerve-racking.

Once at the ranch, John drove us over the hills where possible. Our four horses, which were part of my deal with Windy, grazed on a side hill, pawing the snow away with their front hooves to get at the grass. They were far too thin.

Windy had told us, "They'll come trotting right to you if you shake those oats in the bucket. I left you some there to make it easy for ya." John Jr. tumbled out with the bucket, and Ellen eased out the other side feetfirst. I struggled with a snow boot that had rubbed my heel raw in the few hours I had worn it. John came around the front of the Jeep with his new hat, which had earflaps that hung down, untied. The strings on each flap twirled in the wind.

"Shake that bucket of oats," John reminded Ellen, who now held the bucket against her chest, seemingly afraid it would be snatched away. All the fur-coated horses trotted toward us, down a snow-covered hill in the sunshine, the Bighorn Mountains in the background, their granite peaks against a cerulean sky.

We slid our way down the hill to Piney Creek Road, then drove up to the main road and up onto the small bit of ranch property on the other side of the main road. The view of the mountains from there was lofty; no hill or fence broke the power of those Bighorn Mountains. We drove down to the underpass, slipping there where horses had used the way to get to water in the pond. We crept under the road and stopped. We had been warned by our neighbor Bruce Collins earlier that morning when we stopped by to say hello that this area we were approaching was boggy, not to be trusted with a vehicle.

John said, "Let's try it anyway. I'll race down and across. Speed is the thing over the ice. I think it is thick enough to hold up the Jeep. But let's test it with our bodies to make sure."

We piled out of the car, zipped up against the freezing cold, and put on our gloves and hats. Like the dwarfs in *Snow White*, we heigh-ho, heigh-ho'd down to the pond's mouth and in unison jumped up and down on the snow-covered ice, all four of us in the same spot, breathing out a steamy mist. Not a crack sounded, no movement of ice at all.

"It's a go," John called out as he ran up the hill to the Jeep. The hum of its motor became a roar, then a *crunch*, then nothing. John bellowed, "OH DAMN." The front wheels of the Jeep crashed through the not-so-thick ice and sank nose-down. Not a bird peeped. Not even a whistle from the wind. There was no backing out of this dilemma. I sent the kids, bundled in their warm jackets, hats, and mittens, to walk to the Collinses' house.

A banged-up old pickup stopped on the road as the children disappeared around the corner. "Howdy," an unkempt and unsteady cowboy called out.

"Hi," I said with a bit of distaste. He came up to me with a wide grin and, handing me a pint of whiskey, said, "Have a slug." He had that sour smell of stale alcohol. I didn't take him up on the whiskey.

"I am Leon Hawkey," he said, hand outstretched. I shook his hand, turning my face away. He was a small, wiry man with bad teeth and an engaging smile.

"Looks like you could do with some help," he said as John climbed up onto the highway. The two men began plotting about winches and chains, the best position for Leon's pickup, with no question if the pickup was powerful enough for the job.

I decided I was not needed and walked down the half-mile to join the kids at the Collinses' place. Icy wind lashed at my cheeks, made my eyes water, and swept through my corduroy pants, numbing my legs. Despite the cold, this landscape fed me, opening my mind like a window in springtime. I could feel it as I walked.

Leon and John drove into the Collinses' yard an hour later. We had drinks and sandwiches for lunch, thanks to Bruce and his wife, Mary Jane Collins.

We left at week's end, having talked to the electric company, the telephone company, the bank, the lawyer, and the car dealer. All welcomed us and were helpful with the inevitable snags. There were twenty-six bars but only five or six restaurants in town. Culinary arts had not yet come to Sheridan.

Back in New York, John, the kids, and I all talked about our big move in June, what to take, what we didn't need. The process of disconnecting from our lives on the East Coast was heart-wrenching at times for the kids and me, because this had been our home all our lives. For me, leaving the Catskills home was the hardest. It had been my "security blanket" home. The trees, the beaver pond, the vegetable garden, the mountains, the small streams, the bunchberry that grew in the woods, the oak, maple, ash, and aspen leaves that glowed like a rich Persian rug in the autumn light, all that and more I would lose. My family, except for my sister Pucky, I had already lost. I hadn't spoken to Nelson since he'd cut off my income. He had become someone to fear. The company business was all we'd shared the past five or six years, and often we were on opposing sides. I missed the closeness we had had: "I love you, Nelson," I told him in his office before leaving for Wyoming, "but I don't like you. I don't like the bullying way you behave." He had no answer. I could tell by his blank expression that he didn't understand what I was saying.

Some friends I would keep. They would visit in the years to come, interested to see the wide-open space, the quiet and richness that could come from a walk by the creek. I would miss Mrs. Humphrey, the woman who cooked and cared for our family in the big house for over six years, who could recite Shakespeare from memory. It felt like a lifetime for both of us, we had become so close. And I would miss Bubby, who took care of the outside, mowed the lawn, and fixed broken mechanical things. He would drive my green Chevy station wagon to Wyoming with a full load of items I wanted safe, such as antique furnishings too delicate for a moving van. I gave the house in the Catskills to Synanon, a drug rehabilitation program. Synanon was created and run by Charles Dederich; its main branch was in Santa Monica, California. The house would be a home for New York–area drug addicts who joined the program. Members of the neighboring Onteora Club, a bastion of Republican conservatives, were enraged. "They are not our kind," one of them said to me, and offered to buy my place at whatever price I demanded. I turned him down and made a clay sculpture of his head when I got to Wyoming. I have it still.

In New York there was my sidekick helper, Padget Fredricks, to part from. He was my housekeeper, cook, and friend. He comforted me when loneliness got me down, helped and supported me with my kids, even picked me up at Smiley Blanton's when I had taken LSD. That took courage. Over several years of my marriage, he'd made an amusing joke out of the unbearable, allowing me to keep going. He'd come to us from an employment agency, sent to clean the house. We ended up painting my bedroom for two days instead. Oh, how I would miss Padget.

EIGHTEEN

Why Don't I Learn to Keep My Mouth Shut?

That first summer on the ranch was a day-by-long-day affair of shoveling sheep manure out of the shed. I tried to mow the tall grasses in the backyard but kept finding and throwing out the bones of elk, deer, and antelope buried in the high grasses. I learned to dry jeans by putting them on jean stretchers, then hanging them on the line. The stretchers gave jeans a sharp crease in the front. Wind caught them like sails, tossed them into the ditch. Wicked winds blew dust into every nook, including the insides of kitchen cupboards in the used trailer I had bought to house us. Somehow, we had accumulated seven dogs, which had to be fed and sometimes groomed. John Jr. had a canary named Chirpy. Dozens of feral cats had been fed on the place before the past owners moved off. I like birds, which means no cats. It is a heritage thing. My father's mother wrote a number of bird books, and my father hated cats. Only one wintered with us somewhere in the sheds. We found it frozen on the Chevy's engine block a morning after the temperature during the night had fallen to thirty-five degrees below zero. This could be rough country.

We got warnings and lectures on how to survive if caught in our vehicle in a snowstorm. The following are some of the most sensible: Never leave your vehicle in a snowstorm if stuck. In winter, carry life-support items such as food and chocolate bars for energy, a pot to piss in, water, a flashlight, heavy-duty warm clothes, and a sleeping bag. I follow most of these rules of winter travel now.

House renovation began that summer of 1966, with Oscar Jurosek as contractor, John Kings on design, and a group of plumbers, electricians, stonemasons, Sheetrockers, and painters to complete the job. On August 5, 1966, they were our only wedding guests, save for Bobby Gibbs, who flew his plane in from his ranch on the Powder River, and his wife, Martha, who drove from nearby Buffalo with my children. She had been overnighting the kids. We picked the justice of the peace for his name, Mr. Greenleaf. He married John and me in front of the fireplace in our house, then with no doors or windows. We celebrated afterward on the porch of the studio barn, where John and I slept but which eventually would become our studios. We served beer and pretzels, Coke and cookies. Everyone wore jeans. Ellen was very cross with me for not telling her I was getting married prior to the event. "Darling, we hardly knew the date ourselves until the day before," I told her, but her rancor continued. I had been the one who pushed for marriage, because I sensed John would stray less quickly if we were married. Silly me.

Our neighbors dropped by almost daily to watch the house project. Bob Miller came to bum cigarettes. He had given up smoking but couldn't quit completely. Bruce Collins, our closest neighbor, loaned us equipment we did not yet have. He also helped us with buying cattle from Ray Shreve, an old rancher up north near Ranchester, who had a good reputation for honesty and a fine herd of cattle. His grandson, Cliff, works with me today as carpenter and maintenance man for the houses, barns, and cabins on my properties. He is the finest craftsman, a sometimes poet, a lover of early bluegrass, jazz, and country music, and a most devout reader of *The New Yorker*.

We went to sales and country auctions. John bought stuff, from hammers to a sickle bar, while I sketched people. Ellen and John Jr. climbed fences and trees with other ranch kids, or they complained endlessly, wanting to go home. It was often very hot. We all sweat. The ranch auctions were a country event, fun to attend even if we wanted nothing. We always came home with something—a box of canning jars because we wanted the lids, an assortment of household tools, fence posts, a mailbox. But the true treasure was the gab with neighbors, the swapping of a story or a recipe. With this small bit of conversation came a sense of belonging in a community. We ate good home cooking, ending with pies made by the surrounding ranch ladies. They were great bakers.

The sun shone daily. If it rained, it lasted but a few minutes. I was a sun worshiper. Those clear-sky days of solid sun tanned my face and limbs to a rosy brown. I was anonymous; no Doubleday heiress taint followed me west. Those who knew stayed silent. I breathed so much easier. I talked with the contractor about costs, and with John. I paid the bills for everything. I set John up with a loan at the First National Bank, with my Doubleday stock as collateral. It took more stock than usually required because the stock, impossible to trade, had no market value. John was raising a herd of Hereford cattle to provide him with an income to cover his expenses. Neither of us knew anything about raising cattle, but everyone around us was in the cattle business. It must be possible to earn a living that way, I thought.

During the spring and summer, there was a great deal of news about the Sheridan Inn, which was scheduled for demolition if a buyer couldn't be found. I had heard about the inn, stories of Buffalo Bill and Theodore Roosevelt staying or drinking there. The enormous beams that supported the breadth of the dining room ceiling were famous locally. Because of all the publicity, the train ride, the bake sales, and the tours to save the Sheridan Inn, I felt pressed to write a letter of encouragement to the public in the early summer of 1967. The following is part of that letter I wrote to the editor of the *Sheridan Press*.

> The building is more than the peeling clapboard walls, its importance is more than the fact that Buffalo Bill or any other man slept here. It is our heritage, a symbol of the people who believed in America, believed enough to move West to create a life in the wilderness. They, their spirit, built the Inn and made it a meeting place that became the center of the community.

I felt the Sheridan Inn commanded a place in the community; it was, and is, an architectural and historical site of importance. If we don't know where we have come from, we cannot know who we are, or where we're going. The building stood as a talisman for the community, a well-honored and noteworthy historical structure. While I had been by it many times, I'd never been in it.

On a Sunday afternoon in November 1967, I got a call from Pucky, begging me to go to Hawaii to be with our mother during her cataract surgery. No one else in the family could make it. I left on half a day's notice with my children. John Kings had to mail my letter to the *Sheridan Press*.

He called me in Hawaii a few days later to say they were coming with the wrecking ball the next day to destroy the inn. The landowner supposedly had contracted to put up a gas station on the land. I decided to put my money where my mouth was. By phone from Hawaii, I made an anonymous full-price offer through my lawyer, Henry Burgess, thinking I would turn around and donate the inn to the Sheridan Historical Society, take a tax deduction, and accomplish a good deed. It didn't work out that way. The Historical Society accepted my cash offer but refused to take the inn. Goddammit, now what? I wondered. I came home a week later, befuddled by my purchase, and my stupidity for not getting assurance before the purchase that the Historical Society would accept the inn and surrounds.

A month after I bought it, Henry looked me in the eye over his desk. "Neltje, what are you going to do with the Sheridan Inn?" Henry was a man who commanded attention. He was a power broker in town, I knew. Guilt, panic, and shame at my stupidity paralyzed my mind. I didn't know what to do about the inn. I wanted to be left alone to paint. I have found my voice; now let me be. But I didn't dare say it.

I stalled for time. "Henry, I have no idea. It never occurred to me that the Historical Society would refuse my offer of the inn," I finally said.

Days later, Henry called and said, "Look, I've talked to my wife, Mary. She would be happy to meet with you to talk about what to do with the inn," and he gave me her number. It took me days to get up the courage to call Mary. I felt so stupid. I was now stuck with a broken-down building that the people of Sheridan were waiting to see restored. Mary was knowledgeable about everyone in town, where to get what done. She was an artist herself, a painter, and she well understood my cries of pain over the years while I fixed up the inn. I had a monstrous job before me, one that would take me from my family and devour all my time, allowing none for the painting I'd planned to do. I did not feel I had a choice. I had put my money where my mouth had taken me. A lesson to be learned from that.

I wanted to remain anonymous. Mary Burgess and I came up with the story that we had been hired by the new owner to do the bar remodeling. My first step even before I called Mary was to see the interior of the building. The Historical Society gave tours of the inn for a nominal sum.

On a Tuesday morning in June 1967, I walked up the green-painted wooden stairs of the Sheridan Inn and across the wide covered porch and opened the glass front door. Lyda Campbell, whom I would come to know so well, a thin, frail-appearing woman of a goodly age, took my money and we started the tour together. Her passion for the building was fierce. She told me bits of history, stories of local people and of Miss Kate, the housekeeper at the inn. I asked to see the old kitchen. There in that room, looking up at the thick grease hanging in webbed globules off the old tin ceiling, I saw the years it would take, the hours and hours of planning and decision making, the spending, the stress, everything it would take to give life back to this building. I felt the weight of a massive wave crashing over me. I couldn't breathe. *This is just too much. I am an artist. I need my time to paint,* my heart cried out.

First I decided to redo the bar, then called the Stockade Room. Since bars are said to make money, that would be the sensible way to start. It had booths made with lumpy, diseased wood and fake cowhide, a theme carried throughout the bar. The renovation began with Knute Johnson as carpenter and contractor in charge. An architect, Tom Muth, made drawings, moving the old Buffalo Bill Bar, still owned by the Historical Society, to the other side of the room. He designed paneling for the entire space, including what had been separate gaming rooms. These would become a more intimate area for drinking, partially shielded from view at the street entry. The old rule for Western bars was that upon entry, you had to be able to see everyone in the bar, in case your enemy was there, ready to shoot you.

Mary's friend Buster Metz of Metz Beverage, beer and pop distributors, instructed us on the equipment needed for the actual bar. The list kept growing: beer coolers for extra kegs, triple sinks, and two cash registers. My mind swirled with so much new information to take in, so many decisions to make on the spot. I had to learn on the job. What scared me most was the prospect of doing a shoddy renovation. Would I fail because I was not a local, but a "dude" from New York?

In the meantime at home, John had leased additional acreage, and I had bought the Wolf Ranch on Box Elder Creek so he could run more cattle. Bud Pilch, the plumber, was his cowhand—perhaps working for plumber's wages; I didn't know but thought it possible. I knew I should look into the situation and change that wage scale if I was right. But the business of raising cattle was John's to run, and he was doing a good job of it, from all outward signs. I had to stay out of it. I also knew I could not face the possible consequences of having a row over John's use of the loan money just now. He would probably get angry, think I was interfering and not trusting him. He might leave. He'd left three wives before me. My greatest fear was to be left alone. I didn't know how to cure or stop this overriding panic that undermined every close relationship. I didn't know how to be a grown-up.

John Kings got a show of his paintings in Aspen just beyond the end of our first year in Wyoming. We were both thrilled by the idea of the show and having a bit of a vacation. The kids were with their dad at the end of the summer of 1967, on their monthly summer visit, in accordance with the divorce agreement. John invited me to take my wax sculptures to show Elizabeth, the gallery owner. We drove to Aspen in John's yellow truck. His paintings were under cover in the rear, my sculptures packed carefully in boxes in the backseat. John hung the show with Elizabeth the day after we arrived, while I window-shopped, gawking at the elegance of ski clothes and furs.

Two days after the show opened, I asked John when I could show Elizabeth my work. The following day, John said he would invite her to the condo where we were staying in Aspen, where I had my six wax sculptures and two bronze casts arranged on a table. At the last minute, he called to tell me he was coming to pick me up to take me and the sculptures to Elizabeth's studio. I was disappointed and upset. I had hoped she would see them on my turf, where I felt less intimidated. Elizabeth was a beautiful, statuesque strawberry blonde, charismatic and worldly. She also was a well-known artist here and probably elsewhere. At Elizabeth's large studio, I put my sculptures on a shelf by a window fairly close to the elevator. They seemed small to me now, the emotional tension less apparent. John spoke briefly about each work, defining errors he saw in each one, words he had never said before. He left abruptly. The elevator door swallowed him up. Elizabeth and I faced each other.

There was nothing to say. I was speechless with hurt. I am ashamed I hadn't the courage to lash out at John, as he deserved. My upbringing of "the man is always right," as I saw my mother behave, as I did in my marriage with John Sargent, continued because I did not know how to act otherwise. It would take years to learn another way. Later, John said nothing about his comments, behaved as though nothing had been said.

A few years after the Aspen show, he got a show in San Francisco. He had to drive the art out in his pickup truck. I flew out to join him later. The children were taken care of by Vivian Patterson, an intelligent middle-aged woman who had come to work in the lobby shop at the Sheridan Inn the second year it was open. She quickly became the central chief of protection for me by solving the petty hurts, whines, and complaints of the inn staff. She also became an extra mom to my kids and often came to the house with her husband, Bob, to stay with them when I had to be away. They cared for Ellen and John Jr. as though they were their children.

John Kings's exhibition in San Francisco was at the Herbert Hoover Gallery. I said I wanted no society publicity about me and my family, so no interviews. But when I got off the plane, John met me with, "We are meeting with the society-page editor of the *San Francisco Chronicle* at the gallery in forty-five minutes." It was just as it had been with John Sargent and Wolf. But I did it, even though seething inwardly. I was the dutiful wife. I talked with the society editor. A photograph appeared of me in my fine black cotton dress with long sleeves and high neck, a dress reminiscent of the past century in America, a woman of the early West. My long hair was piled up on my head, with a wisp floating down my neck. The headline read HEIRESS AT ART OPENING. I was furious. My mother phoned from Hawaii and said, "You had cow plop on your head. Why?" There was a line or two in the article about my restoration of the Sheridan Inn, which was the reason I had talked with the society editor. I had thought I could get free publicity about the inn.

As I became more involved with the Sheridan Inn rehabilitation, my days were spent on site in town or afar, searching out light fixtures, furnishings, and equipment. I formed a board of people who advised me on what would interest local people in the way of historical items for decoration, or whether a gift shop in the entry hall would be a travesty. Jim Forrest, a past chairman of the art department at the University of

Wyoming and later director of the Bradford Brinton Memorial Museum in nearby Big Horn, told me the board was a brilliant solution and that "every marriage should have one." The board was a precaution, for John Kings often did not agree with me, leading to bitter fights between us. I sensed he was jealous of the attention I got for doing a good job with the renovation and early running of the inn. "Oh groan," I muttered to myself. "This puffing up of a male ego constantly is a bore."

The saloon opened on April 27, 1968, to a huge crowd of ranchers, town folk, bankers and lawyers and their wives. It was a celebration of perseverance for all those who had worked so long and hard to save the inn before I dropped into the picture. For me, it was a sense of completion of a job well done. I was proud of what I had accomplished in making the saloon a handsome and appealing space. The problem of running the saloon became the job of the manager, Chic Madia. I had hired him away from the American Legion Club in Cheyenne.

Some of the rooms upstairs on the second and third floors of the inn were to be made over into living quarters for Chic, his wife, Dorothy, and their two children. An architect, John Doerr, drew up the plans, Knute Johnson and crew did the work, and Chic was to oversee things on a day-to-day basis. I was exhausted. I needed time off: to paint, to think, to write.

To recuperate, John and I took a trip to Martinique. We lay in the sun on a nudist beach, ate French food, and lazed about. I spent time reading novels beneath the palm trees. We took drives over the mountains and along the sea, and watched the final construction of the first Club Med. John flew off to visit his daughter Tarka in England, and I flew home to the ranch. My children were with their father in New York for Easter vacation. I had my home to myself.

Ellen and John Jr. spent a month with their father every summer and every other Christmas and Easter vacation. I missed them when they were gone, their physical being—their hands at the table, legs on the sofa, anger and happiness evident on their faces. The house was far too quiet. I had never learned to detach enough, not feel a painful sense of loss when I sent them off on the plane to be with their dad. Nor did I like my possessive jealousy, my feeling that they were mine, not his. He had paid so little attention to them when we were together. He didn't do any better now, from what they told me. He always had someone to care for them in summer or a girlfriend to share the care, as when he took them to Aspen skiing or elsewhere for Easter. His inability to connect emotionally played out in all his relationships. I felt for the kids. I told Ellen once when she felt neglected and unloved by her dad, "Darling Ellen, he loves you as much as he loves anybody, as much as he is capable of loving."

"It helps to hear that," she said.

On a trip to New York at Christmastime that year, we all stayed at a hotel on the East Side. Early one morning, the kids walked over to their dad's apartment from the hotel and left me a note. I felt guilty I had not been up earlier to give them something for breakfast. My dream of being the perfect mother showed many cracks. They were growing up. They wanted to do things on their own. I was experiencing separation anxiety. At home I was always so busy at the inn that I had had little time to reflect on what was truly going on.

We flew back home in early January so the kids could be at school on time. I was at the inn one night when we had a piano player in the corner of the saloon playing old Cole Porter tunes. The bar was empty and a Billings salesman came in. I walked down the line of barstools to greet him. We talked for a while before he said, "You know what you need here? You need girls. Girls girls girls. They make a bar profitable."

"I know," I said, "but you see, I have the Historical Society looking down on me; they think they still own the place. In fact, they do own the old back and front bar and the two side cupboards in this room. Besides, there are no rooms ready upstairs." Late-night talk was all it was.

But he went on: "I can get the girls for you; that is no problem. I know a woman in the business in Billings who would run it for you. So you would be clean as far as the locals are concerned. You would make a tidy sum from the business the girls brought in, plus the rent they might pay. What do you think?"

"Hmm, interesting," I replied. I put on my coat to go home. John and the kids were away. I had no one to tell this story to.

"When can you get the Sheetrock on the walls?" he asked, following me toward the swinging saloon doors.

"I don't know. I think it would take maybe three to six months to fix up a few rooms," I said over my shoulder. "Good night all," I called as I passed through the doorway to the front hall. I drove the twenty miles home on that moonless night, thinking about the possibilities of profit for the saloon, moral ethics, and jail time.

In the hall after a luncheon one day, Judge Ilsley asked me what I was going to do with the upstairs rooms. Laughing, I replied, "I'll have girls. They are good for the bar business, you know. What kind of slice would you take, Judge?"

He looked down at me. He was very big and tall. He said, "I don't see paying for what I can get for free," and moved on down the hall, greeting friends and shrugging himself into his blue wool coat.

Six months later, I was asleep at home when the phone woke me. It was ten-thirty at night. I was groggy and did not have any idea of whom I was talking to.

"I am here at the saloon with the merchandise from Billings, Neltje." A male voice rang with excitement.

I remembered now, in the darkness, and knew exactly who this was on the phone. Unbelievable that he'd taken me seriously, without any other contact. What to say to him now? "I haven't gotten the Sheetrock on the walls," I said as I slipped out of bed so I wouldn't wake John.

"Well, then, what do you want me to do with the merchandise? I have to be in Gillette tomorrow," he whined.

"Take the merchandise with you," I said. I put the phone back in its cradle with great care.

The year after opening the saloon, I realized I had to start plans for the major renovation: the front interior of the building needed redesigning, which involved the stairway, the old barbershop I had used for an office, which would become the lobby shop, the ladies' parlor, the main dining room, a banquet room, restrooms, and the kitchen.

I had been asked to serve on the Sheridan Chamber of Commerce's Travel and Convention Committee. I went to various towns with the other committee members, owners of the bars, restaurants, hotels and motels in Sheridan. Our job was to persuade whatever group it was to hold its convention in Sheridan. In Newcastle, we bid on the sheep growers' convention; in Cheyenne, we bid on the Wyoming stock growers' convention. My vision of success was: the Sheridan Inn would need to get most of the convention business, meals, banquets, and the use of meeting rooms. And it happened that way.

I had become friends with Harry and Mildred Smith and their son, Paul. They owned and operated the Hitching Post in Cheyenne, a good-size motel with large convention facilities as well as restaurants to feed the general public at the same time. I knew that the additional banquet room at the inn would mean we could serve five hundred guests when the folding doors were opened, making one big space with the main dining room. There was no room that large in Sheridan. Plus, we could serve meals in the saloon and parlor at the same time for the general public. We could serve up to 250 people for banquets or meetings in the planned new addition, called the Wyoming Room. The town needed these facilities. The Wyoming stock growers were increasing in number. They would need banquet service for over four hundred soon. I wanted to be able to bid for their business. My competitive juices came out from wherever they had been hiding. I was on a roll to make the Sheridan Inn famous beyond Wyoming. At slack times in the local food business, small conventions and daylong business meetings could add to the inn's revenue and provide good publicity locally. In the meantime, I went over the layout plans weekly, prepared by John Doerr and a kitchen consultant from Denver.

I never stopped to question if I really wanted to spend my life this way. I had bought the inn. It was my responsibility to make it work. I made decision after decision, obsessed and determined, with an energy that flowed from who knew where. My natural surroundings fed me and kindled my spirit. I was president of my own company. So there, John Sargent and Nelson. I am not the ditz you tried to make me out to be.

Shortly after I bought the inn, I was appointed by Governor Stanley K. Hathaway to the Wyoming Travel Commission. It was a plum political job. I had always been a Democrat and was appointed as such. However, the local press raised a ruckus because I had supported a Republican in the primary elections years before. I didn't know that would make me a Republican on file. Local Democrats who had worked their way up through the party ranks resented the fact that I, who was not local, had gotten this appointment. I don't blame them. Perhaps they were the ones trying to prove I was really a Republican. They failed.

Because of the notoriety of being the owner of the Sheridan Inn, I met a number of the important people in Wyoming, politicians in state government, motel and restaurant owners, other businesspeople, the statewide economic movers and shakers. They were supportive and generously insightful concerning the restoration. Harry and Paul Smith of the Hitching Post, which housed the legislature when in session in Cheyenne, took me under their wing at the Restaurant Show in Denver. The first booth, right by the entrance, was promoting Hershey chocolate. A young man was telling me the virtues of their new individual packets of sauce, which provided portion control for ice-cream sundaes. I didn't want portion control. That was the opposite of how I thought and how I wanted to run the inn. Gracious plentitude, as I had known in the fine restaurants of New York, was my goal.

"But what if you want to serve a larger portion?" I asked, annoyed.

He did not answer my question. He just asked, "What number scoop do you use?" *Oh my God!* Panic set in. What could I say? Right then, my fantasy of breezing through the show as though I knew what I was doing imploded. I admitted I knew nothing about the food business. I had no idea what size scoop I would use for ice cream or mashed potatoes. "Scoop size" lay bare my terror of all I did not know, from portion control to guest checks, from walk-in freezers to broilers and griddles, from soups to rolls and mashed potatoes, from prime rib to ice cream and apple pie. How the hell was I going to do this? The hall was huge, full of vendors with old and new devices to make a professional commercial kitchen function at its best.

I was out of my depth and needed help but was much too proud to say so to my peers in the business. But they knew. They watched. They said little. A kind sales rep from Green Brothers of Broomfield, Colorado, helped me trim the kitchen budget by choosing different equipment. The soup kettle that would have served five hundred was replaced by a huge roasting pan in which you could cook eighty chicken breasts in a sauce, or meatballs for two hundred. The numbers were frightening. I loved to cook, to create new dishes at home. I read cookbooks like others read novels, and then I cooked a dish, never looking at a recipe, just by my memory of taste. But this was a very different world, where my creative vision needed to be enlarged and curbed at the same time.

NINETEEN

Discovering What I Don't Know

We opened the main dining room on August 2, 1969. I invited members of the community to eat lunch and dinner free of charge for two days to find the flaws in cooking and service.

We opened to the public on August 4. For lunch we offered everything from hamburgers to quiche Lorraine, for dinner prime rib, as the inn had always been famous for it. We also served large shrimp with garlic and parsley, chicken Kiev, and many other simple gourmet items. The dining room filled up at lunchtime, and we had bus tours booked in the Wyoming Room, as well. We raced to keep up. I stayed to watch and help the first night, after being a line cook as an extra hand at lunchtime. We were also serving an informal lunch and dinner in the saloon on paper place mats, instead of on the white linens we had in the dining room.

Paul and Harry Smith called to say they'd read about the opening in the Cheyenne paper and were cross that I hadn't let them know ahead of time. As a surprise, they and Tom Gee, owner of the Washakie Hotel in Worland, Wyoming, a friend and the chairman of the Wyoming Travel Commission, had planned to show up in tuxedos, with white towels over their left arms, to act as waiters for opening night. I was so touched that my competition for conventions had turned out to be such generous friends.

The main dining room continued to fill through hunting season with local folks and tourists. One hundred and fifty-two people could eat in the dining room as it was set up. A woman from North Carolina booked a party of two hundred in the Wyoming Room. She said she was "famous for her yellow parties," and waved her aging arm to sweep the entire room.

"No problem at all," I replied. "We will cover the ceiling with yellow balloons."

Her husband ordered special whiskeys and wines, and their menu included lobster Newburg. I ordered Maine lobsters flown in. On the morning of the banquet, we were notified the lobsters would not arrive in Sheridan at 10:20 that morning, as contracted, but would arrive at the Billings airport, two hours away from the inn, at one in the afternoon. I immediately dispatched a driver to Billings. The entire crew—bartenders, shop manager, business office personnel, and I—worried. We were twitchy and irritable.

Ellen and I had blown up three hundred yellow balloons the day before and pinned them to the ceiling. One came wafting down in midafternoon, and we blanched, certain that a cascade of yellow balloons on the dinner plates was not what the lady "famous for her yellow parties" had in mind. When not snapping at one another, the waitresses and I set the tables, and laughed. The chef made a Newburg sauce I had never tasted before. I wanted a rich, creamy sauce with lots of sherry. I made him redo it. He was not happy. And we waited and waited for the lobsters to arrive.

At 3:45 P.M., more than a dozen crates of lobsters were brought in through the back entry to the kitchen. The kitchen crew, a few waitresses who had come in early, and I undid the packaging with yelps of relief.

"Let's have a race," I said, feeling giddy. "Everyone pick a lobster. We'll line them up by the ovens, and the first lobster to reach the coffee machine wins a prize," I called out. At the sound of crashing pots, the signal to start the race, only five lobsters did a bit more than twitch, creeping a few inches across the terra-cotta tile floor before finding it an alien surface and lying down, despite screams of encouragement.

For me, working in the kitchen, fixing plates of food with the kitchen crew to be taken to banquet tables, was like putting on a theatrical production. We timed ourselves for each event and tried to shave down our time at each subsequent banquet. Mass servings were about the coordination of people working together. Portions had to be equal on each plate and the plate had to look appetizing—no dribbled gravy. The food had to be hot. I had covers for the plates and wheeled carts for fast distribution.

As in everything, it came down to willing human effort. We rolled out the dinner plates one after another from the two entryways to the Wyoming Room. The guests had had drinks downstairs in the Root Cellar and were just finishing the vichyssoise when we entered. Each waitress had a station, where she was responsible for picking up plates, serving, overseeing a busboy, delivering water, and answering all requests promptly. I had to train some waitresses on how to pour without dribbling. Little things like that took up so much time.

The party was a huge success. I passed my first large society event with yellow balloons aloft.

For over a year, I had been putting together the information for a legal battle with my mother and brother over Nelson serving as trustee for all the family trusts. I wanted to replace him with a neutral trustee appointed by the courts, someone who then might consider going public with Doubleday stock. Every Sunday, I worked in my office at home, going through old legal and trust papers, letters, and notes, sending pertinent ones on to my legal team at Vaughan & Vaughan in New York. I had gone back to New York with Henry Burgess to find a lawyer to take my case, as Henry was not licensed to work in New York State. We ran into the problem of finding a firm that had not been involved with Doubleday & Company. One lawyer, from a firm that had done work over fifteen years ago with Doubleday, said, "What you need is an FNJ."

"What does FNJ mean?" I asked.

"A friendly New York judge."

I was not going to buy off a judge. My belief in the integrity of the American legal system faltered.

I had worked many long and painful hours on this legal battle to be heard, to show my trustee, family, and other large stockholders how holding on to Doubleday stock could certainly be looked at as a financial error. Stocks in the major markets had climbed in the past ten years, yet Doubleday stock had not moved at all, and the only buyers for it were Doubleday & Company employees or my brother privately. Several minority stockholders who had either bought or been given stock by my father were in need of cash for serious family reasons, health being the main one. And I wanted more liquidity to enable me to make other investments. My mother had resigned from all the trusts before John Sengstack died, leaving Nelson as sole trustee. He was also vice president of the company now, so his route to the presidency was secure. Hank Taft, Aunt Dorothy's son-in-law, my cousin Sylvia's husband, had left the company years earlier to sail around the world.

In the fall of 1968, I traveled with Governor Hathaway and his wife for the State Travel Commission. We flew to Los Angeles and San Francisco to hustle up business for Wyoming. The group of thirty was composed of state board members from the Travel, Highway, and Economic Development commissions, businessmen, bankers, and politicians from all around the state. We tried to attract businesses to move to Wyoming, stressing the low end-of-year inventory tax. Bobby Hathaway, the governor's wife, and I were the only women. I wore a gray miniskirt with black net stockings and high gray square-heeled shoes that matched my suit. I wore my long brown hair in two braids and topped off my outfit with a high-crowned black Indian hat. At that time, I smoked Between the Act cigars. They were small, and strong. There were twenty to a pack, and I smoked three packs a day, inhaling deeply. I had taken up these small cigars because they were stronger than any cigarette, and I enjoyed shocking people. During the flight, I played gin rummy with Governor Hathaway while Bobby looked on—when she did not have her head bent in a book. Bobby and I knew each other. She had held a small exhibition of John's paintings and my bronze sculptures in Cheyenne shortly after we landed in Wyoming. It was at the Governor's Mansion and was my first exhibition. Governor Hathaway liked my strong cigars. He bummed them by the pack. We enjoyed laughs, and I even won several games of gin.

Back at home, John came to the inn for lunch every workday and we relaxed over a drink and had a bit of quiet time together. We chatted easily about plans, books, people. Not TV, because we didn't have TV. Not available where we lived at that time.

The saloon was almost empty, because we ate late. I worked lunch hours, greeting people, cleaning tables, helping out waitresses who were

swamped in both the dining room and the saloon. During the summer
tourist months, we often served over three hundred lunches in the main
dining area, not counting any bus or banquet meals. I worried I was not
giving enough time to the kids. They often ate frozen chicken potpies at
home with John Kings, instead of my being there to cook dinner, because
I was working.

John had sold some of his cattle to start a poster business of Western
images that he planned to distribute around the state. They were mostly
images of John with his horse Charlie. He was excited about his new
venture, but I was concerned that he was not going to make it, as there
was not enough volume of sales to be had within the state for the miles
that had to be put in. I did not say so, because there was little point. He
was hell-bent on doing it.

Usually, we took the kids skiing on weekends at Meadowlark ski area
west of Buffalo, or the closer one west of Dayton, Antelope Butte. John
patiently waited while the three of us skied until sore ankles and frozen
fingers drove us indoors. On the way down off the mountain one
Saturday, we were caught in a wild wind and snowstorm. John ran off
the road in his Saab with John Jr. I had Ellen and all the ski paraphernalia with me. Ellen and I got to Dayton, where I called Tom Collins,
who owned Bear Lodge, for help. He agreed, unhappily, to go out in his
tractor and pull John out because we were friends. Ellen and I inched
our way to the Trails End Motel in Sheridan, but I was too scared to
try getting home over Jim Creek Hill. Not only was the snow coming
down heavily but wild winds twisted the snow into crazy patterns, from
one direction and then another in seconds, making drifts and whiteouts.
John and John Jr. did make it home. These frightening storms come up
with no warning, and can easily be fatal, through no fault of the driver.
Rarely was I really frightened of road conditions or storms, but coming
down that mountain blind made my mouth dry and my spine ache
with fear.

Within one week, I was to have two soul-destroying events obliterate my
life as I had known it. John had gone to England to visit his daughter
Tarka, so I was alone at the ranch, working at the inn all weekdays.

On a Tuesday in February 1970, I met with my bankers and my lawyer, Henry Burgess, at nine A.M. I was nervous, wondering how this meeting would evolve. Henry told me the Cheyenne Bank, from which I had borrowed money for the original renovation of the Sheridan Inn saloon, wanted to amalgamate my loans. Become my only bank? I wondered. I didn't know why, and did not like the idea. What I did know was that I had reached my limit in terms of borrowing. No banker had to tell me that; I knew because interest rates had escalated from 5 percent to 14 percent, and I could pay only interest, not repay any capital. I was feeling the financial squeeze. Were the banks planning on pulling my lines of credit? Mr. Troutwein, president of the Cheyenne Bank, was standing alongside George Acker, president of the Bank of Commerce, and a vice president of the First National Bank of Sheridan completed the half circle; he was the only banker I did not know. We shook hands and sat down; Henry sat behind his desk. I felt these men to be judges about to sentence me. This collusion of bankers was adversarial. I wasn't sure how to handle it.

I wanted the banks to know my financial position. I was sure they already knew. I had a loan and a credit line at the Bank of Commerce in Sheridan. The loan covered my renovation and major overhaul of the kitchen, banquet rooms, dining rooms, and lobby shop of the Sheridan Inn. The vice president of the First National Bank of Sheridan sat next to me. I had only nodded to him on the street; we had never had a conversation. That bank had given me a small loan to fix up the old ranch house on Piney Creek as a home for us. I had been paying interest and making capital payments monthly on these loans until very recently, when I could pay only interest. The Chemical Bank in New York held an unsecured loan that I had taken out before I began the renovation of the Sheridan Inn. I had borrowed the money to buy a Blue Period Picasso painting entitled *Mother and Child by the Sea*. It would only increase in value, I knew, but that was not the reason I bought it.

The painting had come up at Sotheby's auction house in London. Looking at the catalog, I had seen the rich blue shadings in the woman's garment and the sea beyond, the bent head looking down on the babe in her arms, and felt deeply moved. Picasso had captured in that painting the essence of being a mother. It was the essence I had longed for in my mother but had never seen. And when I actually saw the painting for the first time in New York, I was so moved, I cried. The painting became my touchstone, but I kept it safely in a vault.

At the meeting, the First National Bank's vice president told me the total sum of John Kings's debt. I was stunned. John had maxed out the business loan for moneys that would put him in the cattle business. He'd needed funds to purchase cows and calves and ranch equipment for hay production, such as a tractor, a bailer, et cetera. I had already bought John a pickup. I had agreed to secure the loan up to a certain amount with my Doubleday stock. John was unable to pay off any of it. He had, as well, borrowed against the ranch itself without my knowledge, although he was not on the deed or title insurance, nor had he any other document to show his ownership. Why hadn't the bank investigated John's claim?

My head was swirling in disbelief and hurt. It was the end of my marriage, I knew, and I was frightened. John had also taken out a loan on all the ranch equipment. I knew about that one, but not the size of it. He had never said how much. He had said he just needed a little more till he could sell cattle or paintings, I don't remember which. He had made the transaction sound insignificant and affordable. It was obvious where the banker was heading.

The loans were never processed with due diligence, information available at the courthouse. The loan secured by my Doubleday stock to start John in the cattle business was to provide him with an annual income. I had been very specific with the bank, and my terms were in my collateral agreement, and John and I had the same agreement. I suggested the debt was John's, not mine. The vice president of the First National Bank of Sheridan threatened me with a fire sale of my Doubleday stock. John had never told the bank he had sold virtually all his cattle and invested the money in his new poster business, which involved printing and distributing his Wyoming posters. John had ignored the basic rules of business, lied to the bank, and lied to me as well. He had been so dishonest in the public sphere of business and to me financially and emotionally that I felt sick. My stomach heaved. I knew tears wouldn't help, but they flowed anyway. Henry pushed the box of Kleenex across his desk.

George Acker said, "John Kings has a loan with us, giving ranch equipment as collateral."

"Oh. No. No." I could not take in the extent of John's deceit. Neither bank knew about his arrangements with the other bank. I was enraged because bankers had apparently just assumed the man owned the property. Why had they trusted John? Did they just think he was a good guy? That was enough? Neither bank had bothered to investigate documentation of collateral, records available at the courthouse, because they knew in the end they could get me to cover it all. I was the heiress with the cash flow who would bail out the husband. It smacked of the familiar good old boy society to me. Protect the man, give him what he wants; he's one of us who rules. The banks were negligent, yet in the end I would be held financially responsible. After they all left, Henry told me, "Neltje, legally you don't have to pay off John's debt, but if you don't, you had better leave town." What the hell could I do? I was not going to leave my home.

Then came the next bombshell. I had told the bankers in Henry's office about my loan with the Chemical Bank in New York, which I had used to buy the Picasso painting. I told them how I had to keep the painting hidden because it was so famous and valuable. News of the sale of the painting at Sotheby's had been in all the major newspapers and magazines, even in the local Sheridan paper. The price paid was part of the news. When the painting finally reached Wyoming, I put it in a brown paper bag in my closet. I could not hang it on my wall. Eventually, for safety, in case of fire or theft, I put it in a military-surplus cabinet in the Bank of Commerce's vault because the bank had no safety-deposit box of sufficient size.

Now I learned that a year and a half after I had put the painting in the bank vault, the bank officials had called John, not me. They said they had no record of whose things were in that cabinet, so they had taken a sledgehammer and an ax to open it. When they found historical items marked as given to the Sheridan Inn inside the brown paper bag, as well as the painting, they remembered it belonged to me. Why hadn't the bankers called me? All the paperwork I had signed was in my name only. The historical artifacts showed clearly who owned the contents of the paper bag. I was at the inn, ten blocks away. They knew I worked at the inn every day; they had seen me there. Instead, they called John, who told them I was too busy to go down to the bank—at least that is what they claimed. John immediately went to the bank, but he neglected to call me or bother to tell me he had been at the bank that day. Apparently, according to George Acker, who heard it from two or three of the bank's vice presidents, who had actually been there, John took the painting from where it had been displayed on the gray-painted floor and placed it, along with the historical items belonging to the inn, in the larger metal cabinet, then locked it, pocketing the key. He then signed papers for the bank to the effect that the contents of said metal cabinet belonged to him. No mention from the bank to notify me of this transaction, not even a phone call, let alone a letter.

What to do? I couldn't believe that my husband could be so sneaky, so keenly cruel and dishonest, or that the bank I had trusted could be so careless. What about their allowing John to sign the papers in his name, claiming ownership of the property held in the vault? How did he think he would get away with it? Did he plan to sell the painting behind my back? Was he that kind of a thief? And did he think so little of me that he knowingly would put me in financial jeopardy? How do I handle the fact my husband lied and cheated on a large-enough scale to go to jail if I pressed charges?

How could I sleep in the same bed with John? Why had I ignored warning signs I had sensed? He was always secretive about what things cost, about his financial affairs. We rarely talked about money. He ran his business, and I ran mine. The few money issues that had come up were along the lines of who was going to pay for a hotel room in New York, since I could afford a nicer hotel than John said he could. Once, we stayed at a hotel he could afford, when I was tired of always paying the bill.

"Nobody will love you for your blue eyes," I heard my father saying.

Bile, the acrid bile of betrayal, engorged every moment of everything I thought or did at work or at home. How could I keep this knowledge from the children? They did not need to be involved in this mess. Both banks now looked to me for payment of John's debt.

Half an hour after the meeting in Burgess's office, George Acker called me. I was in the kitchen office at the inn, watching the crew dish up lunch for the Lions Club. Acker told me the painting had been found. It was in John Kings's name. Could I verify it was the Picasso, that the painting had not been switched? I raced to the bank, my heart pounding. George met me at the vault. Three high-ranking bank officers stood uncomfortably to one side. They would not meet my eyes. The Picasso painting was propped up against a military cabinet, bigger than the one I had put it in.

I examined the painting itself. No marks or signs of abuse were evident anywhere on the paint itself. I turned it over, ran my fingers over each edge to examine the nails holding down the canvas. The canvas had not been moved; therefore the painting had not been switched. It was the Picasso I had bought. I wept, turning my face away so the bank officers couldn't see my frailty. George knew. I put the painting back in my name. I was the only one to have access to it. Later I would deal with the vice presidents and other bank officials who had given John access to the painting, and allowed him to put it in his name. "Do you want the bank officers fired?" asked Acker.

"No," I replied after some thought, "but I want the bank board notified of how this situation was handled."

John Kings was in England with Tarka and had been away for two weeks. When he called me from England, I yelled, "You could go to jail for what you have done. How could you think me so stupid as not to find out? Why did you put me at such a financial risk? Did you think my money was available without limit? How could you be so damned dishonest? I feel ashamed of you." He barely replied. I received silence.

After dropping Ellen back at Colorado Rocky Mountain School, I met John, as planned, at the Denver airport. I contained myself until we were in a hotel room. "Why did you do these crooked things with the banks, John? Why? Why didn't you say something before the money situation became dishonest with the double use of collateral?" I asked gently but in anger. He said nothing, gave no explanation. Instead of going to bed nude, as usual, I wore a new long nightgown. When we got home to the ranch, John went to bed, where he basically remained for the next three months, refusing to talk about anything he had done. He stonewalled.

Occasionally, he would come down for dinner with John Jr. and me. He hardly spoke. What do you do with a husband who won't talk about the elephant sitting on the bed? What was going to happen to me? I wanted him away, gone. But I really wanted back the man I had fallen in love with, the love and passion that had flowed between us, the sense of belonging. I was fractured.

I had to wear very dark sunglasses in the meeting ten days later with my husband, George Acker, and the bank officers who had taken part in this potentially criminal deception. I felt violated and said so. My eyes were red from crying. John made up some story about trying to save me trouble. "Why didn't you then tell me what you'd done with *Mother and Child by the Sea*?" I asked. He had no answer. Nor did the bank officials who had allowed John to put the Picasso in his name.

The Picasso was back in my possession, the papers signed in my name only. But even as I had it back in my hands, I knew I would have to sell it. John's debts were huge, and added to mine in these uncertain economic times, the scale tipped. I could not risk losing the ranch, the inn, or my life in Sheridan.

Henry Burgess called. He said, "Neltje, after talking with the banks, I think you had better sell some of your assets."

"Henry, I have already put the Wolf Ranch on Box Elder Creek up for sale. It is a small amount but the most viable asset I own."

"Good," he replied, and hung up.

When John finally decided to leave his bed, he started coming to the inn for lunch again. Most days while waiting for me to finish whatever job I was in the midst of doing, he spent his time impressing and wooing the young girl at the front desk. He told me, maybe after a month, that he loved this young girl and wanted to marry her. It was midwinter of the following year. We would be closing the inn for a month on March 1 for cleaning and to find new kitchen and dining room staff. I had more than too much on my plate. I demanded and got an after-hours meeting with both lovers upstairs in my office at the inn. John repeated in front of this young girl that he loved her and wanted to marry her. I asked her if she felt the same way. She asked to speak to me alone. She sat across the oval mahogany table from me and said, "Oh, Neltje, I was just agog at being wooed by an older, charming man. I have been playing. I meant no harm." She quit her job when the inn closed, and John flew to London to see his daughter again.

John strayed for the last time in 1972. I told Henry Burgess I wanted a separation agreement. He said, "What's the matter with divorce? You have been miserable with John for the last three or four years."

I was divorced the following morning. I had to wear a skirt because Judge Ilsley would not allow a woman to wear pants in his court.

TWENTY

Falling in Love, Picking Up the Pieces

Slowly, I learned to disconnect the strings of a dream. I was alone again. How could that love I had so believed in have become this stinking pile of dishonesty and hurt? John went on to live with a succession of women in the community. I watched him move through and past these relationships and felt nausea, then began to feel better.

Bobby Gibbs helped me sell the few head of cattle left and a stray ewe that had peeled off from the flock as the sheep were being trailed to the mountains for summer pasture from the eastern dry lands of Arvada. We had called the Moores, who had been doing the trailing that day, but they never came to pick up the ewe. She'd become our family pet. I couldn't look the cows and calves in the eye the day they were loaded up from the corrals at Ucross. The ewe was loaded out as well. I felt a traitor.

Ellen was watching *Gone With the Wind* when I got home from the courthouse after the divorce hearing. She said John Kings had told her I was crazy to think he was playing around. "You may be crazy, but you are my mother. I told him I would stick with you. Now, let me watch this movie."

John Kings had given me the name and address of Anthony Rubinstein, a lawyer in London who had connections in the art world. He could possibly be helpful to me in selling the Picasso. Right after the meeting with all the bankers, I had asked Herbert Hoover, of John's gallery in

San Francisco, to get the Picasso into a Sotheby's auction as soon as possible. I put a reserve on it. The painting did not sell, as it didn't meet my reserve price. Now maybe Anthony Rubinstein could help. The painting was already in London.

I met Anthony at the outdoor bar of the Stanhope Hotel in New York a week after my divorce. It was a Thursday in mid-July 1972. I had told him over the phone about my plight with the banks, how John's debts and mine had put me over the edge. I told him where he could find the beautiful Picasso, and what it meant to me. Could he help me sell the painting? He said he'd get on it upon his return to London. He had to go to France for a few days. We talked for over an hour and made a date for dinner the next day.

We had dinner at an Italian restaurant in the midtown area—convenient, just a short walk from Puck's apartment on Fiftieth Street, where I was staying. At dinner, Anthony asked if we could get out of the city the next day. I had nothing on my calendar, so I called my friends Tim and Lee Seldes. They had a weekend house in the Hamptons and would be glad to see me and a friend. Anthony and I had a happy time together and the electricity between us was running on high. We spent the next day with clients of Anthony's, swam in a lake up in Connecticut in a lazy haze of playful adoration. He left the next day for France. He said he'd be in touch.

Anthony called a week later. He asked if I would spend a week with him in Paris. "I have some work to do that shouldn't eat up much time." A playful week in Paris? Perfect, except he was married. Were all attractive men married? Could I manage a brief encounter? "I'd love to be with you in Paris, Anthony. How delicious."

The thought of a magical week, a love affair in Paris, a many-splendored thing, when my world had fallen apart was perfect. Anthony's desire to be with me helped wipe out the sexual insecurity I felt because of John's infidelities. When Anthony called again, I told him I'd meet him at my old friend Jon Schueler's rented apartment. Schueler and his wife, Magda, had been in Paris all summer. He was writing his book, *The Sound of Sleat*, while Magda inhaled history and art for a project of hers. I looked forward to a week of pleasures gastronomic, visual, sensual, and all the rest. I had no further intention other than to spend a slice of time together, and I assumed Anthony was like-minded. I was a bit anxious but couldn't define why. A dash of guilt, I presumed, for dancing off with a married man.

In mid-August, I arrived at Schueler's airy apartment early enough to have time with him. I hadn't seen him in years—not since New York. Before that, I had seen him in Provincetown, when his then-girlfriend, Magda, had left him to get on with her own life. I had listened over those days and nights to a bereaved man who could not understand why a woman would leave him. He wanted Magda to live with him in the northern wilds of Scotland. Why should she want to get a degree in art anyway? he asked. At the time, I left him as disconsolate and miserable as I had found him.

The following winter in New York, we had continued to talk over every nuance of each wintry day Schueler and Magda had spent together in Mallaig. How Magda had, before leaving, completed filing all his slides, a heroic job. That winter, Schueler and I were to have many sorrowful dinners at my small apartment in New York. He bemoaned his lonely state and how the loss of Magda was affecting his painting. When not feeling excruciatingly sorry for himself, he was good company. He took me to many art openings, museum exhibitions, and almost weekly dinners with Bob and Abby Friedman. My awareness and knowledge of contemporary art began with Schueler as guide. He never instructed. He simply voiced his meandering thoughts about a work of art and the artist, or the art scene in general. He rambled on with passion about books or a magazine article, French philosophers or the idiocy of war. And he laughed a lot about human foibles.

Schueler looked happy now, the light back in his eyes. He teased me about getting divorced and then within weeks beginning a love affair in Paris. "No angst or depression for you, baby," he said, hugging me. Schueler never judged, and for that I loved him. He was always, even at his most obsessed, my friend.

We talked, leaning against the tall old French windows and looking out on a courtyard three floors below. The doorbell rang. Anthony stood in the doorway, wearing a bulky brown coat wide open, his dark hair slicked back. He was dressed in a gray pinstripe business suit and had a very large brown duffel at his feet. He took up the entire doorway. We smiled at each other briefly. When we kissed, the electricity almost made me drop to the floor. I looked at his face, his noble nose, his eyes, which made my stomach flip, and his sensuous mouth. We spoke maybe three sentences and then left. Anthony piled my bag onto his as we waited for the elevator; we touched hands, smiled again. I think I said good-bye to Schueler, but I can't be sure.

Anthony and I fell in love that week in Paris. We stayed on the third floor of a charming five-room hotel on the Left Bank. We wandered the cobbled streets of the neighborhood, spent two hours at the Rodin Museum, drinking in the sensual watercolors of nudes. We ate superb meals at intimate neighborhood restaurants, laughed and giggled like young children, and made love with fiery passion. I felt full of curiosity about Anthony, his kids, his work. What he liked and didn't like in people, foods, wines, and decor. I told him about the inn, my children, the ranch, my marriage, and my passion to paint, which lay neglected in some nook in my brain. Anthony was open about his past departures from his wife, which hadn't lasted. He never spoke meanly about her, nor even said what had gone awry between them. I admired his restraint and thoughtfulness with regard to her.

At Anthony's invitation, I traveled to London with him and then the next day on to Finland, where he had a business meeting. The whole time was dreamlike. We talked and talked, disagreed and fumbled in making up. I had never before felt I was part of someone to the degree I felt with Anthony. We went on to Copenhagen for the weekend, where I took a stream of photographs, felt ripe with creative juices: free to explore, abstracting staircases and dripping stains on old stone facades. I said good-bye to Anthony in Paris at the same cozy boudoir hotel with its problematic plumbing.

In Paris I had called my son, John, in Denmark on instinct, something I did not normally do while he was spending the month with his father, but now he was alone in Copenhagen. His dad had arranged for him to spend two of those four weeks there with a woman friend of his and her three sons. She was a working member of the Church of Scientology, on board the ship outside the harbor where L. Ron Hubbard, the Scientology guru, lived and worked.

My instinct to reach out to John was on the nose. I finally got through to him. He sounded upset. I changed my plans to go home and flew back to Copenhagen instead to meet him and see what was going on. He was recovering from a broken leg and was meant to be canoeing on the canals of northern Denmark with his hostess's eldest son, a skiing friend. It was obvious from the restrained answers to my questions that he couldn't talk on the telephone and that he was not happy.

I sat on the bed in my bland Scandinavian hotel room in downtown Copenhagen, waiting until the time when I could call John and arrange a meeting. I felt solitary, aware of the space about me, no honking horns or shrill sirens to distract my mind. The past two weeks and the emotional impact of falling in love had obliterated my life at home. I had no idea what would happen next with Anthony, and the not knowing did not disturb me one bit. I was filled with the memories on so many levels of intimacy and desire. Yet life decisions needed to be made, and my dreamy mind just couldn't take stock of them. When I finally got John on the phone, he whispered for me to meet him outside the house where he was staying. He needed to know exactly the time I would be there, so we could talk. He sounded anxious, even frightened. I felt for him.

I met him in an arched doorway halfway down the block from where he was staying. He was fifteen years old now. He looked a bit disheveled, his hair needing a cut. He was thin, having lost some weight. "What is going on?" I asked after we hugged.

"Get me out of here, please, Mom. They don't have enough food. You will see at dinner, so don't take much." The words tumbled out of his mouth like spring thaw racing down a creek bed.

I asked John if he had been canoeing on the canals with his friend Tony, as planned. "No," he said. "Tony has to spend every day going to banks for money." Was it for donations for Scientology or because the family was broke? I wondered but did not ask. John went on: "Tony has to do everything—the household shopping as well. The other boys, Tony's brothers, are too young to do business with bankers and figure out what to cook for dinner. So Tony does it all. I just tag along."

The family dinner was a scene of sad tension. There were three mid-size fillets of whitefish, a very small bowl of rice, and another of green peas for four large boys and two adult women. I didn't inquire why this woman was nearly starving her children. After the dinner, I took John to the hotel to call home, and the brothers all came along, but they stayed downstairs while we phoned Ellen from my room. Ellen was in tears. She had stayed in Wyoming to be with her boyfriend, giving up time with her father, and the boyfriend had dumped her. Our family world had turned upside down and sideways. We were all anxious.

I flew back to the States with John, reluctantly leaving him to recuperate and spend time with his dad on Long Island, and went on home to Wyoming. John called the next day, saying he would be on the flight that got in at three the following afternoon. I unpacked, wrestled with the dogs, and cooked sloppy meals for Ellen and me, cobbled together from what we liked—no meat, potato, and vegetables. We ate a good deal of ice cream. She felt rejected, that hideous feeling of diminishment. Her boyfriend, Jim, was contemplating the priesthood. How do you respond to that after dating for over half a year?

Only a few days passed before Anthony called, asking to come visit. He had had hideous scenes with his family in France after he told them about being with me. He arrived two days later, bearing a huge smoked salmon, and was disappointed for a moment that neither of my children ate fish. However, my coworkers at the Sheridan Inn were delighted with their share. Anthony jumped right to work in the inn's kitchen. He helped with several banquets that were to take place on the same day and at the same time. The two chefs had walked out during the night, stealing the inn's knives and all my good cookbooks from home. I shared my newfound skills on the meat saw with Anthony, who then cut up four crates of chicken into eight pieces each. He learned how to open large cans of tomatoes for a sauce, how to prepare prime rib for the oven, and how to use the dishwasher. "On to the broiler next," I said, laughing.

At home he quickly became a member of the family. He was funny and fun to be around. Anthony, sensitive to my children's wariness, included Ellen and John in daily life, as though he had lived with us from the beginning of time. He stayed for weeks, long enough to win my heart again and get me pregnant.

I could get an abortion in New York State but not in Wyoming. To be with Anthony, I chose to fly to London for the abortion in November 1972. On the plane, I mulled over my decision any number of times. I did not want to be put in the position of needing to marry Anthony because I didn't want to raise a child alone. And as much as I felt love for Anthony, I knew I had neither the patience nor the desire to have another child at this time in my life. I felt selfish. I wanted time for me: to work in the studio, to grow, not to care for others. Anthony wanted to marry; I didn't. The responsibilities of commitment in the role of wife were not for me anymore. I wanted to live with Anthony, not feel the entrapment of marriage. My marriages had both been terminated due to some form of abuse.

Anthony had moved out of the house with his wife and was now living with his best friend, Ralph, who was semi-living with Ann Kings, John Kings's wife before me. Surreally, after the abortion, I was in Anthony's bed in Ralph's apartment at one end of the hall, with Ann Kings in bed with Ralph at the other end. The toilet was right opposite their bedroom. Anthony told me I was to hide. Ann was not to know I was there, as she was hypersensitive because John Kings had left her and Tarka. She was having a good deal of emotional problems and instability. What a bizarre time that was. I felt like a culprit, the enemy in Ann's eyes, and I didn't blame her at all. How strange that Ralph's apartment was their love nest and also my place to recuperate. Of course she didn't want me at the end of the hall. I read in bed, peeked out the doorway to listen if their door opened, then dashed to the toilet. I had a nightmare about being caught out by both Ann and Ralph, in my nightie in the hallway. And what could I say? A scene of great comedy or potential war.

The pending lawsuit with my family had not resulted in any agreement satisfactory to me. They offered me the option to choose my own trustee, but that still left me like all minority stockholders, coping with the diminished stock value and no viable market for the stock. Nelson kept that value low in order to reduce inheritance taxes when my mother died, he said. (She was seventy-four in 1972.) However, it did offer him an opportunity not available to others: to increase his investment in the company at a very low cost by buying any shares a stockholder wanted or needed to sell at whatever price Nelson set. He knew how the company was doing financially, what the future should hold for the next few years at least. The price would go up. It was around three or four hundred dollars per share at the time. The rest of the stockholders had only the financials given out at the stockholders' meetings to inform them, and I knew those to be limited in accuracy in order to keep stockholders in the dark. This had always been the policy of the company, as was true in many privately held companies.

To get a fair value of the stock from Doubleday & Company was impossible. So for many of us minority stockholders, a number of whom I had been in touch with, the problem was that when money was needed for a loan, for illness, or for investment, banks shied away from using the stock as collateral because there was no way of liquidating it. I found this blockade of information and financial resources infuriating. It was bondage, and possibly for Nelson's profit.

When Anthony was with me in Wyoming, he took on the task of putting all the legal papers from two years of negotiations in order. Once this was done, although I did not go through them all, I had a far better sense of how the fight in court would or could develop. Anthony never gave me advice; he simply made information available. My mother called. She threatened to disinherit me if I went on with the suit, which told me that she was insecure about winning the case. I told her to cut me out of her will if she felt like it. I was doing what I believed was right. Her use of money as power had always bothered me. I had had plenty of opportunities to see it since my early childhood, and see the pleasure she got in using her power.

My anger came out of the closet. After age thirty, I owned a quarter of my trust outright but was in the trap of having nowhere to go with that quarter share. Nelson had full use of his entire trust once he reached thirty, but I had been forced to go to court to get my share. That was when Nelson had cut off my income and refused to give me the quarter share from the trust. I was emotionally strung out now by the imminent trial date, and that along with my financial position while trying to pay off John Kings's debts and the pressures of work at the inn made me a mess of a companion. Anthony didn't mind. It was his presence beside me, his love and patient support, coupled with his joie de vivre and quick sense of humor, that helped sustain me for my day in court.

I went up to my mother to say hello in the corridor outside the courtroom. My mother literally did not recognize me, or chose not to, and my brother refused to speak to me. At the end of the court day, as Nelson had made it evident that he did not know the difference between one trust and another, my mother's lawyer went up to the judge and pleaded that if they removed Nelson as trustee, either Nelson himself or my mother's attorneys could select his replacement. I, and my team of lawyers, felt this was a good sign. Nelson's inability to have any insight into the structures of my mother's trust, my two sisters' trusts, or my trust had been painful for me to watch. On the stand, he sounded either drunk or hungover, out of it. Ultimately, the court ruled to give me the right to appoint my trustee but left Nelson as trustee on all other family trusts.

Eventually, I took the case to the New York State Supreme Court, because I thought the court had been biased in retaining Nelson as trustee for all those other trusts, giving him huge voting power in the way the company was run, without any consideration for the position of minority stockholders who were entrapped financially. The judgment from the Supreme Court of New York agreed with that of the lower court. I did get to choose my own trustee, but I lost the bigger battle. Were the years of legal hassle, the emotional tearing, the family tensions, and the financial stresses worth this final court decision? Yes. I followed my sense of right all the way. This in itself gave me confidence. And I saw in the open what I had always known deep inside—that Nelson, financially and emotionally, would always be protected by my mother, and given all. Her own financial liquidity was compromised by this decision; she could not sell or borrow against her stock, either. Her emotional need to pass along the power at Doubleday from father to son made her oblivious to other business considerations. The intricacies of family were a Galsworthian tale. I grew up during this court battle in ways that triggered change in my future. The disregard of my mother and brother hurt, yet it set me free. I stopped thinking I couldn't do this or that because of their disapproval or emotional pain. I no longer felt I had a family save for my half sisters.

The end of summer in 1973 was a slower time at the inn. Ellen went off to college in Bozeman, Montana. I watched her drive down Piney Road with a sharp pain in my solar plexus. Ellen, my daughter, friend, and companion, was grown up and gone. She wouldn't come back as the young girl she was now. John went to Pomfret School in Connecticut that fall. I thought he'd do better at boarding school than at high school in Sheridan and home alone with me. I hadn't known that Anthony would become a factor in all our lives at the time the decision was made. Our house echoed in emptiness. Sunlight splashed on the Mexican tile floor, leaves began to tumble as I watched, and a sadness, deeper and thicker than bone marrow, choked me.

I left Wyoming later that fall to live with Anthony in the English countryside. I arrived at Heathrow Airport, outside London, with a thirty-five-pound bag full of vegetables from my garden and three rolled-up canvases that I was working on. I had left the Sheridan Inn in good managerial hands and would phone in weekly for reports. My housekeeper, Clara Harbel, and ranch hand Bruno were taking care of the ranch, horses, and dogs. They had been with me for so many years.

The house that Anthony had found for us, Ben Ezra, was in Sussex at the end of a gravel road, with an open meadow at the back. The kitchen was built in the fourteenth century, I was told. The very small stove under the back stairs had only two burners that worked by turning a dial. The third burner required a heavy-duty wrench with muscles to match. The living room became my studio, its furniture sent off to storage and plastic sheeting taped down on the handsome wood flooring. The Snuggery, a small room that seated four or maybe five at a squeeze, had a fireplace almost tall enough to stand in and wide enough to spit-roast a good-size pig. Anthony and I spent our evenings there over cocktails and, later, coffee. We bedded down early because Anthony left for the train to work in London before six.

I painted every weekday morning, as I had started again the past few weeks in Wyoming. I drank cheap white wine to boost my creative spirits, to make me feel less lonely. It was an unsettled feeling I had, a dis-ease, wandering about in the rooms of this old house, wondering about its past and my future. I walked in the snapping afternoon wind, sometimes rain, too, to visit a horse about a mile down the road. I nuzzled his nose like I had that of my horse, Little Dan, at Bonny Hall. I talked to him and scratched the back of his ears, then faced the weather going home. But I didn't feel it was home, despite having bought magenta and deep purple sheets for our bed. I napped drizzly afternoons away after consuming too much wine. It passed the time, which hung heavily without Anthony. I knew no one. I began doing pen-and-ink drawings at the dinner table, which seemed a less challenging endeavor than painting. Then there was dinner to prepare in the awkward little kitchen.

Anthony did not get home until seven-thirty. I drank bourbon—expensive in England, Anthony told me—and orange juice. "A lazy lady's whiskey sour," I called it. I was homesick, lonely for a sense of belonging, and despite loving Anthony, I became depressed. I had a life back in Wyoming. Here I had a belonging only at night.

Eventually we got an apartment in London, and quite often Anthony came home for lunch. I spent a good deal of time shopping at the green-grocer's, the cheese and egg shop, the pastry shop. In the afternoons, I drew with a pen at the round dinner table for four. Our apartment on Marylebone Street shimmered with light all day and was furnished American-style, with an open decor. Ellen came over from New York. She had abandoned college for the moment but went to the Davis School in London right away, where she took a number of literature classes. It was such fun to have her close again. She and Anthony teased and laughed with each other; they hugged, and my heart lifted. Finally, she had a father. She and I hid out at the American Hotel for lunch occasionally just to hear American voices and eat a hamburger. I was close to happy but was aware I was drinking too much, a sign of serious trouble. I saw myself change into a mean woman, become raging angry at something, often something insignificant, when I drank too much. My humor altered often enough in this cyclical pattern to frighten me. When Anthony locked the liquor closet at Ben Ezra, where we spent weekends now, I split for home. His attempt to be helpful brought on an internal panic in me, a sense of being hemmed in, trapped—by whom, I didn't know. My need to be free was intense.

I bought an airline ticket home, with a stop in New York to see Madeleine and Puck. I would go home and drink when and where I wanted to without censure. Ellen stayed on in London with Anthony. My mind seemed to shift in squares like the game of concentration. If I picked up a wrong card and turned it over, I was capable of verbal cruelty. Where did this come from? I worried about what Ellen thought. There goes crazy Mom again? I shivered with guilt.

On the flight across the Atlantic, I sat next to the mother of a magazine editor I knew from the John Sargent era. I felt I had to be careful not to drink too much in her presence, although I really needed a drink. I was nervous traveling alone. A drink always made that anxiety of nerves soften or even vanish. The balance was what was tricky. The second drink could start a downward slide.

I stayed in Puck's apartment that night in New York, as she was in the country, where I would visit the next day. Madeleine and her husband, Pete Martin, a wildly funny, bright man, had dinner with me at a restaurant on Fiftieth Street between Third and Second avenues. The rich Italian dinner was a while coming, allowing for several rounds of drinks. I could have only two, as I had had a drink at Puck's to make me comfortable. We ate far too much while listening to Pete tell hilarious stories about his wayward time in Ireland, when he was supposedly writing the "great American novel."

Madeleine had been drinking steadily. "You don't play the guitar with any passion, and why don't you play jazzy tunes instead of damn ballads?" she yelled at the guitar player. His soft face froze.

Pete and I were astonished. She rose up queenlike and in a theatrical tone announced, "I am going to the ladies'," as if she were going on a trip to another continent. In a stilted yet elegant manner, she staggered off to the ladies'. Pete continued right on with another story.

Madeleine came up in back of Pete. She looked at me, bleary-eyed, then banged Pete on the head with her purse from behind. "You bastard, you're not going to have that girl so you can screw. You are coming home with me."

"Madeleine, Madeleine," Pete said, his arms protecting his face. "This woman is your sister, Neltje. Sit down, Madeleine."

Madeleine had thought I was Pete's girlfriend. I knew she was in a booze blackout. I could see myself headed down that road, and I was ashamed. I was also scared. I had to stop drinking. I had tried, by myself, telling myself to have willpower, not to be like my father or my mother. Snippets of embarrassing moments in my past resurfaced, times when I'd felt ashamed, questioned my behavior. I remember one night in Jamaica with Anthony: I had been dancing, laughing, having a wonderful time, and because of some small thing Anthony said to a waiter, I went ballistic; the rush of anger grew and kept coming until sleep blocked it. Horrid things I'd said, I barely remembered. The out-of-proportion rage I felt was what terrified me.

I had promised my son, John, when I visited him at Pomfret earlier that year that I would cut back on my drinking when I went to England and was away from the pressures of the inn. He had replied quietly, "Mom, you can't."

Oh God, how those words hurt, and how right he was. They came back to me as I drove to Puck's house in the morning.

When I got to Puck's out in the country the next day, I felt at home. In the late afternoon, Puck called out from the kitchen, "Grab yourself a drink, Nelch, I'm getting out the ice."

"I have a drinking problem, Puck. I need AA, not a drink," I replied as lightly as I could. "Well, damn," she said. "You could have told me before I got that big bottle of whiskey for you."

She came around the corner from the kitchen, held out her arms, and said, "I am so sorry you, too, are stuck with the booze problem." She had been sober for decades. She was my friend and helper in the struggle to get there myself. Puck called an AA friend I'd known at school, and we went to a meeting that evening. How fragile are moments like this, how serendipitous.

That was over thirty years ago, and I have been sober ever since. But it has taken me many more years to be comfortable in my skin.

I no longer kept a bottle of Jim Beam under the front seat of whichever car I was driving. I no longer drank three Manhattans at the saloon before going home. I have had no white wine to enhance the creative juices in the studio. The oblivion I'd searched for in booze was gone. What was left was me. I did not like what I saw. AA meetings, alcoholic counseling, therapies, from Jungian to primal scream—they all helped uncover a sense of abandonment, of being unloved, and the continuing sense of being "lesser than" because I was a woman. All these emotions were coupled with the rage of a wounded tiger.

I boiled with rage. How I hated to admit it. As a child I had been locked in the closet if I got angry. "Women don't behave that way. We keep everything running smoothly," I heard over and over again. The dichotomies between my upbringing and who I really was were at war. I was learning I could not change the hateful past, but I could do something about what I felt and how I acted. The person responsible for me was me, and what a revelation that was. I felt alone yet connected to others in AA meetings. All of us with behavior in the past, and touching moments as well, were trying to stay sober. I felt apart. I rarely spoke at meetings, and it took me seven years to find a sponsor, which should happen within months of going to AA. I continue to feel apart in groups, can feel the space around me like a cool cocoon.

Anthony and Ellen came over from London for Christmas of 1973, and my son, John, came home from the East Coast. We went to Aspen, where the kids wanted to ski. In fact, we all skied, but the two young ones put us in our aged places. I told Anthony that my whole secret world of demons was erupting, at times on a daily basis. I felt too rocky to have a relationship with anyone. I could barely manage living with myself. He was loving, as always, and wanted to help, but he felt rebuffed and useless. Quietly and with sadness, I told him I had to cut loose from our relationship, that he should go find a wife, which was what he really wanted, and that I was sorry it could not be me. We were tearful, but Anthony and I parted as close friends. My children continued to love him and he them. He had told them early on to call him Pater Vite, "father in life." That was what he continued to be to them until his too-early death.

He agreed to be my trustee and the children's trustee after the court case was settled in 1972. In that role, he came to New York once a year to deal with trustee business and to visit us. He brought his new wife, Molly, who became part of our Rubinstein family. Memories of him make me smile, and they appear at the oddest times, when I am walking by the creek, or in a store buying groceries, and I hear his voice, see his eyes crinkle in merriment. He was a love.

TWENTY-ONE

Anger to Action

Still in a vague fog of sobering up, I decided to focus on my art by taking classes in design, drawing, and Sumi-e painting (Japanese ink painting on rice paper) at Sheridan College. The fear of being a failure was ever present, but I learned I could live with that feeling. As weeks built into months, then years, that panic gradually became something I could converse with and manage, not something that I had to flee from.

I started a gallery at the inn on a whim after talking to a local artist, Ed Smyth, who had no place in Sheridan to show his work. "Sheridan needs a good gallery," he said.

"Okay, I'll create one in the apartment over the dining room," I told him. The Madia family was long gone. We were sitting by the fire in the front hall of the inn on a windy, gray November afternoon. We went on talking about the possible mission of the gallery, the publicity that needed to be created in order to get good artists. I wanted a judging panel, which I would not be on, because I didn't want any artist to feel I was deciding who got in and who didn't. I had enough envy and backbiting to deal with because I had money. Besides, I was just beginning to think of myself as an artist. Who should we have? Not artists—the possibility of jealousy and envy was far too predictable. And how best to set up the business of commissions and what length of time to hold a work of art? Ideas flooded in. I had a hard time staying on track with one idea; my mind leaped like a frog on a rolling beer can. It was late when we left the inn.

The next day, I bought an old used black paneled Suburban to ferry artwork, the "Black Mariah." I contacted my artist friend Barbara Margoff in Boulder, Colorado, a university town with an artists' community. She would be my art guide. I took my first trip to Boulder the following month in the Black Mariah. Barbara introduced me to over a dozen fine artists, all thrilled to loan paintings on consignment. I was stunned and touched by their trust in me. I drove home elated, with a full load of work ready to hang. I took a quick trip to New York, where I gathered paintings from galleries and more artist friends and carried them home in my luggage. Buffalo Kaplinski, a landscape painter from Denver, was our featured artist for the opening. His paintings had a vitality that was unique; by the smallest slice of color perfectly placed, they made the viewer feel the grasses, rolling foothills, and mountains in earliest sunlight.

Hundreds came to the opening from a two-hundred-mile range. The beautiful nude watercolor by Lennart Anderson shocked one mother, who fled with her young son, screaming, "Lewd. Pornography. Disgusting." Fortunately, the gallery was empty at the time, save for the staff. Another detractor claimed there was not sufficient paint on a watercolor by my beloved old friend Jon Schueler to make it worth the marked price of five hundred dollars. These were the extremes, but exhibiting contemporary art, which was the mission of the gallery, proved an uphill struggle worthy of Sisyphus. I seemed to enjoy swimming against ocean currents.

In Boulder I met a string of talented artists, most doing watercolors. Betty Woodman, the well-known ceramicist, gave me some wild vases and a few bowls. We eventually did a solo exhibition of her work. Betty is a dedicated artist who was among those who elevated ceramics, and therefore crafts, to the position of *art* when she was given a retrospective exhibition of her work at the Metropolitan Museum in New York in 2006. What an extraordinary achievement. I think back now to all the talented people I met, laughed with, and learned from over those gallery years. They never knew how scared I was of their rejection.

On one of the early trips to Boulder, I was led by the Margoff daughters to look at the work of a friend, Gordon Krause. He painted and made pencil drawings of parts of the female body—a shoulder, a hand, crossed legs, or a face—in an unusually realistic manner. I found his work exquisitely crafted, detached yet pulsing with humanity. On my way back to Sheridan, I stopped by to visit with him in Laramie, where he was in his junior year at the University of Wyoming. I found him to be silent except for what interested him, no side chatter. Gordon explained to me his method of painting by projecting the image onto the canvas in the dark. It was a difficult and painstaking process, one that fit his quiet personality. His father told him it took too long and that he had to find another way to paint, "because you can't earn enough the way you are working now." That attitude infuriated me. "Do not create the way you want and need to do. Be like me" was what I heard. His father was a doctor in Casper—a left-brainer.

I gave Gordon a show at the inn gallery in 1974. We became friends, and he often drove up from Laramie when he had time. We would talk about art, the dedication it took, how different artists worked, and how essential it was to be true to oneself, not to copy. The more we talked, the more time I put in on my work in the studio. I so needed a voice. I worked with collage, making a meaningful form and pattern of the detritus I had found on the streets of New York. These were small pieces, some quite tentative; others resonated immediately in strong constructs on paper. In Sumi-e it was the mark of black ink that glided, danced, raced, or pounced across the rice paper. What I learned and continue to learn about mark making is the foundation of my painting.

Clyfford Still wrote, "It is the moral duty of the artist to create a work to impact the viewer."

I thought about Still's comment often. My paintings, fueled by anger, were daunting to viewers. People said my paintings made them uncomfortable. I could understand this comment, because they scared me, too, made me turn away; they were so in-your-face painful. I have learned to let them be, asking knowledgeable artist friends only, "Does it work?" That is what matters. Gordon pressed me to try painting big canvases. I started with oils again but quickly shifted to acrylics, which I could manipulate to mimic oil painting. I had no patience for oils, which took so long to dry. Eventually, I learned to use my whole body, even when my hands danced with the touch of butterfly wings on six-foot-square canvases.

Gordon introduced me to the work of Joan Mitchell. Her powerful abstract paintings, brilliant in color, are explosive with passion. The landscapes surrounding her home outside Paris often were their inspiration, and her works were fueled by rage. They taught me that anger could be translated. I researched her earlier work, traced how she had dropped representational work, opening her unconscious mind for the deeper truth of Abstract Expressionism. I learned from her work and from De Kooning and Franz Kline, as well as Milton Resnick, Richard Diebenkorn, and others. All these Abstract Expressionists talked to me. I came upon the writings of Anaïs Nin, the journals that recorded her way of life—the freedom to explore the sensual and sexual parts of our being, the creative and artistic—so different from the way I had been raised, uptight Victorian/Edwardian, never sexual. Anaïs Nin was a revelation, someone who felt the sensual as I did. Her writings set me free.

Gordon was very much my mentor, even though there were twenty years between us—he was twenty, and I was forty. I was not scared of him as I was of many other men. We eventually became lovers. I still suffered fear about sex, guilt and fiery anger in response to my early abuse. Being vulnerable scared me. I felt battle-scarred by the relationships I had had. Memories implanted in my nine-year-old mind—"If you tell anyone, I will come kill you"—rattle in my head to this day. The men I had chosen in my adult life added to my fears and insecurities. I overcame many of my early terrors and guilt associations in my relationship with Gordon because when I reacted in fear or flash anger, particularly about sex, he would say, "I am not the man who abused you." I owe him a good deal for his quiet patience as well as for his mentoring of my art over twelve years.

Evenings, I went to AA meetings in Sheridan. During the day, I became involved with the Women's Center, as well as running the Sheridan Inn. The Women's Center's office, above Tucker's store on Main Street, was run by Diane Wilcoxson, a dynamic, caring woman with a dream. Her mission was to help women get out of abusive situations, support them as they learned to become self-sustaining. A number of self-help programs needed to be coalesced and put into action. There were no rape kits at the Sheridan hospital, and the police were not helpful to abused women. The tone of some legislators was, "If you can't rape your wife, who can you rape?" Programs aimed at providing the value of women began locally. Two rapes occurred that summer of 1975. When I went to a city official and asked him what he was planning to do about the rapes, his answer was, "Women should be off the streets at sundown."

I retorted, "This is 1975, not 1875. What are you saying?" It was part of the old-time attitude that women were play toys, cooks, cleaners, and brood mares who should know their place. I had heard a version of this all my life, had lived under the belittlement-of-women rule. One evening at home in the library, my father had offered me five thousand dollars if I would elope. I was ten at the time. I knew he didn't want the expense of a wedding. It was said only half in jest, I think. I joined in the local efforts to help women. My rage gave me incredible energy.

Early in our love affair, Gordon invited me to a weekend at his folks'. His mother was having a dinner party Saturday night. She was a conservative woman, dark-haired and sensibly dressed. I offended her sense of propriety by having sex with her son. She was above us in the kitchen, washing dishes after the dinner party, when she heard the crash of his bed breaking. Gordon woke me the following morning at seven with fresh orange juice. He handed it to me, saying, "My mother wants you to leave immediately." I was a forty-year-old woman being booted out of the house for having sex. Gordon's eyes were wide with fear. What should he do?

Steve Nicholas, Gordon's best friend, came to the rescue and gave us his house for Sunday night. I liked Steve. He had been up to the ranch with Gordon to keep Ellen occupied, giving Gordon and me time alone. Steve was intelligent, well read, and on his way to becoming a pediatric doctor. Many years later, after both had had love affairs and breakups, Ellen and Steve married. She was thirty. My daughter is a woman of strong will, outspoken in her views, yet a tenderly aware and concerned mother. She has always been caring from earliest times, from protecting Johnny in the sandbox to babysitting the Collins kids. She's an avid reader and has read all the classics in English literature and those of other countries, some more than once if her probing mind was tweaked. So often she has been the person I have turned to for support. She has always been sensitive and cognizant well beyond her years in the intricate foibles of the human spirit.

It was Gordon who believed that I had talent, helped me train my eye, exposed me to the larger art world, and pushed me to grow, to expand my horizons, to persevere and create the best possible. He was there to tell me when to let a piece rest, when to push it further. I owe him.

I exhibited my paintings, collages, and monotypes in shows all over Wyoming for the next two years. They were small shows, but each year the standard was raised by which competitions I tried to get in. During the summertime, after my children had graduated from school and were working either in New York or at the Sheridan Inn, I took workshops at the Anderson Ranch in the mountains of Colorado. Nationally well-known artists taught two-week workshops in photography, oil and acrylic painting, printing, ceramics, and woodworking. The ranch was alive with creative energy. Most workshops were open to visitors. I took monotype, painting, and ceramic workshops taught by various artists.

The process of creating a monotype demands an acceptance of error, luck, and a willingness to lose control. Although I have seen some very precise work done by passing paper multiple times through a press, I started off with an idea of a subject, such as the figure of a woman or an abstraction of a landscape, which I would then paint on the bed of the press with lithographic inks. I had to recognize and remember that the last color applied would be the most buried. Everything would be printed out in reverse. What was placed on the right would appear on the left. I then positioned the paper very carefully and precisely over the image and dropped it in place. The paper passed under the roller or the bar of an electric lithography press, imprinting the ink onto the paper, which created a monotype. Sometimes I included a paper collage element. When the print was pinned up on the wall, I made fine marks with the angled edge of a brayer (a barrel-shaped tool that moves ink over a flat surface), my index finger, an old credit card, or a paintbrush, texturing the flatness of the print. At the Anderson Ranch, I would get up at two in the morning and go down to the press, so that I had time alone and a clear space to work. I finished my day when my classmates came in to work at ten A.M. I then visited other workshops, listened to lectures, read, or went to galleries in nearby Aspen for the rest of the day.

Another year, I learned to stretch six-by-six-foot canvases of jute, and paint in those dimensions at a class with the painter Roberto Juarez. It was difficult to overcome my shyness when painting these large canvases in front of other students. I feared being judged and felt exposed and vulnerable. I found a front-corner spot at the bottom of the staircase for privacy and did not join in class revelry. Over the two-week period, I finished four of these huge canvases and felt a soaring sense of pride in my accomplishment. The large size gave me the freedom to think big, move forward, make tighter, bolder statements. Open space has always let me breathe free.

My serious professional art career began at that workshop. Monotypes were considered a secondary art form. In order to get into a gallery or museum show of note, painting was the medium required.

Within a few years, I was invited to show two works at the Yellowstone Art Center. It was for their annual auction, a goal to achieve. A monotype and a painting of mine were selected for the auction in March. Pete Stremmel was the auctioneer. He and his wife, Turkey, have a large and well-respected contemporary art gallery in Reno, Nevada. At the auction, my colorful monotype sold for a good price. The large painting did not. Pete Stremmel came over to me after the auction and said, "Don't worry that your big painting didn't sell. It is a fine painting, just too powerful for this audience. You are the best painter in Wyoming." Pete was a tall man, large in mind and heart. To this day, I am grateful for his comment. His statement gave me confidence.

I taste color sometimes when I am deeply concentrating in the beginning, middle, or toward the end of a painting. It does not always come to me succinctly, I have to murmur it, caress it, place my brush or rag (I use both) on the glass door palette, poke at the colors laid out before me, let my eye rove over the generous mounds of paint. The sensation, palpably lush, invites my whole being to choose color. The choosing feels so intense, but in the end the choice is random. I try one, then another hue, thin it down with gel or matte medium, slap the brush on the canvas, let the paint fly, the drips roll. Sometimes I find I have held my breath until I lift my brush off the canvas. I gulp air, return to my palette for more paint, more colors in the dance, wild and wide, sensitive, bold there, sensuous everywhere. A dream. Zydeco music beats. Is the painting beginning to work? Well, maybe, but it needs just a mark, a big one, of purple blended with blue, which demands Hansa Yellow, a cold yellow like a lemon, then strong, warm orange next to cobalt blue. I blend colors on the canvas, using my whole body, my arm outstretched in sweeping gestures, now all muscles taut, then the tender lines or the soft blend of lush alfalfa fields and sun-soaked terra-cotta, like Moroccan sands.

Donna Forbes, the director of the Yellowstone Art Center, worked in the converted old jailhouse in Billings for years. She turned the center into a nationally accredited art museum, well known across the country by dealers, collectors, and art professionals. The exhibitions she put on were exciting, showing the best artists of the region, thereby fulfilling the museum's mission. Donna and her curator, Gordon McConnell, traveled not only to adjoining states but also to New York, Seattle, Houston, and other large cities to keep in touch with what was going on in the art world. They both had excellent contacts in the American art market. Both liked my work.

In 1987 I was invited to have a solo exhibition at the Yellowstone Art Center, downstairs and upstairs, the entire space. I wallowed in prideful joy. I had spent the winter in New York City, painted every day in the New York studio I found on Houston Street. My newest work was open Sumi-e-like paintings: large and lyrical.

My relationship with Gordon Krause lasted on and off for twelve years. The twenty-year gap in our ages made a bigger difference as the years passed. I wanted a different relationship and sadly told him he had to find another place to live and another life unattached to mine. I had started out wanting to help his art career. Ultimately, he helped mine.

At the inn, Vivian Patterson had said to me when I first became involved with Gordon, "You are a rescuer of the downtrodden, the sick, the hurting, and the broken." I had replied, "Maybe I am." I will always be grateful for Gordon's tender help training my eye and supporting my talent.

I lived with Lou Peterson for two years in New York City, where I spent the winter months. We traded nights at each other's apartments, his in Chelsea, mine on Sixty-first Street near Third Avenue. He was a black playwright who had written an important play, *Take a Giant Step*, and taught at SUNY at Stony Brook, on Long Island. We went to AA meetings nightly and played Spite and Malice at my kitchen table.

At the end of our love affair, I spent more time in Wyoming and began to have a sense of myself. I wanted to be home. I began taking tennis lessons because I had started dating a local jock who would not play with me. "You don't play well enough," he had said in the hot tub of a now-defunct tennis club. His attitude pissed me off. I'll get good enough so that you will ask me to play in a state tournament, I said to myself. I wanted to get in shape, so I jogged a couple of miles down Piney Creek Road every morning, took exercise classes every weekday at the YMCA, had an hour tennis lesson daily, and then played tennis with whoever would play with me. I got good enough to win some prizes and moved on to play in tournaments around the state. The jock and I played mixed doubles in the state tournament in 1985. We won. I gave up tennis.

In October 1984, I reached the mellow age of fifty. I gave myself the birthday present of a two-and-a-half-week trekking adventure in Nepal with a group called Women in the Wilderness; I had seen the trip advertised in *The New Yorker*. To climb the Himalayas had been a dream of mine since I first read about Shangri-La in James Hilton's book. I thought that to be surrounded by nature's natural giants was to be at peace. The director, China Galland, had dinner with us in San Francisco the night before we left and told us her goal was to make women at ease in the wild, confident, not fearful. She found that when she taught women to be comfortable and how to take care of themselves in the wild, the confidence they acquired there passed on into their business and professional lives, and even altered their perspective within the home. To be "at one" in various settings in the wild, either alone or with a companion, added great joy and interest to women's lives.

Many years later, I was to use her idea with some of my grandchildren. I would spend a day or days with them playing in among the ponderosa pine and the spruce, or on the open meadows of the Bighorn Mountains. I had resurrected two small cabins on my property, which extended up to Bighorn National Forest. They nestled in among aspen and pine trees close to a pond. It was a private area, where access was hidden from public view. My goal was to make my grandkids at ease in natural, wild surroundings; I knew that the confidence gained would serve them in other experiences throughout their lives. I slept in the bed, while my grandchildren got the floor. I took one or two at a time, occasionally as many as four. We told ghost stories and raced boats made of fallen leaves in the thin stream that flowed from the pond. We built fires, cooked hamburgers or soup, ate apples and cookies. We skipped stones in the pond and scooped out space in the earth by the cabin, named Sweetwater, so I could fill a gallon jug from water trickling down through rocks beneath the cabin. This delicious water came from a spring in the hillside, but we never have found exactly where it is. We were happy talking to squirrels and birds, salamanders and frogs.

TWENTY-TWO

Cancer Once More

My mother called in early spring of 1977 to say she had been diagnosed with an inoperable and fatal tumor in the back of her throat. She said she was moving back to New York and had taken an apartment at the Carlyle Hotel. She didn't think she had long to live and wanted to be back where her children lived. All her furniture had already been shipped by boat to the Carlyle to furnish "an apartment almost exactly like the one we had when you lived with Nana and Puck." My mind quickly went back to those years when I'd felt so abandoned by my family and the man who I thought had loved me. Scenes of his touch became palpable, the pleasure at being held, the shame, my cowardice.

My mother said she was going to Doctors Hospital when she arrived in New York.

"What are you going there for?" I asked.

"A second opinion on the tumor. But I think it is a waste of money. I know the doctor here in Hawaii is right. I can feel it. But Nelson, Puck, and Madeleine think I should get a second opinion, so I will do it to please them," she said. She started to cough.

My mother continued saying how she looked forward to seeing her friends and having her family close by. Her spirits were obviously elevated, at least on the surface. I wondered how she truly felt. She had never confided in me and wouldn't now, but she might to Puck. I assumed she was frightened—I would have been—but she was determined not to let her fear show, to be stalwart and brave. I told her I would meet her in the city the week she got there in late June, before her appointment at Doctors Hospital. I was the member of the family who dealt with hospitals, nurses, anywhere human management skills were needed. Puck was my mother's confidante and was good at sensing what was going on with her emotionally. Madeleine and her husband, Pete, would enjoy the luxuries at the Carlyle. Nelson had been a presence at my mother's hospital bedside only once before she left for Hawaii, and that was when he had some maneuvering about her will that he wanted to accomplish. She had had some trouble with her heart then and was passing out and falling in her house on Long Island. He had been so angry with her as a young boy for interfering in his budding social life. Once married, he had become hideously rude to her when she tried to be part of his life. He was working for the company, married with three daughters, and had no time for his mother. The interaction between them was classic and icky. Nelson would send flowers but not be helpful.

I set the phone back in its cradle and looked out my kitchen window. I watched a flock of rosy-breasted finch swoop down from on high in a triangular formation. They swarmed all over the bird feeder and the ground beneath, pecking feverishly. For no visible reason, they took off in unison, like flame.

I had to start layering up my walls of defense before I could begin to deal with my family, particularly my mother. The thought of having to care for her, smooth her way in and out of hospitals, depressed me. At first I couldn't feel anything about her dying. Her physical presence in my life, even by phone, was not worth the mention. Because I wanted someone to care for me when I needed it, it was essential I do the caring now. Once I realized the truth, at least in part, about my caring behavior, some of the frustration and anger I always felt in her presence, or when I thought about her, seemed to lessen. My job was to retain a detachment and be kind. The deeper I searched, the more I realized that my need for her love was still there. How amazing at my age. My mother would die soon. I felt a sense of relief, a freedom from emotional shackles that had constrained me since early childhood, the little girl of eight who gave up who she was because she couldn't fight anymore. I felt ashamed that I wanted her dead.

In late June I walked into a familiar space at the Carlyle Hotel. This time, it was decorated with my mother's furniture, her adornments of fabrics and decoration. The layout was almost identical to that of the apartment I had lived in with Puck and Nana, then Aunt Virginia and Uncle Uzal. My mother was still sleeping in the old four-poster mahogany bed she had given me when I was thirteen. When she had moved out of the big house at Oyster Bay, after Nelson and I each were married, and into the smaller one she had built at the end of the property, she told me she wanted the bed. So I swapped the bed for a folding dining room table, which I could use. Now the bed was decorated in English chintz, with a fitted bedcover, pillow roll, and a band of the same material around the top of all four posts. The room looked so like my mother, acceptably old-world. I went out for coffee, and when I returned, she was sitting up in bed, looking like Marie Antoinette, bespectacled and wearing a pink frothy bed jacket, reading *The New York Times*, a sapphire ring on her right hand and a three-strand choker of pearls around her neck, left on from the previous night.

"Hello, darling," she said, putting down the paper and peering at me over her glasses. "I was just about to get up and dressed. How are you?" The words seemed rushed together. I hugged her gently and went around the bed to sit in the pale blue velvet lounge chair. She was to go to Doctors Hospital the next day for a CT scan of the tumor and a biopsy to find out if this tumor would be fatal. My mother told me she liked her new doctor, who had been in to visit her at the Carlyle. This was unheard of. Doctors no longer made house calls, as far as I knew. Her eyes sparkled when she spoke of him, which signaled to me that she was having a flirt. Good for her.

The reports came back in a week, confirming the original diagnosis. Her doctor told us, her three daughters, she probably had three months to live and, if lucky, perhaps a little more. Nelson did not come down from his summer home in Nantucket to be part of the family group. Instead, he sent a charming floral token with a "Love, Nelson" card. I was furious with him for not showing up. What could he do? Nothing. Just be there, *dammit* ran through my head. But I said nothing. To start a family fuss now would only hurt my mother. She would only defend Nelson.

I went back to Wyoming in mid-July for the remainder of the summer. I had been in New York for only a month, yet I already felt the twitching anger and frustration I always felt when dealing with my family. They liked me only when I was doing what they wanted me to do—get them out of a hole. My son, John, was home at the ranch, working for Don Knox, laying cement foundations for houses next to the airport. Knox had become a mentor for John; he had been teaching him how to fly-fish (a sport John continues to enjoy now in his mid-fifties). Ellen was home as well. That summer she worked in the gallery of the Sheridan Inn, where her ability to put people at ease, interest and amuse them, was a great asset. She had ideas on how to make the gallery more appealing to a wider public. Her quick sense of humor delighted everyone, and her caustic insights either frightened me or made me laugh. Summer was always a frantic rush at the inn. We never knew when busloads of tourists would arrive or what other events might alter the number of people we would feed at any given meal. Most weekday lunch hours, if we had banquets or busloads of people, I helped the cooks on the main line in the kitchen get the orders out. In summertime, we often served between three and five hundred people for lunch. Panic set in if a cook didn't show, or if one of the more elegant ladies in town wanted a private lunch in the parlor at the last minute and we did not have enough waitresses to handle the job. But we managed to accommodate everyone. When we had only young people working the night shift in the kitchen, all bases were always covered, because those kids sent a friend if they couldn't show up as scheduled. Another pair of hands to cover their slot was what we needed, and it didn't matter if the person had never been in a kitchen before, as someone could show him or her the ropes. Those few months, not one person in the kitchen was over twenty years old. They pulled together to make meals happen. The inn continued to be a success in the community, and its popularity was growing statewide. I felt driven to make it work and work well. I had been at the job for twelve years and the time would come when I needed to sell the inn and get my life back.

That September, I answered Puck's latest call for help in caring for our mother. Puck had a novel to finish, a deadline to meet. I flew to New York a week later. Ellen had left to begin her sophomore year at Redlands College in California. John was in his freshman year at Stanford. I was free of responsibilities, except for the inn. I stayed at my rented apartment in the city and spent the days or evenings with my mother, took her to doctors' appointments, played backgammon with her, or listened quietly to her social concerns, such as "What should I feed my bridge group next Tuesday?" The fact that she was dying did not seem to be upsetting to her. She never spoke to me about her coming end. I intuited her thoughts occasionally, once by reciting the Twenty-third Psalm when she had seen a flock of sheep in a magazine about the stately homes of England. That was very near the end, when she couldn't speak. She smiled sweetly during my recital; her tiny frame and bright eyes looked doll-like. I went on automatic pilot as caregiver, meaning I gave up everything to be with my mother, making her comfortable when needed. It was what I knew, how I could give of myself, how I could love.

Madeleine, the eldest child, responded to my mother's illness like a needy young girl, teary-eyed and sniffling. She wanted to talk in person or on the phone daily, sometimes several times a day. "What are we going to do without Mummy?" Madeleine whined. "Mummy" was mean to her on many nights when she and her husband, Pete, stayed at the Carlyle. Most likely, everyone had had too much to drink and our mother's claws came out. Madeleine was dependent on our mother emotionally and financially, an unfortunate place to settle. Although Madeleine had been the earliest renegade in the family, the one who joined the navy and welded planes during World War II to be with the boys, the one who became a fine painter, the one who joined the Communists in San Francisco, and the one who, while being a cocktail waitress, danced on tabletops, she now yearned for the comforts my mother's wealth occasionally provided for her. On our mother's death, Madeleine would lose her emotional and financial guardian, and I wondered how she would manage.

My mother could and would turn vicious with any of us daughters when she wanted to declare her power. Puck and I snapped back. But Madeleine wasn't strong enough. My mother would ridicule Madeleine about her financial failures, the way she dressed, her failure as Maggie's mother—anything to belittle the adversary. Was it female jealousy that made my mother so mean? Is that what triggered her viciousness? This broad streak of Irish cruelty overtook my mother, as it had her father. He used to belittle his wife in this same manner when he had too much to drink on some holiday like Thanksgiving. After crucifying his wife, Grandma, he would fall in love with her all over again, serenade her with Irish love songs at the dining table, and cry, shedding real tears.

I stayed well out of my mother's way. She had done all the damage I would allow. I lost patience with poor Madeleine. I talked more with Puck, who tuned in to the family saga when she could. Nelson never communicated with me or any of us caretakers, nor did he visit his mother. He only sent small but elegant bouquets of flowers.

To save my sanity, I pressed on with my art in any free time I had. I took a class in figure drawing from Bob Hale at the Art Students League that autumn. Although I did not do figurative work, Hale was famous for this class; therefore, it was an opportunity I should not miss. I could learn the importance of line, the threads and nuances of the female nude. Hale stood before a class of twenty-five with a stick over a yard long, a bit of white chalk bound to the tip with string. He used it to draw on a blackboard fastened to the ceiling, so we pupils in the back could see without stretching our necks to peer around the pupils in front who had gotten to class on time. Slowly moving his outstretched arm with only the slightest bend in the elbow, he drew an outline of the nude model before us. It was a display of extraordinary talent combined with a passionate knowledge of the female body, which he re-created on the board. I can still see him now, thirty-six years later, in gray sweater and tweed jacket, standing before the blackboard, creating a female with limbs, hips, and head, but no facial features, as though his fingertips were tracing the outline of her body. I took an evening class in drawing the human body from Giorgio Cavallon and other artists at the Studio School on West Eighth Street, in Greenwich Village. I had won an honorable mention at the Art Students League in Hale's class, and wanted to draw and draw and draw. I found fascinating the many different views of the nude in the same pose you could create by how you structured the body. Experiencing a number of teachers and the inevitable art conversations that followed opened a doorway that I could translate into the abstract. It gave me another push forward.

As fall progressed, my mother's condition worsened. Eating became more of a problem for her. She never ate much anyway, just pushed food around the plate to look like she had tried everything, but now she really could only manage pureed soups. By Thanksgiving, we had to hire round-the-clock nurses on twelve-hour shifts. My mother wanted reassurance in case anything happened to her—if she fell or the tumor started to bleed. She had never been good at taking care of herself, such as doing exercises for her arthritic knees, things like that. Now that she was so fragile, I think she was terrified of being alone.

My mother wanted one of her daughters to stay with her every night in the guest bedroom on the floor above hers, accessible by an internal staircase. We took turns. Madeleine and Pete spent weekends willingly. They enjoyed the elegant attentions of Yaeko, the housekeeper and cook. Puck and I were not so keen to be guests. Puck's mate, Tommy Thomas, was stalwart help. She took the strain off Puck by making us all laugh. We sisters imagined disaster and would stew about things together, creating more of a mountain than the molehill deserved. Puck was the one who talked with our mother about dying. I would talk with Puck most days, going over the stresses and upsets, analyzing moods and intentions, the details of caring for the aged and dying. Madeleine continued to be fragile in her response to daily problems. I felt sorry for her, when I was not annoyed. Our conversations were not kind. I was worn-out long before Christmas. I remembered the tension and stress I had felt from the brief time I was home from school before my father died, waiting for the other shoe to drop.

My mother was also set on getting medications to enable her to let herself out of this life. Her panic to do so came on a Saturday, when no doctor could be found in the city. Eventually we got a prescription for something (I assumed for sleeping pills but never checked) and got it filled at the local chemist. The bottle remained in her bathroom for almost two months. The subject only came up again in mid-February. I told her I would get the pills from the bathroom for her, mash them up, and get the apricot juice, which she could still swallow, and set these on the bed tray. I would not feed them to her. She had to do that herself. This dialogue was repeated again and again.

One of the nurses overheard us talking and reported our conversation to her nurses' agency. She said I was planning to kill my mother. She threatened to go to the police. Fortunately, my mother's doctor took the nurse off the case, and the subject never came up again.

My job was to keep the household staff and the nurses on schedule, and to ensure that good and varied food was produced daily for nurses and guests by Yaeko; I was to keep Yaeko sober, too. My other responsibility was to ensure that all medical matters took place quickly and efficiently.

I lived alone at my apartment on Sixty-first Street, next to a busy Third Avenue restaurant. The eatery generously shared their dog-size cockroaches with me—in my bathroom and kitchen on the ground floor. When I turned on the kitchen light, the roaches paraded back into the walls as if they were the queen's guards. I gave the shiny big bastards names as I smashed them with an iron frying pan. I was quite successful. The light, the easy street access, and the fact that I had two floors of space gave this apartment character and made the roaches somewhat bearable. A guest room and bath, small but adequate, provided room for Ellen when she came home on vacation. John slept on the sofa in the big upstairs living room, which had a fireplace and wide, tall windows that faced south onto the garden, thick with trees. In winter, their branches cast strange sculptural shadows on my bedroom wall below. I loved watching the gray shadows slide across the white wall. My bedroom took in a little sun in midmorning and was absolutely quiet. No sound of city life intruded. The kitchen, on the same floor as the bedroom, faced the street and was noisy. The art classes I attended helped me stay steady, engaged in my artwork.

At two different crisis moments when doctors told us my mother was at the end, my children came to be with their grandmother and to help me. I was warmed by their generous caring; both were in their early twenties, usually not the most thoughtful time in the lives of young people. They paid for their own air tickets and never asked me to refund the money.

The potential crisis didn't happen. Day and night vigils continued. We three sisters snapped at one another because we were tired; each had her own agenda. Besides, we couldn't snap at our mother, whose care ate into our lives, soured our humors, and eventually poisoned the affection between us for a time.

My mother shrank into skeletal form. In mid-March, she had been on an intravenous feeding of sugar water for a month. I scooted home for a week off, and when I returned on Sunday, Puck took off for a week in the Caribbean. We knew the end was near. My mother slept most of the time. Madeleine and I watched over her. At the end of the workweek, on Thursday, I tried to reach Puck to tell her to hurry back; our mother was sinking fast. I was unable to connect because the phone lines to the island where she was staying weren't working. A doctor had come on Thursday afternoon to check her IV. He struggled for almost two hours to find a vein in my mother's leg where he could insert a needle, but her veins had shrunk. "I can't find a vein. I am so sorry," he said as he packed up his small black bag. I thought of Beenie and Divine, the funeral directors who had embalmed my father. A knot tightened in my chest.

"You know what that means, Ma, don't you?" I said, looking down at her tiny frame in the blue velvet chair. She looked up at me with childlike, questioning eyes. "You will die in a couple of days." She nodded.

My mother had had a tracheotomy so that she could continue to breathe and talk, but she had never mastered the talking part. She wrote the doctor a sketchy note—"All right"—and then went to sleep, sitting up in her blue lounge chair. The following day was March 31, a gray, blustery Friday. My mother slept a good deal of the time. She opened her eyes occasionally, looking startled and confused, and then went back to the comfort of sleep. I tried to phone Puck again and again, without success. Saturday, my mother seemed to be in a coma. I was scared she would die before Puck got back. If that happened, Puck would be paralyzed with guilt. After her great friend died from an aneurysm years ago, Puck continued to blame herself, without reason. On Sunday morning, April 2, I arrived at ten. Miss Feyer, the day nurse who had been with us since November, told me she didn't think my mother could possibly last till noon.

I did not tell Miss Feyer that Puck's plane was not due in until 1:20 P.M. I sat in the blue velvet chair, dressed in jeans and a sweater. I sipped at a cup of coffee in my right hand. In my left, I held my mother's withered hand. There simply was no flesh there. I said to her in a firm but kind voice, "Stay with me, Ma. Puck is coming. She will have a fit if you die before she gets here. Stay with me. Hold my hand for strength. Stay with me." I chanted the message over and over for more than three hours, stroked my mother's arm, and beseeched her. I looked at my watch, then out the thirty-second-story window of the Carlyle Hotel at the heavy gray skies, then back to my mother's face. She looked peaceful, but so tiny and wrinkled.

At 2:24 P.M., Puck burst into the room, dropping her coat on the floor as she came in. I had sent a limousine to fetch her at Kennedy Airport.

"She is alive," I said as my eyes locked in with hers. I quickly got out of the blue chair so Puck could sit. I passed my mother's hand over to her and took a deep breath. "Thank you, gods and goddesses, who have watched over this scene," I said to myself, looking up to the gray heavens. Only a minute passed. It seemed far longer, as though the second hand had not moved in a timely way, each second stretching too long. My mother took an audible breath and let out a soft rumble of air. She was gone. I had told her she was doing a great job, waiting to die till after Puck arrived. I went to the window to look out on the city. My mother's lawyer, Bruce Hecker, came into the bedroom. He had at one time been my lawyer, but now he represented both my mother and Nelson. His presence sickened me. I felt something between disgust and revulsion.

The funeral was delayed three days because my brother, Nelson, and my ex-husband John Sargent were playing in a golf tournament in Hobe Sound, Florida. Nelson had a winter home there. Nelson came up from the South to see his mother only once, just after Christmas, at a crisis moment. He had visited her two other times during the ten months she had been ill. I did not pretend to guess at the intricacies of their relationship, but it angered me that we sisters were the ones left with end-of-life care for our mother, when the only child she loved, for whom she had worked so tirelessly, ignored her.

I sat in the waiting area reserved for families attending funerals or weddings at St. James's Church on Madison Avenue. I waited for the organ music to begin. My mother's will was delivered to me there by Bruce Hecker, at Nelson's request. I knew Nelson. I knew how he calculated hurting someone, demeaning them, or crucifying them verbally. I had watched him be abusively rude both socially and in business. Delivering my mother's will to me in the church before her funeral was his way of getting even with me—for suing him as trustee, possibly. The contents of the will showed him getting half of my mother's estate and the three women sharing the other half, a change from an earlier, fairer distribution for all of us that I had known about. If there were to be any dispute over her will, that person was to be cut out of the will. That line had been inserted for me. A final thrust from my mother and a final bid for Nelson's love and gratitude. I sighed and willed myself not to be upset. My friend Lou Peterson was sitting in a pew somewhere in the church. I concentrated on him, his caring.

After the graveside ceremony, Nelson and his wife, Sandy, gave a luncheon at their house nearby, in Locust Valley. Cousins of varying ages, whom I hadn't seen in twenty years, gathered with us to again be part of the McCarter/Doubleday family. My mother was the last McCarter of that generation to die. Now we were the elders. I felt apart, a viewer, except for an honest talk with my cousin Sue Tift. She had been my best friend until she and John Sargent had something going on while I was in Europe. I never faced her at the time of the event. I just vanished out of her life. I was not happy with how I had treated her.

TWENTY-THREE

Liquidity Matters

Within the week, I fled back to Wyoming, leaving good AA friends who had supported me during the long haul the past ten months. Lou Peterson had talked with me daily, taken me to meetings, and made me laugh. I had finally gotten a sponsor after seven years of sobriety—something I should have done the first year.

Alone at home, the first hint of green forecast the possibility of an early spring. The upshoots on the hills brought life back into my veins, and the sense of nature's cycle warmed me. From the top of Jim Creek Hill on my way to work at the inn, I often pulled over at the peak of that crest to let the landscape flood into me. From there, I looked over a sea of hills, waves washing their rhythmic way west to the Bighorn Mountains. I wondered in awe at the lushness of green in late May, when the burnt oranges and red oxides of the scoria-topped hills perfectly balanced that wild intensity of green. Hay fields sported a much lighter green coat a bit later. Anything seemed possible on those days. Nature's vibrancy quickened my heartbeat.

I needed time apart from everyone now. I painted long hours on weekends, played tennis, hit the ball with every ounce of energy I had stored up. For the minutes and hours when I could not speak, I cried, not for the loss of my mother, for she and I had never been friends, but for the child-like need I had for her love. I cried for a love that would fill me. When I was not feeling sorry for myself, I was hugely pissed off at her neglect.

In 1984 I had a rotator cuff operation on my right shoulder, necessitating my wearing a sling for weeks. It was an injury many tennis players suffer. I was worried about the inn, which was having a hard time because a Holiday Inn had opened up in town. They bested the Sheridan Inn's prices on banquet meals every time, which left our facilities half-empty, when they had been full for years. The Holiday Inn had the income from rooms to compensate for any loss in food sales, so they could afford to lowball banquet prices. The inn did not have that capability. Just as we were about to clear a profit, the inn was taking a big loss. I thought there was no marketing I could do to increase business. The Sheridan Inn could not compete with chain-hotel prices.

I was dating a surgeon during this time. One night, he said, "You had better get the inn sold, or you will go broke." His bluntness was painful but I knew it true. I thought of the Rockefeller family, who owned Teton Lodge in western Wyoming. They might be interested in expanding their investment in the state. John Sargent was friends with Laurance Rockefeller and had stayed with him in Jackson years ago, before he came over the mountains to check on the children. I had met Laurance at some party when I was married to John, but my memory could not bring up his face. I called John to see if he would give me an introduction to Rockefeller. John and I were now on easily polite terms with each other. I had stayed that way throughout because of Ellen and John.

I walked into the Rockefeller offices in Rockefeller Plaza two weeks later, in late June 1984; my arm was still in a sling. My accountant had sent financial information along with territorial and community details the week before. I had nothing to carry but my wits. I was escorted to Mr. Rockefeller's office by a youthful man dressed in gray pinstripes, who had probably just fallen out of Harvard Business School. His shoes were polished to perfection. My nerves began twitching. This was not my favorite milieu; formality frightened me. We took a left, and there behind his desk, the New York skyline in the background, sat Mr. Rockefeller. Three other men in the room moved toward me in greeting. Mr. Rockefeller got up and came around his desk. In a relaxed yet formal manner, he introduced me to his subordinates, the three men standing now in a half circle in front of his desk. One was in charge of the Rockefeller hotel, restaurant, and real estate business in the United

States, another had direct oversight of Teton Lodge, and the third was his chief financial officer.

"It is a pleasure to see you again, Neltje," Mr. Rockefeller said, extending his hand.

"Likewise, Mr. Rockefeller," I replied. "It has been many years. You look well. And you have a handsome office. Thank you for taking time to see me."

When Mr. Rockefeller sat back down at his desk, he lifted a stack of papers in his thin right hand and turned to me. "Congratulations, Neltje."

"For what, Mr. Rockefeller?" I replied, wondering what approach he was about to take.

"You have lost less money in this sort of business than anyone I know of," he replied. We laughed.

In the end, the Rockefeller Group was not interested in acquiring further investments in Wyoming. I knew the visit was a long shot, but I needed to explore every avenue to find a buyer for the inn. I was physically and emotionally exhausted and becoming resentful of folks in Sheridan who brought their guests to enjoy the decorations of historical significance but did not even buy a cup of coffee. Scenes of the inn's early beginnings filled my mind: the day we opened the saloon; the morning I got the call the chefs had split; the special dinners we did throughout one winter, including Polish night, with the Polish women arguing about which town in Poland had the best latkes, and a luau night; the donations of furnishings from all over the state. I remembered small kindnesses, like the local town kids cutting the grass and washing windows when I first opened.

After discussions about the difficulty of making a profit in the food business, I made my excuses to leave Mr. Rockefeller's office, then turned as though with an afterthought. "Would you know Charlie Duell? I understand he has had some real estate connections in Wyoming. He is from somewhere in the South—Virginia or maybe South Carolina?" I questioned.

"Oh yes, indeed. Charlie, I know him well. He lives in Charleston, South Carolina. We would be happy to get in touch with him for you. If he is interested, we will send him on these materials. If he shows no interest and we can come up with no other prospects, we will return the materials to you," said Mr. Rockefeller.

I thanked all the gentlemen for their time and concern. One of them escorted me to the elevator. I have forgotten all their names but can see their faces. Mr. Rockefeller's earlier compliment gave me strength, helped dispel the gloom of being stuck with the inn for the rest of my life.

I pressed on, realizing that I had to find an entity that could put the money into developing a motel, either in the old Cook Ford building and lot across the street or on the inn lot itself. I did not have the cash to expand the facilities, nor the energy, will, or desire to get involved in such a project. I wanted the freedom to paint. I was on a schedule, as I had been for some years, of painting every morning, then racing to the inn to be there for the lunch crowd. This schedule had my body and mind flying in one direction, then slamming to a halt and reversing.

Twice I had purchase offers. One progressed to the point where we began taking inventory, from dishes to booze. That buyer had had the liquor license transferred to his company's name. At the scheduled morning meeting at eight A.M. in April 1984 to go over plates and glasses, pots and pans, liquors and foods, the buyer never showed up. He just disappeared, left town. We got the liquor license back. The other buyer backed off when his investors didn't show up with the cash down payment. By this time, I was a hardened shopper for a way out. I hired a manager whom I did not like but who would serve. I could no longer be at the inn on a day-to-day basis.

In 1986 I got in touch with the National Trust for Historic Preservation, first regionally, then in Washington, D.C. The people there said they would accept the inn but wanted me to pay them a quarter of a million dollars to take care of the building for two years. Their financial figures for overseeing the protection of the inn were excessive. They bore no relation to the true cost. I was looking for financial help, and a way to ensure the Sheridan Inn would be preserved, but I did not plan on being taken advantage of financially. I was livid and depressed. I had thought that the National Trust for Historic Preservation raised money nationally to help out in the kind of situation I found myself.

I asked my son, John, who was now married and living in New York, working at Simon & Schuster, to go with me to their headquarters in Washington, D.C. I told him to kick me under the table if I started to behave in a way that would squash the deal. I knew my temper could fly at inappropriate times, and I was not a good negotiator when my back was against the wall. I had racked my mind trying to come up with an alternative to the National Trust for Historic Preservation without even a whisper of a solid idea. For now, I needed this organization to be my safety net while I continued the search for a buyer.

At the meeting in Washington, D.C., I remained quiet. John did all the negotiating. He said he would tend to all the telephoning, and the organizing of all financial and legal matters. I hadn't known he was actually going to take all these matters into his hands, relieving me. Listening to him discuss and negotiate possible terms of an arrangement with the National Trust, I nearly wept with pride and awe at his negotiating skills. Anger often got in my way when an issue under negotiation had any emotional content, as this did. We flew back to New York together, with me sputtering outrage at the attitude of dismissal that had prevailed throughout the meeting. As he ran off to catch a subway home, John told me, "Cool it. I will deal with them."

Two nights later in my New York City hotel room over by the East River and the UN, I awoke from a deep sleep. I'd had a long good dream about the man who had appraised the inn for me years before. I had needed the "fair value" price for the inn in order to sell it. We had been having lunch in the inn dining room when we discussed possibilities for sale in Wyoming, or possibly Colorado. At that time, I asked him if he knew any charitable institution in the Denver area who might be interested were I to gift the inn. He had said he had a friend on the Children's Hospital board in Denver and could ask him. First thing that morning in New York, I got the appraiser's number from the office at the inn. I phoned him in Denver, excited at the possibility of an alternate avenue to the National Trust. He was glad to hear from me, and we talked a bit, caught up with each other. He said that of course he would be happy to call his friend.

I told him, "I have an hour and a half between my flights tomorrow. Maybe your friend could meet me at Stapleton Airport. We could do some preliminary discussion at least, if he is interested."

He called me back within the hour. I had been out for a fast jog up and down First Avenue, mostly breathing in gas fumes from traffic, circling around Sutton Place, where I had lived when first married. I longed for the Wyoming air, the wide views and the mountains that changed color and even seemed to change structure in the altering light. He said, "My friend on the board of Denver's Children's Hospital is a handsome white-haired and blue-eyed guy, about six feet tall. He will meet your plane at Stapleton, and will arrange a private area for you to talk."

I walked off the plane in Denver, and right there in front of me was a good-looking man with white hair and intense dancing blue eyes. I threw my arms around him and held him as though I had known him well for a long time. The Sheridan Inn was transferred to the Children's Hospital of Denver a month later. And I danced.

I was free from my mother's unrelenting voice of disapproval and annoyance in my head: "Why don't you ever look where you are going? Why do you wear that awful cow plop on your head? You have lovely long hair, but it's too bushy. You should have it thinned." Endless therapies and good counsel helped me see her insecurities and jealousies. I had been a threat to her, a visible reminder she was getting older. These jealousies were mostly based on the fact that I was born a Doubleday.

Yes, I was fortunate. I have had a place in society because my father was well known in the literary and business world. He made the Doubleday book-publishing company a huge success through his imaginative marketing and his will to win. Thanks to the trusts he created for his children upon their births, and for his wife and children upon his death, I am financially independent, and that means I've been free to make art and to live as I wish. For that, I was and am grateful beyond knowable measure.

In 1986, eight years after my mother's death, Doubleday & Company contracted to sell its assets to Bertelsmann, a German publishing company that John Sargent and I had visited on our first trip to Germany, in the early 1950s. Nelson and Fred Wilpon bought the Mets baseball team from Doubleday before the sale to Bertelsmann. Finally, Nelson could do what he had always wanted. I applauded both sales with enthusiasm.

At last there would be assets in the trusts that could be bought and sold. The share price was fair. And I congratulated Nelson and John Sargent for getting the job done. Nelson was where he belonged, in baseball. His passion had resided there since childhood, not in books. John Sargent retired into the land of directorships.

After the sale, I felt separation, like the loss of a family member, which surprised me. Since childhood, I had railed against treating the Doubleday business like a human being, giving it that kind of concern and attention, to the exclusion of people, children particularly. Yet when the Doubleday bookstores existed, I could not pass them without a sense of pride. My relationship to the family firm had always been complicated.

Money from the sale allowed me to buy the two ranches adjacent to mine on Piney Creek. It happened right after the sale of the company, and I now felt my home place safe from development. The possibility of rooftops and fences cutting off my view of the mountains had troubled me. The properties belonged to my good neighbors, the Collinses and the Millers, my poker-playing buddies when I was married to John Kings. Many a winter night, we had played cards at one another's houses, with good drinks and eats, teasing and laughter. The timing was right. Major remodeling was required to prop up the main Collins house, an old wood and stone ranch house that had passed through generations of the Collins family. The purchase was bittersweet for them, I'm sure. Kathy, my housekeeper, cook, and friend, and her husband, Ray Daly, would live there. Ray leased the ranch land and hay fields for his cattle, and took care of my cattle as well. He proved to be a good manager of the hills and hay lands. David Schreiber, my assistant, who has been with me for years, moved into the log house by the creek, where Marge and Byron Collins used to live. While growing up, my son, John, fished the creek, especially the big pool by the Collinses' log house. He would leave his catch of trout on the kitchen table for their dinner, and Marge Collins would give him a pie she had baked in exchange, with a note if she wasn't at home when he stopped by. He would gobble it down as he walked the half-mile home. Apple was his favorite. I just learned of their sharing this past summer, when John and his family were visiting, forty years after the fact. The story made me smile.

Once the Sheridan Inn was gone, I could spend the whole winter in

New York City. I walked to my studio on Houston Street every morning from my apartment on West Fourth Street, in the Village. I had a two-story garden apartment in an old brick house. The landlady controlled the thermostat for my apartment in her apartment on the second floor. I was often cold, but the space suited me. The high-ceilinged living room/dining room had two fireplaces and lots of wall space for my large paintings. But I found myself lonely in the city in a way I had never been at home in Wyoming. My back began to give me trouble, and my legs felt like ice water was running through my veins; the doctor thought it came from some pinched nerve in my back. All the city delights, like dance and theater, became a painful struggle. I had occasional dinners with Jack Marquand, an old friend of John Sargent's. He was a writer and society figure from days past. His cynical views of contemporary "nonsociety" amused me. He sounded so like an old 78 recording, but his wit was worthy.

In 1990 I decided I wanted a home situation in the city, not a rental on a yearly basis. I purchased an open loft in an old building on West Seventeenth Street, in Chelsea. It needed an extensive remodel, but my eighth-floor bedroom windows looked down on the breadth of lower Manhattan, with a spectacular view of the Twin Towers. Sun flooded the interior from morning until the often-blazing sunset that streamed over the Hudson River into my living room. Once installed, I watched my very young grandchildren play, have temper fits, laugh and giggle, hug me and wrap their tiny fingers around mine. My children and I flounced about with pride. My back failed me the second winter, forcing me to stay flat on my back in bed for months. The pain, like a dentist's drill bearing down on a nerve in my spine twenty-four hours a day, scared me. Could I bear to live with this pain all day, every day with not a moment's relief? I did not know. Ultimately, I found a pain-management doctor at Ellen's suggestion, and within a year I gave up the loft and went home to Wyoming. My back still hurt the same in Wyoming, but I felt at home on the ranch, with help close by. I just am not a city person.

Someone at a Christmas party in Sheridan told me about the most beautiful place he had just seen, and wanted, but could not live in because it was too far away from his business. Was it the passion in his voice that stirred interest in me? I think so. His lavish description enticed me to search out the property. I immediately fell in love with the land, the protective hills, the enormous granite outcropping, heaved out of the earth millions of years ago. The red clay hills and roadway reminded me of the red clay roadways at Bonny Hall. The Realtor John Gibbs, son of my schoolmate Martha, drove me in his truck along the Little North Fork of Crazy Woman Creek to the mouth of the canyon, where we came to an old log cabin, filled with manly (what I call Y-chromosome) furnishings of a fishing camp that belonged to the CEO of the Apache Oil Corporation, Raymond Plank. John told me of a waterfall higher up in the canyon, but for now my back could not be put under the strain of a climb. I wanted to touch every blade of grass or weed, every tree, shrub, and stone. I marveled at the creek waters, bubbling even in winter, half frozen over with ice and snow. I bought this piece of paradise at the base of the Bighorn Mountains, just south of Buffalo. I stayed out there on weekends for the whole next year, in the fisherman's hideaway. I changed the decor to a futon with lots of bright pillows. The old wood cookstove had been ruined by a thoughtless someone who had built a fire in the stove's oven. I bought a camp stove, a three-burner, which answered my cooking needs for the moment. There was no electricity, but there was an outhouse. I survived on pain pills and grit, walked just a bit farther every day, got stronger, and my will to live grew. It took over four years for the pain not to be a constant companion.

With the help of good craftsmen, I restored the log house on the property, a simple two-story structure atop a knoll, with a view eighty-five miles eastward on a clear day. A dead cow lay in mouse, pack-rat, and cow dung next to the woodstove in the living room. There were no doors or windows, just gaping holes. The structure was sound, but friends and contractors suggested I would be better off bulldozing it. I couldn't bear the thought. Those logs held the history of a family that had grown up within its walls.

I call the house and property Little Crazy. The house can sleep nine, with the addition a few years ago of my downstairs octagonal bedroom and bath. A redwood deck, sometimes covered, mostly bare to the elements, makes a beautiful living space in summer, in sun or shade. Little Crazy is my haven, a place apart, where my spirit is enlivened by the trees, the grasses, a wildflower, or a thistle, and my soul is fed.

After my back healed somewhat, I braved traveling again. I went to Bali with my friend Mary Jane Edwards. At the time, she was head of the art department of the University of Wyoming. She was on a six-month sabbatical in the winter of 1998, which allowed us time to have a month's stay on the island. MJ, as she likes to be called, and I have been friends since we met at Artspeak in Cheyenne in 1991. Over the years she would often come up from Laramie just to get away, to be with someone who was not an academic. At Little Crazy, we climbed around Sisters Hill, sought out new pathways in the forests, some already sculpted by wild game, some just a whim. Or we took wild Jeep rides to hidden mountain meadows along barely hacked-out trails with downed trees and scraggly brush impairments. We laughed and screamed till we wet our pants as we thumped over rocks, tree trunks, or slid sideways into hollows. At night we ate and watched movies till we dropped off to sleep, woke to sore muscles and blessed the goddess of hot water. I have no other friend I can be at play with in my paradise at Little Crazy. MJ's equal delight in all forms of nature validates mine. I am so grateful, but too shy to tell her so.

I took MJ on an ATV ride along Piney Creek a month or more before our departure for Bali. I wanted to show off my new vehicle and my prowess at maneuvering this "boy toy" over terrain just like a rancher, a male rancher. Me, too, "I CAN DO IT." The one thing you are not meant to do in an ATV is traverse a hillside. You can go up a hill, or down, but you cannot travel across it. The vehicle will tip over, no matter how stable it seems. We crossed the creek beyond the Piney Road Bridge and the far corrals on the old Collins place, then started up the steep hillside. I came to a knob on the hill, where I turned a bit to the left. The land seemed less steep that way. We were fine one moment; the next second, the angle of the terrain changed, became dramatically steeper. Instead of stopping and backing up to find a new route, I continued on, hoping the steep hillside angle would soften.

I watched in excruciating slow motion as the ATV rolled over my head. Every second elongated itself into a ribbon of horrifying possibilities. I observed the event from a place apart in my mind, as a helpless bystander or voyeur in a movie. I heard the machine thump and clunk in repeated rhythm down the hill. Then silence. I was breathing. My head, arms, and legs seem undamaged. MJ, when I got to her partially down the hill, was not so lucky. She lay on her back, crying in pain. What had I done, me and my show-off self? Fortunately, Sean, who worked on my ranch, had watched from the old corrals below. He yelled he was coming. I went to shut off the ATV, which lay between Mary Jane and the corrals at the base of the hill. By the time I got back to MJ, Sean was there in the truck. MJ had broken her upper arm or shoulder, I thought. She was in agonizing pain. In the emergency room at Sheridan Hospital, she was diagnosed with a broken arm bone at her left shoulder. I put her in my bed, a disguised hospital bed with moving parts, a holdover from my bad-back days. Pain pills and sleep for two days burrowed into pillows was all MJ wanted. She did not complain or become angry with me, as I might have. I was horrified at my stupidity and bravura. My assistant, David, drove her home to Laramie the third day after the accident, at her insistence.

Her doctors agreed she could not drive a car in Bali. It was an order MJ tolerated with growing displeasure once on the island. In Bali they drive on the left-hand side of the road. That was the first scary bit of news I got when we arrived. We rented a Jeep; a small car was a necessity, I found out, because of the narrow two-lane roads and crazed traffic. Every human, animal, or vehicle coming onto the road you traveled on had the right-of-way, no matter which direction they wanted to go. To say the driving experience was bizarre, terrifying, and funny all rolled into one was a valid description of trying to get from point A to point B without killing a fat pig in the road or being killed in a rollover.

MJ navigated for me, with maps on her lap, while I shrieked at old men pushing far-too-heavy food carts up mild inclines, begging them to get out of my way. A string of ducks waddled slowly across the road in front of me on a tight curve, stopping traffic in both directions on this two-lane road. When the last duck reached safety on the far side of the road, a line of Vespas, both behind me and coming at me in the other lane, flew by, weaving past one another in both directions, honking madly, an inch of space between them and me.

Our hotel on a hill outside Ubud had not more than ten rooms, each with an outdoor bathroom. The showers had a wall of rock with blooming orchids and a resident gecko. The staff brought coffee and croissants to the small terrace outside our room every morning. This happened after MJ twisted her ankle while coming back to our room in the dark after dinner. She hobbled and jumped with the aid of a crutch to get from bedroom to poolside, where she read under an umbrella. I took a series of photographs of the bottom of the pool at different times of day, as the markings in the cement interested me. Years later, I used those photos in an art installation.

Afternoons, we searched out visual feasts in stores, ancient buildings, and ruins, watched monkeys scamper about while trying to steal any edibles we might have. We delighted ourselves with the textures of ancient wood carvings worn smooth by sun, rain, or seawater, or in clothes from outer islands, the fabric the softest cotton, the colors like a basket of fruits and flowers. We watched a funeral ceremony where kids raced around with the name and dates of birth and death of the deceased imprinted on their T-shirts. Everyone ate. Balinese music by a variety of bands blared. The coffin was handsomely carved and painted. We were told the funeral had to be delayed a week to give the artist time to complete it.

That was the beginning of many trips together for MJ and me, from the icy waters of Antarctica to the flea markets in Beijing, from the plains of East Africa to Samarkand and Tashkent, in Uzbekistan. We saw tigers and textiles in India, visited Senegal, Gambia, Swaziland, and South Africa, Togo and Benin, Ghana and Mali, and Morocco, beautiful, passionate Morocco. Years before, I had taken a train across Siberia to Lake Baikal, on to Ulan Bator, in Mongolia, and then to Beijing. I had traveled with the daughter of a friend. She was a treat, and she spoke Russian. In 1981, I walked the thick jungle undergrowth to see Dian Fossey's gorillas in Rwanda. How like them we are. But I did not climb Kilimanjaro, in Tanzania, because I was frightened to do it while traveling alone. I did trek up the Khumbu Valley in the Himalaya Mountains in Nepal, and later, during one trip, MJ and I took in Machu Picchu, the Galápagos, and the Amazon River. A piranha jumped into our boat for no reason while we were fishing. It was small. We returned the sharp-toothed fish to its familiar waters. I longed for a one-room cabin on stilts by the river, completely separate from the populated world. It was there as we sailed upriver. A dugout canoe was tied to a dead tree trunk. A woman and three small children stood on the deck and waved.

TWENTY-FOUR

Anger, Art, and a Family of Friends

I was adding an extension to my house on Piney in 1992, because Ellen was producing children at a speedy rate and I wanted a space where I could live with my art, hang my big paintings, some more than twelve feet long. My friend and architect, Ross Iverson, took me to meet his steel-bending, welding friend, Butch Jellis. We were looking for a welder with a strong artistic eye to make gates and a set of stairs. Butch stood in his shop by the railroad tracks on Lower Goose Creek, welder's cap on like a baseball catcher's, bill to the nape of the neck. I had been told he was a maverick, a man who did not fit any occupational slot or any one place in society. He could do most anything, from running an excavator to welding a complex table.

We planned, changed plans; looked at finishes, rejected them. Eventually, Butch created the structure for the cherrywood stairs that curl around my round bathroom to fly in the air like a deck of gambling cards flung high and far out. He made broad free-form iron gates to keep my dogs in or out of certain areas and painted them a bright yellow and an even brighter red.

A year later, I took a welding class at Sheridan College. I had no place at home to create what I really wanted to make in steel. I imagined the sculptures I had sketchily drawn when flat on my back as ten feet high, not two-foot-tall pieces for the desktop. Could Butch help me?

Butch and I made Styrofoam models in workable small scale from my three charcoal drawings. I scraped in nuances of line again and again, until each piece became alive. From that point, Butch took over, multiplying numbers for coordinate sizes, and with chains and cranes, he moved, cut, and lifted thousands of pounds of steel plate. He carved the sides of each piece to scale with his laser cutter and welded them together with a MIG welder. I completed the finish on the three sculptures that winter in that icy metal shed, bundled in fleece and welders' clothes.

During earlier autumn months, I had made two other steel sculptures using scrap pieces of steel from Butch's boneyard. Once the second sculpture went up at home, when the ropes and cables came off, Butch said, "Hey. That piece there belongs on my tractor."

"Too late now," I replied, and we laughed.

Butch and a team of his helpers, Chuck and Donny, brought out two of my large steel sculptures, *The Couple* and *Woman*. They raised them from the deck of the flatbed truck with cables and ropes, eased them onto the uneven grassland, which had been a hay field the prior summer. The sculptures shone a soft black, with undertones of burnished color in the waning sun. I stood on the terrace, three hundred feet away, in front of the big window in the living room. I felt so proud and so grateful. To create a work of that size, to finish a dream in a medium as difficult as steel, was not something I could have done alone. I learned to ask for help, something that did not come easily to me. I got it done.

We celebrated by going to a big welding operation in Gillette, where Butch's friend allowed us the run of his yard, which had neat piles of a great number of odd-shaped pieces of steel. I became a bag lady, collecting large and small pieces of rusted and painted steel. My idea of a sensual treat was to go to a junk dealer and come home with a truckload of others' unwanted leftovers. The best one I found was at Jimmy Flipowitz's Steel Etc. in Great Falls, Montana. There, I got yards of copper pulled from a burned-out electric company, a beat-up old saxophone, square nails from a past century, and the flat bottom of a freight car to use as a bridge over Piney Creek. I resisted a caboose, something I had always wanted. The caboose would have been a memento from the time when I watched freight trains rumble through the Green Pond railroad station in South Carolina, while my father was busy sending telegrams to his office up north. He had liked spending time with the telegraph operator. I had liked watching the different-colored freight cars, and listening to the *clickity-click* sound the wheels made when rolling over the tracks.

When I was in New York, I often wandered about SoHo and the East or West Village with a canvas bag to hold scraps of wood, wire, or paper that I tore off posters stuck up on buildings and lampposts everywhere. The glue on the backside of old posters was a thick brownish-black mosslike goo, which provided texture for a collage. The right side of posters provided diverse color scraps, and any street was a source of old bits—tickets, string, or strands of wool, slim bits of aluminum chain or crushed beer cans. Once, on the Lower East Side, I was actually caught inside a Dumpster, looking for interesting wood or plaster scraps. The Dumpster sat by the owner's house nearby. The man came running down the steps of his brownstone, screaming, "Get outta my gawbage."

I incorporate papers and even three-dimensional pieces into my paintings, creating sculptural depth on a flat canvas. Color floods my soul. When painting, I often sense that I taste the need for a change in hue, rather than think or feel it. I move brush, rag, or the heel of my hand across the canvas with instinctual speed, as though following the rhythms of a symphonic dance. This movement, primal and unstoppable, is like the power of a twenty-foot ocean wave relentlessly moving forward. Anger was an ally in my creativity, helping to define the unsayable, make visible the haunting or explosive, in rage, or the deepest grief, in delight and exultation, or in curiosity, tenderness, or just flat boredom. I used, and still use, my visceral reaction to nature as a fundamental in my life, to be explored, nurtured, and translated. The anger that fired and tortured me with its power, the guilt that swept in behind it, and the fear that coated every emotion were the rats that gnawed at my guts, made me scream. They were also the ones that gave me the courage to face my past, take it in, recognize it for what it was, and change the way I felt about it. Queen Elizabeth I said quite simply, "The past cannot be changed." She was a bright lady.

Peace in my valley is created by many things, from an African sculpture to a glass sink, but the consistent sources of support and caring come from Kathy, my housekeeper, and my assistant, David. Kathy's husband, Ray, is half ghost, rarely seen but evident in how the grasses grow and the cattle fatten. Cliff is the carpenter-builder who makes anything wood whistle a symphony, and the rest of the crew makes my home a place filled with ease and beauty.

Kathy creates tasty dishes that keep my freezer and refrigerator full. She can cook gourmet delights for a horde of guests or toss up a hamburger feast for the entire valley. She keeps my life organized and my house in order and polished in spite of the restless way I live and travel. She fixes the furnace or the garage door opener when a power failure has screwed up the mechanical workings. She also manages Turned Antiques Etc., the antique home-furnishing and much more store I opened in 2007.

David copes with all facets in my life. He is the photographer of my artwork, my assistant when I teach, the keeper of my art schedule, my general secretary, and a warm entertainer who discusses far-flung ideas and happenings worldwide. His ranging knowledge and interests, his wit, and his talent at storytelling are a constant source of delight to me over coffee at 7:30 A.M. or a Diet Coke at 3:00 P.M. He makes me laugh. He is also a fabulous cook and treats me to strange dishes on occasion, like pickled tongue or Thai melon shrimp. He and Kathy have been with me for twenty-six years. I can't think of us all not being together.

In managing the rangelands, Ray moves the cattle from pasture to pasture in an environmentally sound way, and over the years the grasses have improved significantly. He has taught my grandchildren Texas Hold'em, as well as good manners around horses and cattle, and has rescued many a buried car or pickup from the depths of a snowbank for me. Ray has been a whiz at the barbecue when help was needed, and told stories that made us all laugh. He gives good hugs and has won my heart except at the poker table. He cooks liver and onions to rare perfection.

I have lived in my sculptural home on Piney Creek for forty-nine years. The original stone house now extends way west, with vast windows that take in views of the Piney Creek Valley and the Bighorn Mountains in every season. My large living room is sunken, so views start waist-high beneath cathedral-high peaks. Despite the sprawl of the room, the intimate groupings of furniture, the massive stone fireplace, the variety of art, and the sense of being belowground make the room cozy. Warm wood flooring, the ficus tree, a totem pole, rugs, a ceramic wall piece by Betty Woodman, and sculptures—one of wood, one in clay over eight feet tall, and one of tractor tires made of cow intestines—that hide bulbs that light up and provide soft illumination in the evening.

Back in 1964, I was the model for a large-scale nude painting by my friend Jon Schueler, and it now hangs at the end of my dining table, sometimes to the surprise of a dinner guest. The top of the dining table was made from my corral fence when the original top split and curled in Wyoming's dry air. A quiet painting portrays the broad nothingness and peace of the Australian outback in midday sunlight. It was done by an Aboriginal woman and her two daughters in Australia. I bought it there, rolled it up, and brought it home. All the bits and pieces that surround me, everything from an Asmat wood sculpture to an assemblage of Coldwater Creek catalogs mushed into palm-size varnished balls, have tales to tell, personal memories that fill my life with happiness. I always mean to switch around my own enormous paintings but often forget, partly because I worry whether I have an equally good canvas of the right size to use in replacement and partly because when I think of it, no one is there to help, like at night. By morning, my mind is entangled with something else. Isn't that the way life rolls?

I have watched the seasons change and learned the tempo of life alone. Kathy, Ray, David, and I have become an extended family. We count on one another to break the loneliness of a winter night with a game of Scrabble, to help take care of one or six dogs, to give a hand at loading or unloading a truckful of paintings. We have a Christmas lobster dinner celebration at my house when we can, usually the first week of January. That starts the New Year with hugs and love, laughter, and a certain tenderness.

For quite some time, I have been thinking about what will happen to this house and land I love after I die. Who will be here to take in the special feeling of this valley, the peace to be found in this invigorating setting for mind and soul? All my adult life, I have felt an obligation to repay those who made my financial life so comfortable, the authors who wrote the books. Without them, there would never have been a book-publishing business. Always, it was the authors who interested me, not the business or socializing.

I talked with my friend Mary Jane about starting a residency program for writers and visual artists. How difficult would it be to set up? I didn't want my children to have to cope with the idea when I was dead; I wanted to make it happen in my lifetime. "That could happen," she said, "and I would be happy to help. Just tell me when."

MJ and I traveled up and down the West Coast area visiting artist residencies. I quickly found out what I liked and didn't like, and that pretty well defined what I built. Ross Iverson became the architect for buildings I envisioned at the southern end of the Collins ranch. It took eighteen months from start to finish. Even before we broke ground, I started buying antique American furniture for both the writers' studios and the bedrooms and the living area of the main building to create a homelike feel for the writers and artists. The name of the residency program was to be Jentel, a scramble of my name.

The Jentel Artist Residency Program takes two writers and four visual artists for a month each year. They are given a handsome place to live, a separate place to work, and a stipend for food or travel expenses. They cook for themselves, which has become a bonding experience, a happy surprise for us all. The residents participate in Jentel Presents, an evening where the writers and visual artists share their work with the public in Sheridan. Up to fifty or sixty people listen and observe on the first Tuesday of each month at an art center in town. A few guests join the artists and staff for dinner after the program is over and the conversations have dribbled down. The interaction between the residents and the public provides a rewarding experience for both: an eye-opener for the public and, for the residents, an interest in their work.

Mary Jane Edwards is the director of Jentel. Lynn Reeves is the program manager; she, along with others, makes the operation run smoothly. That team creates an atmosphere of interest and peace for the residents. Everyone is helpful, but they don't mother the residents; they do bring joy and laughter to work. Mary Jane, Lynn, and I have gotten many letters and presents from residents since Jentel's inception, praising staff, the landscape, the weather, the creek and, most of all, the time apart to work, think, and dream.

I like doing things in a big way, and I guess I overbought. Two years after I finished decorating all the Jentel Artist Residency facilities—office, house, studios, and, to some extent, Mary Jane's house—MJ reminded me that sixteen pieces of Early American furniture were still stored in the barn at Jentel, and that space was needed for equipment. It was during this process of mulling over what to do with those pieces that my store Turned Antiques Etc. was born. The choices were: get smaller and sell off the pieces, or get bigger and acquire more.

I built a large metal building for Turned Antiques Etc. at the corner of Route 14 and County Road 149 on the border of my ranch, nineteen miles from Sheridan. Windows let in light and overhead doors provided easy access for bringing in and taking out the furnishings. The building provided ten thousand square feet of space, ultimately not enough for my craven taste. I found over the years I needed space for new inventory of both home decorations and antiques. Mary Jane joined me on the quest for unusual early painted antique items: a canning cupboard or a dry sink, a pine dining table or a step-back cupboard—none needing big repairs. We traveled all over Nebraska and then to Iowa and Kansas, searching out and getting tips on locating dealers. It was a treasure hunt for furniture and friends. We were told by all the dealers that the Round Top Show in Round Top, Texas, was where we would find the largest and best collections of antiques. That was a long distance away. The Round Top Show covered over three hundred acres of antiques and just plain junk. MJ and I flew down on a Monday in late March. I selected the antiques; MJ inventoried with tape, pen, camera, and notebook. We each drove home a twenty-five-foot truck packed full. We covered 1,386 miles in two days. Not bad.

Once Turned Antiques Etc. opened, semitrucks loaded with Early American, English or Welsh, and a few French country antique pieces arrived and needed unloading. I bought a worn pine kitchen table with shallow hollows, where a laboring housewife had once pounded and rolled out the daily bread, and a workbench lovingly restored with two vises and two drawers. Many different sizes of step-back cupboards, benches, bureaus, canning cupboards, trunks, and iron beds became the foundation of rooms to be decorated in the vast square footage. Lamps, mirrors, an entire section of silk flowers, table linens, and new and old kitchen necessities and flavorings together made the store sing. Could it work way out of town, on my ranch, a store catering to sophisticated tastes in everything from lotions to ladies' blouses, the newest kitchen gadget to an Early American corner cupboard, or a European bidet to use as a dog's water bowl? Was I mad to do this? Probably, but I thought it would be a success just because of the unusual and varied merchandise; it would draw people from hundreds of miles away. It has proved so, even though we are open only on Saturdays from May to Labor Day, and on Fridays and Saturdays from November until Christmas, as well as by appointment. The store is closed all winter.

I started commercial land development of the Wrench Ranch just a few years ago, but I bought the ranch on February 14, 1995. It was to be a sound land investment over time, and time it has taken. Land development means meetings, meetings, meetings—to bring sewers, water, electricity, and roadways, and to design hundreds of acres of residential and commercial lands. From the time I bought this ranch, I have run a herd of black Angus and leased out a majority of the land to other people in the cattle business. The borders of the Wrench Ranch stretch east and west on the northern border of the city of Sheridan. Butch Jellis, my steel-sculpture friend and teacher, is the one who brought the ranch to my attention, and he has done an excellent job as my managing partner. With his help, I have developed and sold residential subdivisions that I had designed, with houses stepped back from the road and a walking/riding path of two miles for horses or bikes, but no motored vehicles. All such matters demand my attention and face me at my kitchen table over coffee in the early morning, before I get dressed. With the telephone ringing, friends visiting, a dentist appointment or other daily activities, and queries about the store, there is no time to think. Besides the actual time I spend painting, there is the making and shipping of crates of my artwork, perhaps an exhibition load of paintings and monotypes to pack up in the trailer and hitch to my Suburban or truck and drive to a museum in Montana, where I'll give a talk and a workshop over the weekend, then drive the five hours home. And there are new dogs to train, a trip to pack for, or a dinner for artist friends to prepare. I am lucky to be busy. Visits from my children and their families are the best.

My house is an old stone ranch house built in 1898, right after the Spanish-American War. It has grown like a wandering sculpture over the years. I have since added wings to the house, but never subtracted. My first addition was to make room for my daughter's arriving babies; she had four on the fast track, so I built a large living room with cathedral ceilings and a spacious bedroom wing for me, far away from baby activities. Space for both my children and grandchildren was enhanced by an indoor pool, where in winter I can swim during a snowstorm, and where in summertime we all plunge and play. In 1982 my studio complex also grew to allow for a press, storage space for paintings, collages, monotypes, and other works on paper, and an enlarged work space for painting. At least it was large enough until I decided to make really huge canvases. I am a prolific painter. I paint in chunks of time.

Normally, I work with three or four canvases, trading back and forth, giving drying time as needed. I bring each canvas up to a point, then go to the next canvas and bring that one to be on par with the earlier one. This rhythm of moving a group of paintings to a finish bit by bit creates a small exhibition of the moment. I paint from the unconscious, moving color and brush mark in a rhythmic dance, a pulse beat. The seed is sown; the layers grow. The lushness or sparseness of paint on a brush alters the density of the mark. The angle and strength of the mark laid down, the erasure or wipe-down, the threading out of the paint to gossamer—all create or diminish density, texture, and the sensual layering of the work. Memory flows straight and sideways, becomes abstract; passion felt must translate in color, mark, and form. I react in the second that passes, allowing my arm to swing and touch brush hairs to canvas, a stream from my subconscious mind. I plan hardly anything; maybe it is a color that sets me in motion, or the sound of flowing water the past weekend at Little Crazy. My visual responses to ideological thoughts, memories, or immediate emotions live together—not in a linear fashion of time or even subject matter, but melding together—touched off by who knows what word or seen object. I use shards of experience and emotion to create a whole. To write about painting is an absurd effort.

Two years ago, Tom and Jacque Buchanan came up to visit me from the University of Wyoming in Laramie. Tom was president of the university. I had sent out feelers through Mary Jane and Susan Moldenhauer, director of the University of Wyoming Art Museum, to see if the university might be interested if I offered to gift them my house, all my treasures, my paintings, and Jentel, the artist residency program that I began six years ago. We walked about the buildings: my house, Mary Jane's house and studio, Turned Antiques Etc., my studio. Tom was silent; only twice did he write a few words in a small notebook he held close to his chest. Who I am lay about us, in my surroundings. We sat at my dining table in the old part of my house, Tom across from Susan, Jacque, and me, with Mary Jane close by at table's end. Tom glanced in his little book, now on the table, and said, looking me in the eye, "Neltje, you have created a world-class living museum. The University of Wyoming would be proud to accept the gift of your home and art collection upon your death." There was no sound for a few seconds.

I was crying. I raised my tear-streaked face and said, "Thank you, Tom. How is it that someone who has known me for barely twenty-four hours can know me better than anyone else?" The paperwork and then the ceremonies came later, but the words said by Tom Buchanan in those few moments have stayed with me, a mantra, a means to fly. My home will become the Neltje Center for the Literary and Visual Arts. Jentel is included and will continue operation as is. My home, my interests in the arts will continue to grow and be a resource for education and development in Wyoming. I am filled with gratitude for Tom Buchanan and the University of Wyoming Foundation.

In May 2012, Susan Moldenhauer asked if I could paint a ten-by-thirty-foot painting for the rear wall of the main-floor gallery, where I was to have a retrospective exhibition in September 2013. Well, why not, I thought to myself.

"Sure, I'll try," I told her.

Being me, I painted not one, but four ten-by-thirty-foot canvases. I titled them *The Moroccan Suite*. They were on exhibit in a room built specially for them at the University of Wyoming Art Museum from September to the end of the year.

Epilogue

From my red lounge chair in the living room at Little Crazy, I look west toward the mountains. Bare trees and a tawny hillside, bouncing ponderosa pines and blue spruce are now a landscape in whirlwind turmoil, and in a few seconds it will be smoothed in stillness. I let my mind wander in the past, see myself as a young girl in a flat-bottomed boat, fishing with my pal Jimmy. Or there I am on my horse, cantering along the red clay roads of Bonny Hall. I feel my wild spirit, my drive for perfection, and my boundless energy.

In my first marriage, I learned I could not be who I wasn't. The corporate wife was not in me, though I had been trained in that role and did it well for almost ten years. I needed more food for my soul and more love for my heart.

Delights, such as my time with Anthony over those few years; my children, who tantalized me and drove me crazy with their bright minds; my grandchildren, now almost all grown up, who have encouraged me, to my great happiness, to remain a child at heart. As for the failure I felt at being a not-so-good mother, I know now that I wasn't so bad. Both my children have been happily married for more than twenty years. I never made ten!

I wanted to live a full life, rich with challenges around the corner, just out of sight. They came, those challenges, because I learned to put my mouth where my heart directed. Is my delight in new adventures born of the fear of abandonment? Yes. I keep having to prove myself. But it comes even more from a curiosity to know how those around the world live in a day-to-day environment: the pots they use to make soup, the clothes they wear—perhaps some handwoven textiles made out of necessity—the wooden sculptures they create to honor their gods, all tell tales that become part of me. Remembrances of animals and peoples in their native surrounds connect me in a spiritual way worldwide, especially to those in the more primitive societies. I have wanted to make difficult ventures work my way. My grandchildren and my children provide me—and they'd better continue to do so—with a sense of belonging that has minimized the apartness I've felt since babyhood. And the most significant risks have been choices to feed my soul, like becoming an artist. In finding my truth, there are fragments still afloat, and living every day has been a dynamic, though complex, adventure. I speak my mind, unafraid (most of the time!), and try to take each moment as it comes. Just don't hurt my dogs!

I reconnected with my brother before he died in 2015, put to bed the angers and jealousies that consumed me. I reconnected with Aunt Dorothy's daughter Sylvia Weaver by visiting her in Florida. What a loving treat for both of us.

Do I worry? Of course I do. Do I feel lonely? Rarely. Do I miss being held close against a man's body? Mmm-hmm. But a cheap roll in the hay is exactly that. I've been there and come away feeling grubby. When not painting, writing, or being held hostage by Wrench Ranch problems, I read a book from stacks by my chair. Books are an addiction. Or I call a friend or my kids, pick up one of several knitting projects—hand warmers, sweaters, a vest, all idling on the counter in my bedroom at home on Piney Creek, waiting to be finished. Then I watch the *NewsHour* on PBS at five and sometimes, till far too late, *Criminal Minds* or *CSI*. When weather allows, I walk the hills, the creek bed, the canyon trail, and in the summertime, I wander through the mountain forests and meadows with my dogs, two basset hounds, one Australian shepherd mix.

Through the window I see pine and spruce, the pinks, reds, and oranges of peonies and poppies. I wonder whether butterflies mate in flight. For two days, I have watched the same two swallow-tailed butterflies chase each other in wild patterns, flying next to each other like mates. Then once again they zigzag crazily, darting back and forth and sideways, dipping down, then driving straight up as high as the top of the blue spruce. They remind me of teenage love, the innocent freshness of first-time coupling. I delight in them each day, enjoying their freedom. What a gift they are with their bright yellow wings, framed in black, with a black tail at the bottom of each wing. They vanish as they came.

My delight in the natural world is so often enhanced by memories of my early-childhood capers in the gardens and woods of Oyster Bay and even more by dreamy playtimes with frogs and bugs along the canal banks at Bonny Hall. Visual memories, scenes, survive to serve as a firm structure in my being. Even the painful bits that harmed me have their place. When my father died, I was so young, only fourteen. I had to with-hold my grief then, and the gut-wrenching rage that filled me. Now, safe at Little Crazy, I weep—great racking sobs for the father who vanished just as he became a father. Goddamn! How unfair. I love you, I need you, I miss you. Come back, be with me. You might even like me now.

— ACKNOWLEDGMENTS —

My thanks go to many people: Jane Wohl, professor of English Literature at Sheridan College—you had the courage to take me through the first stages of my manuscript with vast patience, great good humor, and incisive intelligence. Beena Kamlani—you shaped my story after work and on weekends with dedication and an ear for rhythm. Courtney Hodell—with empathy and a caring awareness you encouraged and supported me through the final stage of my memoir. And many, many thanks to editor in chief George Witte.

There were others without whom the manuscript and I might have fizzled: My assistant, David Schreiber, kept me on target and relatively sane through the years as I tumbled about with thoughts and no words that fit. Readers Hank Siegel, Jacquelin Buchanan, Patty Kemper, David Lombardi, and my good friend Mary Jane Edwards—many thanks for the hours and effort you spent reading and the responses you made. And to my extended family in Wyoming and all of my Eastern family—thanks for putting up with me.